The Coldest Harbour of the Land
Simon Stock and Lord Baltimore's Colony in
Newfoundland,
1621–1649

In 1624 Simon Stock, a missionary priest of the Discalced Carmelite order in England, began correspondence with the recently founded Sacred Congregation "de Propaganda Fide" in Rome in an attempt to interest it in the establishment of a novitiate for English priests of his order. While Propaganda was unwilling to do this, Stock was encouraged to continue his correspondence because of the information it provided on Lord Baltimore's attempts to found a colony in North America. Luca Codignola draws on these letters of Simon Stock and material in archives in Rome (Propaganda Fide and the Carmelite order) and London to present a fascinating picture of seventeenth-century Catholic colonization.

Lord Baltimore planned to establish his Avalon colony in Newfoundland and to provide its settlers with Catholic missionaries. Stock, however, was concerned with much more than providing a single colony with missionaries: because of his belief in the existence of a northwest passage, he saw "Avalon" as a gateway to China, India, and Japan, and to the establishment of other Catholic colonies. Despite his repeated appeals for aid, Propaganda was slow to react and Stock's letters leave no doubt about his sense of frustration. However, as Propaganda's main source of information on North America, Stock had an important influence on the development of their colonization policy.

The second half of the book provides full translations or summaries of all Simon Stock's letters and enclosures during 1622 to 1649. These letters are particularly important in detailing his activities as a priest, giving his perception of events in England during this period, and providing new information on the Avalon colony. Stock's letters and Codignola's essay greatly expand our knowledge of the Catholic communities and their reaction to colonization.

Luca Codignola is a member of the Department of History, University of Pisa.

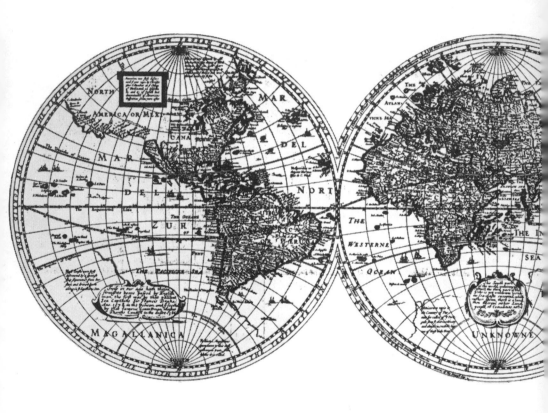

Luca Codignola

# THE COLDEST HARBOUR OF THE LAND

*Simon Stock and Lord Baltimore's Colony in Newfoundland, 1621–1649*

TRANSLATED BY
ANITA WESTON

McGill-Queen's University Press
KINGSTON AND MONTREAL

© McGill-Queen's University Press 1988
ISBN 0-7735-0540-7
Legal deposit 1st quarter 1988
Bibliothèque nationale du Québec

Printed in Canada

Printed on acid-free paper

This work was originally published in Italian in 1982 by Marsilio Editori
under the title *Terre d'America e burocrazia romana: Simon Stock,
Propaganda Fide e la colonia di Lord Baltimore a Terranova, 1621–1649.*
This translation has been published with the help of a grant from the
Canadian Federation for the Humanities, using funds provided by the
Social Sciences and Humanities Research Council of Canada.

Cover illustration: Peter Rindisbacher, *A Drifting Iceberg Strikes the Ship
in the Night of June 19, 1821.* (Public Archives of Canada, C-1904)

**Canadian Cataloguing in Publication Data**

Codignola, Luca, 1947–
    The coldest harbour of the land
    Translation of: Terre d'America e burocrazia romana.
    Includes letters by Simon Stock to the Congregation
    "de Propaganda Fide" in Rome.
    Includes bibliographical references and index.
    ISBN 0-7735-0540-7
    1. Catholic Church – Newfoundland – History – 17th
    century. 2. Stock, Simon. fl. 1621–1649.
    3. Baltimore, George Calvert, Baron, 1580–1632.
    I. Stock, Simon, fl. 1621–1649. II. Title.

BX1422.N4C6313 1988   282'.718   C87-094336-7

*For Federica*

# Contents

# Preface to the
# English Edition

Preparing the English translation of this book with my friend and colleague Anita Weston provided me with the opportunity to double-check and revise the Italian text, published in March 1982 by Marsilio Editori of Venice.

I have added two documents to those published in the Italian edition and corrected a few inconsistencies and errors pointed out by colleagues and friends. Otherwise, this version is the same as the original. All documents and citations in the text have been translated into English. The Italian edition will still be useful to those who wish to check the English translation against the original documents.

Little has appeared on the topic in the interval between this and the Italian edition. The bibliography has been updated, and includes a number of books and articles published between 1982 and 1986, as well as others I did not know about at the time the original version was published. Some of these works are very important. They include all of John Krugler's articles, except "Calvert's Resignation" (1973) which I referred to earlier, David Quinn's *New American World* (1979), Gillian Cell's *Newfoundland Discovered* (1982), and John Smith's *Complete Works* edited by the late Philip Barbour (1986). My own *Calendar 1622–1799* of Propaganda Fide documents was published in microfiche (1983), as was my general interpretation of the relationship between the history of early North America and the Holy See which appeared as "Rome and North America 1622–1799. The Interpretive Framework" (1984).

Finally, I wish to acknowledge, with deep gratitude, Jane Fredeman's help in the production of the Canadian edition of this book. Without her support, the audience for my book and Simon Stock's letters would still be limited to those who read Italian.

# Preface and Acknowledgments

In 1980, while working in the archives of the Sacred Congregation "de Propaganda Fide" in Rome, I came across a number of letters written from England by the English missionary Simon Stock. Some of these seemed of great importance to the early history of European expansion in North America. After finding the first seventy-three letters, my research logically progressed to the General Archives of the Order of the Discalced Carmelites (Stock's order) where I found twenty more of Stock's letters, plus a quantity from his confrères which considerably amplified the significance of the letters preserved in Propaganda. Later, I found two more letters written by Stock, one in the Vatican Secret Archives and one in the Westminster Diocesan Archives. A quick probe into the available historical literature proved that only a small fraction of those letters (and none of those preserved by the order) was known to historians.

With regret I soon realized that reasons of security had obliged the author of the correspondence to omit the names of the protagonists whose activity in America he was eager to relate to Propaganda. Only one name recurred in his letters, "Avalon," the name of the place where the missionary's friends had founded their colony. Starting with it, I attempted to reconstruct the events in which Stock was involved. Although the extant documentation is scanty, I was determined to publish this wealth of unknown detail concerning Avalon's history.

Part One of this book tells the events of the history of Avalon. It is not, however, a history of the colony, nor a history of Propaganda's first moves concerning it. Neither is it a biography of Simon Stock. I have dwelt upon those facts in Avalon's history which Stock himself deals with or gives new information about, but I have only briefly touched upon well-known facts which Stock does not mention. I do examine Stock's life and personality in general, but I have concentrated mainly on the years of his involvement in America. The vicissitudes of his mission in England are only touched upon insofar as they explain Stock's background. I have described Propaganda's attitude towards Stock and towards Avalon, although a complete analysis of Propaganda policies would require consideration of a much vaster geographical area and time-span. This book is, therefore, mainly the history of the relationship between Stock, Propaganda, and North America and of the reciprocal changes and transformations which came about.

Part Two contains ninety-five of Stock's letters, some translated and given in full, others—of lesser or no interest to North American history—summarized. For the editing rules adopted in the volume, I refer the reader to the Introductory Note to Part Two. Full details of the works cited in shortened form in the footnotes are to be found in the Bibliography. Dates are given according to the New Style calendar. When sources use the Old Style calendar, I give both systems (for example, 7 March 1624/17 March 1625).

I could not have completed this work without the help and co-operation of many friends and colleagues. In 1979 I was awarded a fellowship by the Social Sciences and Humanities Research Council of Canada which enabled me to work for four months in the Public Archives of Canada, Ottawa, where I took advantage of the assistance of Robert S. Gordon and Victorin Chabot. In 1980 I obtained a fellowship from the Wolfson Foundation, administered by the British Academy, and was able to work in archives and libraries in London, in particular at the University of London Library, the British Library (Department of Manuscripts, Department of Printed Books, Map Library), and the Public Record Office. On that occasion I received a most welcome invitation from the Institute of United States Studies in London, directed by Esmond Wright, to work there as Honorary Research Fellow in the 1981–82 academic year. I thus had access to the IUSS library and to the hospitality of its very helpful staff. I would also like to thank the Facoltà di Lettere of the Università di Pisa for granting me a sabbatical year in 1980–81, which enabled me to complete this book.

William J. Eccles (University of Toronto), Raimondo Luraghi (Università di Genova), H.C. Porter (Cambridge University), David Beers Quinn (University of Liverpool), Richard Simmons (University of Birmingham), and Sarah Tyacke (The Map Library, The British Library) have read portions of the manuscript and discussed points which presented particular difficulty. Tiziano Bonazzi (Università di Bologna) and Piero Del Negro (Università di Padova) have given me continual advice and assistance, which I hope I have put to good use. Similar assistance and co-operation has been forthcoming from the cultural offices of the Canadian Embassy (David Anido and Gilbert Reid) and the American Embassy (Roberto Bolzoni) in Rome.

*Preface*

I take this opportunity to thank all those who, in various ways, have offered help. Franco Angiolini (Università di Pisa), Didi Biglia, Alan and Susan Budd, Gillian T. Cell (University of North Carolina), Sean Conlon (Teresianum, Rome), Anton Debevec, Bede Edwards (St. Luke's Priory, Wincanton), Hugh Fenning (Collegio San Clemente, Rome), Birkin Haward, Pierre Hurtubise (Université Saint-Paul, Ottawa), John D. Krugler (Marquette University), Raymond J. Lahey (Memorial University of Newfoundland), Valentino Macca, Angelo Mitri, Terrence Murphy (Memorial University of Newfoundland), Oliver McGettigan (Carmelite Priory, London), Michael McGiffert (College of William and Mary), Juliet Mitchell, Liam S. O'Breartuin (Carmelite Priory, London), Emma Piper, Alison Quinn, Martin Rossdale, Pierre Savard (Université d'Ottawa), Alessandra Surdi (Centro Italiano di Studi Americani, Rome), Joanna van Heyningen, Leo van Wijmen (Collegio Internazionale Sant'Alberto).

The greater part of this work was carried out in the archives of Propaganda in Rome, which are so efficiently run that to work there is a pleasure. Josef Metzler, former archivist, could not have been more helpful or obliging. Sister Maria Margherita Villaluz of the Oblates of the Holy Spirit and Signor Ercole Giordano have done everything possible to remove any existing difficulties throughout the years of my research. Finally, my thanks to Antonio Frotes, archivist of the General Archives of the Order of the Discalced Carmelites, whose courtesy and competence allowed me to amplify the results of the research carried out in the archives of Propaganda.

Pisa, 1st January 1982

# Abbreviations

| | |
|---|---|
| *Acta CGF* | AOCD, series *Acta Capituli Generalis* |
| AOCD | General Archives of the Discalced Carmelites |
| *APC* | *Acts of the Privy Council* |
| APF | Archives of the Sacred Congregation "de Propaganda Fide" |
| ASV | Archivio Segreto Vaticano |
| B | blank |
| BL | British Library |
| BV | Biblioteca Apostolica Vaticana |
| CO | Colonial Office |
| *CP* | APF, series *Congregazioni Particolari* |
| *CSP, Dom.* | *Calendar of State Papers, Domestic* |
| CSP, Ven. | *Calendar of State Papers, Venetian* |
| DCB | *Dictionary of Canadian Biography* |
| DNB | *Dictionary of National Biography* |
| HMC | Historical Manuscripts Commission |
| *Litterae, Bede* | AOCD, series "P. Beda a SS. Sacr.: Litterae & relationes 1625/27" |
| *Litterae, Stock* | AOCD, series "P. Simon Stock: Litterae & relationes 1622/35" |
| OCD | Discalced Brothers of the Blessed Virgin Mary of Mount Carmel (Discalced Carmelites) |
| OFM | Order of Friars Minor (Franciscans) |
| OFM Cap | Order of Friars Minor Capuchin (Capuchins) |
| OFM Rec | Order of Friars Minor Recollet (Recollets) |
| OMinim | Order of the Minims (Minims) |
| OP | Order of Friars Preacher (Dominicans) |
| OSB | Order of St. Benedict (Benedictines) |
| PF | Sacred Congregation "de Propaganda Fide" |

## Abbreviations

| | |
|---|---|
| PRO | Public Record Office |
| *SOCG* | APF, series *Scritture Originali riferite nelle Congregazioni Generali* |
| SJ | Society of Jesus (Jesuits) |
| SS | Simon Stock |
| WDA | Westminster Diocesan Archives |

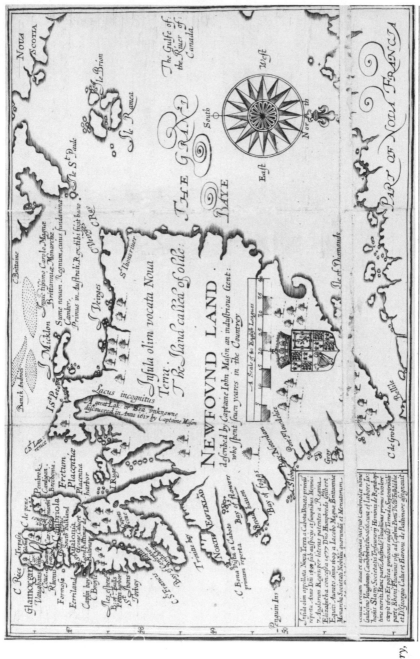

John Mason,
Newfovnd
Land, 1625.
British Library,
c.122.b.2.(2).

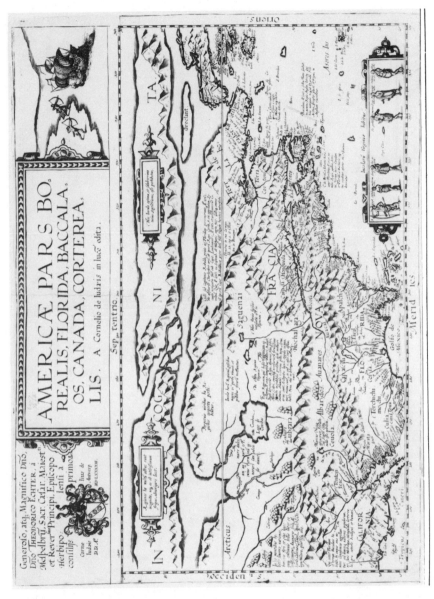

*Cornelis de Jode,*
*Americae Pars*
*Borealis, Florida,*
*Baccalaos, Canada,*
*Corterealis, 1593.*
*British Library,*
*69917.(21).*

*Gerard de Jode,
Totivs Orbis
Cogniti
Vniversalis
Descriptio,
1589. British
Library,
C.7.c.13.*

*Abraham Ortelius,
Americae Sive Novi
Orbis, Nova
Descriptio, 1587.
Biblioteca Apostolica
Vaticana, Chigi, S. 122*

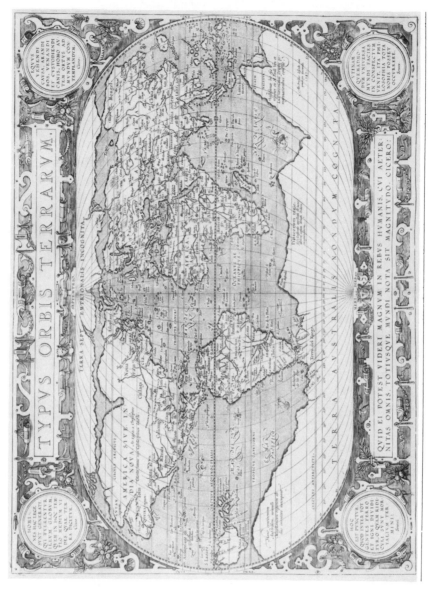

*Abraham Ortelius,*
*Typvs Orbis*
*Terrarvm, 1587.*
*Biblioteca Apostolica*
*Vaticana, Chigi, S.122*

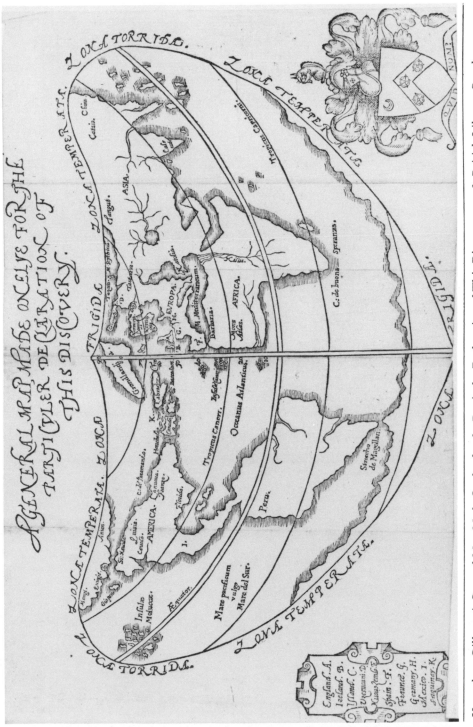

*Humphrey Gilbert, A General Map Made Onelye for the Particvler Declaration of This Discovery, 1576. British Library, C.32.b.29.*

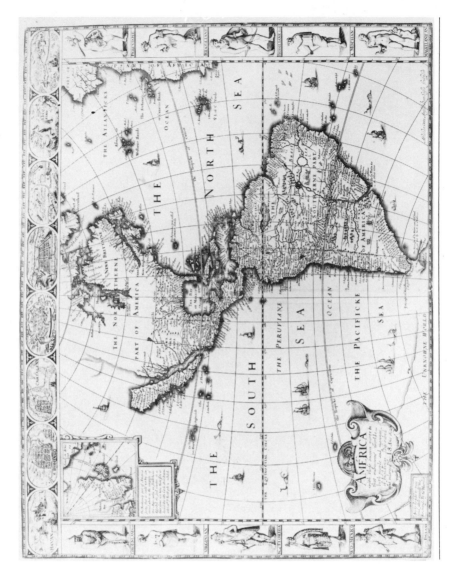

*John Speed, America
with those known parts,
1626. British Library,
69810.(89).*

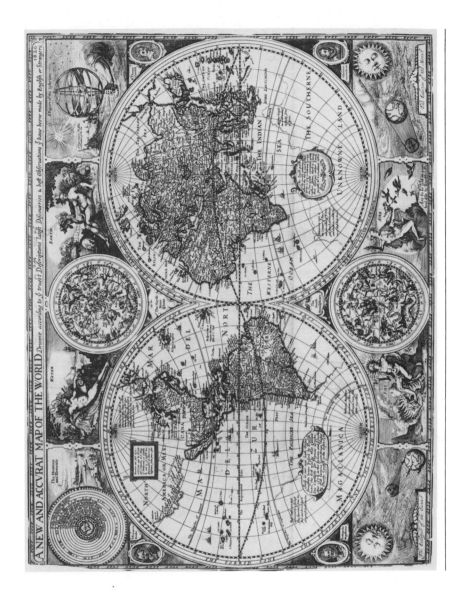

*John Speed,* A New and Accvrat Map of the World, *1626. British Library, 920.(47).*

*Henry Briggs,* The North part of America, *1625.*
*British Library, 69915. (10).*

Ill.mi et R.mi Sig.ri miei Col.mi

La lra di VV.SS. Ill.me del 15 di Novemb: non l'ho ricevuto sin
al 3 di marzo. sopra quel negotio di più facilmente plantare la s.
fede in China, come nò ho havuto risposta. l'ho communicato con il
sig.r Bruneau residente di sua Maestà catholica. per essere bono
catholico et zeloso del honore d'Iddio, et credo che l'avanzerà quanto sia possibile. non è negotio di poca difficultà, o spesa, massimamen
per la prima volta.

Questo pilloto del qual desideranno di sapere VV.SS. Ill.me con
suo fratello maggiore furano sempre levati in quell'arte. et questo
ha sentito spesso dire che suo fratello è vivo adesso morto, che fu passo
to per quelli parti, et così ha una desiderio di provarlo. si subito
volse di buscare trafico procurava che li fu dato uno capitano, et
alcuni soldati per andare in una nave sua propria. Passando per quelli
populi. Il capitano essendo più valoroso, che discreto, volva lasciare
la nave, et saccagiare uno loco delli infideli: et fu amozzato con
tutti li soi genti. Il Piloto essendo liberato di loro passava più
oltra con li soi marinari et uno suo figliolo, et passava tanto, che
poiche havevano passato per molta agua fresca nel mezzo, arrivava
a agua salata l'altra parte, et andava seguitando quel agua salata,
fin a tanto che nò solamente luy ma li soi marinari vedevano una nave
del altra parte; così per coprire meglio re il suo intento, lasciava
la sua nave, et andando un poco più per terra non solamente vedeva
la nave, ma anchora li homeni di quella nave, et così tornava,

Io ho dato più credito a questo Piloto, perche l'ho trovato bono
catholico, et tiene uno suo figliolo religioso. et per questa sua curi-
osità, fu posto in grande travaglio, essendo accusato per spia, et
li sapev più ch'ogni altro lelli scenti et pali di quelli mari, et
così marini, et fu posto in prigione, et con spendere multi denari
fu liberato, però con obligatione d'una grande summa, che non
andasse più sopra quelli cosi. et di questo sono certo, perche lo
visitava in prigione. et da me nò haveva cosa alcuna, perche dove-
va dire bugie, et l'ho trovato homo vertuoso, dito più che 50 anni
et l'ho dimandato multe altre cose di quelli populi d'America settentrionale, et delle plantationi delli inglesi: et ho trovato che tutto quello
che mi disse fosse vero.

Io l'ho dimandato perche nò publicava questo suo passo, scrito.
et mi disse che sarra la ruina della christianità, si fusse cognosso
to alli infideli, et curresa rischia della sua vita: perche ha cognosciuto
uno che scoprendo uno simile secreto, fu preso, et poi nò si ho lle mai
più novo di luy.

Et quanto alla probabilità, multi affirma nò che sia passo, et l'ho
trovato stampato in alcuni scritori: ma nò ho cognosciuto altro, che
ha:

*Francesco Ingoli's comments on Stock's letter to Propaganda, London, 7 March 1626, APF, SOCG, vol. 101, ff. 18v*

# Part One

*Simon Stock, Propaganda Fide, and Lord Baltimore's Colony in Newfoundland*

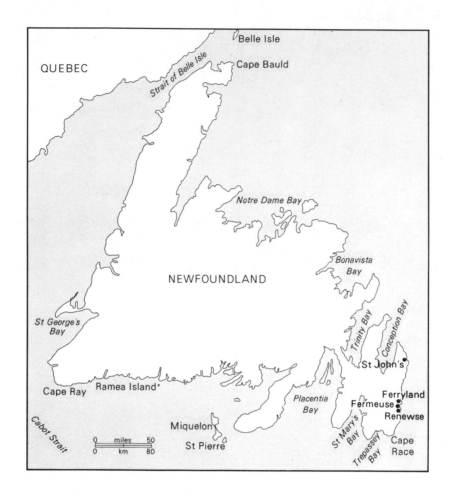

*Newfoundland, early seventeenth century. Source: Gillian T. Cell,* English Enterprise in Newfoundland 1577–1660. *University of Toronto Press, 1969, facing frontispiece.*

### CHAPTER ONE

# Introduction

This book recounts events in the history of the colony of Avalon in Newfoundland, which flourished between 1621 and 1630. It can be read from three different viewpoints. The first is that of a missionary, the Discalced Carmelite Simon Stock (1576–1652), who lived through one of the most difficult moments of English Catholicism, caught as he was between the persecution of the Protestant establishment and the serious national crisis which was to lead to Cromwell's revolution. The second viewpoint is not that of an individual but of a ministry, then only recently established under the name of the Sacred Congregation "de Propaganda Fide" (1622). Its officials had received from the pope the enormous but stimulating task of spreading the True Faith around the globe. The third viewpoint is that of America, a real place inhabited by a handful of Europeans and an unknown number of Indians and, at the same time, an idea, an image, in the minds of Europeans who were never to set foot on the other side of the Atlantic Ocean or who had not yet gone there. The New World had been discovered over a century previously, but for the most part it was still unknown and surrounded by myth—the object of military occupation in the south and the centre of avid and pious hopes in the north.

Stock is certainly not a key figure in English history or even in English Catholic history. His long life was characterized by a certain monotony, in action as in intention, and by a steady concern with survival in the difficult conditions of an England that was both unstable and dangerous. The five years (1625–30) in which Stock was actively involved in American matters and discussed them with Propaganda were not many out of his lifetime, but they were undoubtedly those in which he lived most intensely, when new and unimagined horizons were opened to him. It was his meeting in 1624 with George Calvert, the future Lord Baltimore, which drew Stock's attention away from the affairs of England to the other side of the Atlantic.

Calvert spent long years at court as a high-ranking politician, but he is much better known for his part in the colonization of North America. The history of Maryland is linked with his name, and the southeast peninsula of Newfoundland is still called Avalon today, preserving the name of the colony that Calvert founded there at the beginning of the seventeenth century.

Stock's America is more invention than reality. Never to set foot there himself, he busily reconstructed it using the accounts of those who had, the commonplaces in general circulation, some books he had read, and a limited number of maps he had consulted. For the historian, the interest in analysing Stock's American correspondence lies as much in sorting out actual detail from the superimposition of myth and legend as in following Stock's elaboration of a few data at his disposal into a model and image of America—and of Avalon.

In Stock's case, the historian has not merely to retrace the cultural itinerary of an individual, but also to consider it in the light of his public function. For the whole of the time Stock was in contact with Lord Baltimore and took part in the Avalon affair, he kept up a steady correspondence with Propaganda, becoming their informer, confidant, and "American" agent. For want of other sources, Roman officials gave considerable weight to Stock's information, descriptions, and suggestions. He thus directly contributed to the shaping of their consciousness of America and indirectly influenced the decisions they took concerning the New World. That these decisions failed to come up to Stock's expectations and did not bring about concrete results in no way alters the fact that Propaganda's American policy in the early years was modelled sharply on Stock's vision and interpretive framework.

As is the case with Stock, Propaganda is also doubly interesting to the historian. One has to verify how much of Stock's proposed model was accepted, filtered, and modified by Propaganda, but Propaganda's American policy itself is a subject of interest—what decisions were taken, why, and what effect did they have on the history of America and its inhabitants.

Obviously, the same criteria of analysis cannot be applied to Stock and Propaganda. Stock was an individual, and his history of common and somewhat generalizable attitudes and opinions cannot be taken beyond the limits of his existence, concentrating on the five years of his American experience. Propaganda, however, was not an individual but an office, a body of individuals acting collectively as a bureaucracy within the more general political and administrative machine of the Holy See. On the one hand, Propaganda officials acted, made decisions, and actuated one policy rather than another. In this sense it is legitimate, indeed mandatory, for the historian to ask how and to what extent Propaganda modified the history of Avalon and the development of North American events in general. On the other hand, and precisely because the rhythms of a bureaucracy are not those of an individual, the historian must recognize that the Congregation's actions are to be judged from the long-term perspective and within larger contexts. One should ask, for example, how these early years influenced the whole future of Propaganda's American policy, whether Stock's interpretation of events continued to bear weight with its officials once its relationship with him had come to an end, and what place Avalon and North America in general occupied in the scale of geographical and political priorities both of Propaganda and of the Holy See. While only a general study of the history of Propaganda could give a complete answer to such questions, even a short work such as this can show that these first five years were particularly formative, precisely because they were the first, and that they established guidelines which were still operative years later.

At the beginning of the seventeenth century, the time of these events, America was just taking her first steps. Port-Royal was founded in 1605, Jamestown in 1607, Québec in 1608, Cuper's Cove in Newfoundland in 1610. Bermuda was first colonized in 1612, and in 1620 the Pilgrim Fathers landed at Plymouth. By 1625 there were still only two thousand Europeans in North America. Avalon and its inhabitants form part of these settlement activities.

### CHAPTER TWO

# Simon Stock, Discalced Carmelite, Meets Lord Baltimore, 1621-24

Relatively little is known of the Discalced Carmelite Simon Stock, born Thomas Doughty. Yet Stock wrote books, had access to the diplomatic and political circles of the London area, and was a person of some importance in the Catholic community of early seventeenth-century England. His confrère Benedict Zimmerman wrote a brief biography of him at the end of the nineteenth century,[1] and all subsequent mention of Stock is based, without exception, on Zimmerman's work. The Carmelite historian, in turn, based his work entirely on a manuscript history of the English mission compiled in 1705 by another confrère, Biagio della Purificazione,[2] and on a short autobiographical letter that Stock had written between 1641 and 1643 at the request of his superiors, of which Zimmerman gives the most salient points.[3] According to the custom of the time, this is necessarily a kind of spiritual autobiography and says very little about the facts of its author's life. It remains, however, the only source of information about Stock's movements in the years preceding his entry into the Venerable English College in Rome[4] and the period between his departure from the English College and his final return to England.

Born in Plombey, England, around 1576,[5] Thomas Doughty was either born of Catholic parents or was soon converted to Catholicism. Undecided between a military or an academic career[6] and already persecuted for religious reasons by English law, Doughty travelled extensively in Europe until, in October 1606, he entered the English College in Rome to study theology, with the idea of returning to England as a missionary.[7] He visited England once, though for how long is not known, between the end of his stay in Rome (1610) and 6 October 1613, when he completed his novitiate with the Discalced Carmelites in Brussels and made his profession of faith, taking the name Simon Stock.[8] In 1614 the order decided to open a mission in England,[9] and

Stock was chosen as the first missionary. In April 1615, he returned to England for good. He was followed by his confrères Eliseus of St. Michael, as provincial vicar, in 1618[10] and Edmund of St. Martin in 1621.[11] Others came later, but the Discalced Carmelites were never numerous in England. Only a few years later, a careful observer, the papal envoy extraordinary Gregorio Panzani (1634–36), mentioned only five of them. For approximately 150,000 Catholics Panzani's catalogue also mentioned 500 secular priests, as many as 160 Jesuits and 100 Benedictines, 20 Franciscans, 9 French Capuchins, 7 Dominicans, 2 Mimins, and 1 Carthusian monk.[12]

Here Stock's autobiography ends and with it Zimmerman's biography. Few details are available with which to attempt a reconstruction of Stock's life between 1615 and 1622, when he began to correspond with the Roman authorities. He apparently devoted much time to his writing, and five of his seven known books were published between 1618 and 1623.[13] Through Genoese merchants living in London, he established contact with the Spanish Embassy, at that time the centre of frenetic negotiations regarding the proposed marriage between Prince Charles, son of James I, king of England, and the Infanta Maria, daughter of Philip III, king of Spain. In October 1620 Stock replaced the Dominican Diego de La Fuente as embassy chaplain, and he was subsequently the confessor of Diego Sarmiento de Acuñas, Count Gondomar, the Spanish ambassador, and of his successors, Carlos Coloma and Jacques Bruneau.[14] His Italian, increasingly spaniolate over the years, is further proof of his integration into the Spanish milieu, and certainly these contacts explain, in part, Stock's great freedom of movement after his return to England.[15]

In London Stock lived, at least for a while, in the "lower end of Holborn."[16] The residence of the Spanish ambassador was at that time also in Holborn, at Ely House, and Stock may have lived, either then or afterwards, at the residence.[17] What is certain is that he went through the embassy in forwarding and receiving correspondence. It is also possible, as Zimmerman suggests,[18] that Stock lived with the Roper family, with whom he was to remain in close contact.[19]

Stock's correspondence with his order began in 1622. In 1623 he established contact with the nuncio in Flanders, Giovanni Francesco Guidi di Bagno, archbishop of Patras, who put him in touch with the Sacred Congregation "de Propaganda Fide." In 1624 he began to correspond with the Congregation. Little of Stock's correspondence with Rome, which was to continue until 1649, is published.[20] His letters afford a detailed picture of Stock's life and interests, and they are of particular significance with regard to the 1620s for what they reveal about the history of North America.

One of Stock's greatest concerns at this period was a project to found a novitiate for Discalced Carmelites in Saint-Omer, Belgium, which was to be made responsible for recruiting new members for the English mission. Unlike the seculars and the other religious orders in England, the Discalced Carmelites had no novitiate specifically devoted to the care of English novices, who were thus obliged to receive their education from other orders. Some were educated overseas in houses of their own order, but these were dominated politically by monks of different nationalities, keener to pursue interests other than those of the English mission. Stock took up this project after his return to England in 1615[21] and continued to fight for it throughout his lifetime, even though he continually met opposition from the order's superiors. In his early letters he dealt equally with the project itself and with his strained relationship with his superiors. He accused them of boycotting the project because they had little interest in the success of the English mission in a time when ongoing persecution of Catholics called for the greatest possible effort in missionary activity.

Initially Stock addressed himself, not to Propaganda, but to the nuncio in Flanders, Guidi di Bagno, asking his help in the matter of the novitiate, since his order had been essentially negative.[22] The nuncio forwarded Stock's letters to the newly founded Propaganda. Its officials certainly discussed them with Diego de La Fuente, who was in Rome from 1621 to 1624 to negotiate the Spanish marriage, and whose chaplaincy Stock had taken over. During his last visit to England (April–July 1624), La Fuente himself informed Stock that Propaganda had received his requests and was considering them.[23] From that time on, Stock addressed himself directly to Propaganda.

While dealing minutely with, and replying conscientiously to, Stock's letters, the cardinals of the Congregation do not seem to have devoted any real attention to them. Stock's requests seemed to make sense, but in the delicate period following its foundation, Propaganda was forced to pass over Stock's arguments. The Congregation considered it more important to keep on the best possible terms with the religious orders, which until then had held a monopoly in the field of missionary activities and whose hostility could well bring about Propaganda's failure. Stock's problems with his superiors were thus considered a matter internal to the order. Propaganda could advise, but it would not intervene in favour of either party.[24] It was also true that the Congregation was interested in maintaining good relations with Stock, who, like many others, had of his own accord referred himself to them and who could both become an unconscious agent of their policies and also provide a precious source of unofficial information.[25] In fact, as long as Stock continued to bombard Propaganda with letters, Propaganda took good care to consider and reply punctually to them.

---

The Sacred Congregation "de Propaganda Fide" was officially established by Gregory XV on 22 June 1622 with the bull *Inscrutabili divinae providentiae*. It had the double mission of spreading the True Faith among the infidels and of protecting it where Catholics lived side by side with non-Catholics; and ultimately its aim was to achieve union with the Protestant and the Orthodox churches. Propaganda was meant to pursue these goals by co-ordinating all missionary activities and centralizing information on foreign lands.[26] The new Congregation had thus taken upon itself an enormous task, lightened to some extent by their good fortune in having the active and efficient guidance of Francesco Ingoli, Propaganda's first secretary.[27] On the global chessboard on which Propaganda was operating,[28] England was one of its most difficult problems. After the break with Rome, the English authorities had practically destroyed the Catholic hierarchy within their own dominions. They had not, however, managed to eliminate observants totally from the kingdom, and secular and regular priests continued to operate secretly. On the death of Cardinal William Allen (1594), Rome had preferred to avoid the creation of a bishop and instead appointed an archpriest, George Blackwell (1598–1608), who was supported by the Jesuits. Blackwell was subsequently replaced by George Birkhead (1608–14), who was followed by William Harrison (1615–21). The archpriest regime came in for severe criticism, especially from the seculars, one of whose chief representatives, William Bishop, appointed bishop *in partibus* of Chalcedon, finally arrived in England on 1 August 1623. Bishop died soon after (16 April 1624), and the problem of the succession again presented itself.[29] As a territory governed by Protestants, England was considered as much in need of missionary activity as a country in Africa or Asia. It thus came under the jurisdiction of Propaganda, which was responsible for the state of the Catholic religion in the kingdom. Any direct (and unofficial) source of information on the situation in England was therefore bound to be of interest to Propaganda, which lost no time in accepting and furthering a relationship which Stock had offered on his own accord.

It is difficult today not to associate Newfoundland's rugged natural beauty with images of foggy skies and frozen waters. Four centuries ago, although at the time that America was discovered[30] Portuguese, Spanish, Basque, French, and English fishing-boats made it their favoured objective, no one, as far as we know, had ever passed a winter there, and reports about the island were unconditional in its praise.[31] It was not until 1610 that serious attempts were made to establish a colony there. On 2/12 May 1610, James I granted the Company of Adventurers and Planters of the City of London and Bristol a concession for the whole island of Newfoundland. That same year Captain John Guy, with thirty-nine settlers, set off to found the company's first colony at Cuper's Cove, today Cupid's Cove. The colony was something of a disappointment, and between 1616 and 1621 the company alienated five portions of its territory, four to individuals and one to a group of people.

The first concession was granted to the Welshman William Vaughan, who in 1616 received the portion of the Avalon peninsula which lies to the south of Caplin Bay and Placentia Bay and included the ports of Ferryland, Fermeuse and Renews. Vaughan's first settlers went out in 1617, with Captain Richard Whitbourne as their commander. The colony probably did not last beyond 1619, and it was certainly no longer in existence by 1625. The Bristol and London associates of the Company of Adventurers split, giving rise to the colony of Bristol's Hope at Conception Bay. The new colony was established no later than 1618, with its main quarters at Harbour Grace. The venture went well, and the colony was still in existence in 1631. The Company's third concession was granted to Henry Cary, Viscount Falkland, who obtained a vast stretch of land situated between the latitudes of Penguin Island and Trinity Bay in 1620. At the same time, Falkland had obtained from Vaughan a narrow stretch of land reaching from the east coast of the Avalon peninsula to Placentia Bay. Its northern border was a place midway between Ferryland and Aquaforte; its southern, the port of Renews. Sir Francis Tanfield was appointed governor of the Falkland's colony, and he took possession in 1623. It too was to undergo some difficulties and definitely ceased to exist in 1628, although it was probably still active in 1625–26. The fourth concession will be dealt with below. The fifth was granted to Sir William Alexander, who bought an extensive stretch of land on the south coast from the company in 1621. The venture ended before it had begun, and Alexander turned his interest to the North American mainland and to his plan to found a New Scotland.[32]

Vaughan allotted the fourth concession to George Calvert in 1620. It consisted of a piece of land whose main settlement was to be Ferryland,[33] bordering Falkland's territory on the south and extending north from some point between Aquaforte and Fermeuse up to Caplin Bay.[34] Calvert was not new to colonial enterprises. In 1609 he had invested in the Virginia Company of London. A few years later he had become member and an investor in the East India Company. In 1622, after his agreement with Vaughan, he became a member of the New England Company, taking up silk trading at the same time.[35] Earlier in 1619 he had procured lands in Ireland, though he had since done little with them.[36] Calvert's first settlers landed at Ferryland on 4/14 August 1621 under the guidance of Captain Edward Wynne. The first two winters went so well for the community that Calvert decided on a thorough commitment.[37] On 31 December 1622/10 January 1623 he obtained in concession from James I nothing less than the whole of Newfoundland.[38] No doubt because it was in conflict with the original concession granted to the Company of Adventurers, this grant was soon quite reasonably reduced to the territory of the Avalon peninsula.[39] Nothing more is recorded about Ferryland or the settlers until the beginning of 1625, when Calvert decided to go there in person.

Until at least 1624, Simon Stock had probably never heard of Avalon or Newfoundland, and America was far from his mind. The presence of the Jesuit Robert Persons as rector of the English College in Rome (1597–1610) would not have done much to awaken Stock's interest in the New World. When Stock studied there from 1606 to 1610, Persons was no longer concerned with the idea of Catholic expansion in America and showed only a lukewarm interest in the possibility of converting the Indians.[40] Thus, mentions of America in Stock's books are always stereotyped, more a matter of literary convention than of any real sensitivity towards the horizons of the New World.[41] Until his meeting with Calvert, then, Stock was only one of the many members of the Catholic clergy fighting to withstand the perils of religious persecution in England while following their vocations as missionaries as best they could. Stock had been more fortunate than many in obtaining the protection of the Spanish Embassy, through whose channels he met Calvert. Together, politician and missionary turned their eyes to the other side of the Atlantic Ocean, the possibility of a Catholic mission in Avalon taking shape before their eyes.

In his long letter of 15 November 1624 to Propaganda, Stock no longer confined himself to the project of the novitiate. This time there was something new, something which would give prestige to his missionary activity in the eyes of the Roman officials:

> I have gained for Our Lord, by His Grace, two councillors of the King's Privy Council, the most intelligent and sufficient men that are of the Royal Council. And not since the time of the Queen Mary, which is now some sixty years, has other councillor been gained but these two. And most religious men are they, and live beneath our government.[42]

Stock had managed, probably thanks to his acquaintances in Spanish circles, to reach the highest ranks of the Privy Council and to convert two councillors. Nothing can be known with certainty about the identity of the first, though I am inclined to believe it was James, Marquis Hamilton. The question is, however, of little importance, since this councillor disappeared from Stock's life as rapidly as he had appeared in it and is never mentioned, even incidentally, in the whole of his correspondence.[43]

The second councillor can be identified without the slightest doubt as George Calvert,[44] soon to be named Baron Baltimore of Baltimore, secretary of state and a member of the Privy Council since 1619.[45] After a slow but steady rise to political power within the ranks of the London bureaucracy, steadfastly loyal to the king, Calvert was going through a period of serious difficulty. The negotiations for the Spanish marriage had fallen through and with them the political strategy that Calvert had backed. His fortunes at court had thus suffered a considerable setback. Furthermore, the new rising star of English politics, George Villiers, Duke of Buckingham, was against him.

Disillusioned and bitter with this course of events, Calvert resigned within a few months from his post as secretary of state, declared himself a Catholic, withdrew from the Privy Council, and started to devote himself exclusively to his lands in Ireland and the New World. What relation is there between one dramatic event and the other? In what sort of time span did they occur, and in what succession? Since Stock's correspondence furnishes new elements to help complete the picture and since Calvert's and Stock's interest in Newfoundland is directly related to these events, I shall devote some space to the more obscure points.

Rumours of Calvert's forthcoming resignation from his post as secretary of state were circulating at the beginning of 1624.[46] It seems likely that he had already resigned by 8/18 January 1624/1625, when John Coke is mentioned as his successor.[47] Albertus Morton, Calvert's actual successor, was sworn in as the new secretary on 9/19 February.[48] On 12/22 February, Calvert handed over the seals to Morton, in exchange for £3,000 and the promise of a barony in Ireland.[49] On 16/26 February, in recompense for past services, James I appointed Calvert Baron Baltimore of Baltimore, in County Longford, Ireland.[50] The king's promise to keep him on as member of the Privy Council[51] was not to be maintained by his successor, Charles I, to whom Lord Baltimore refused to swear loyalty.[52]

What relation is there between Calvert's resignation and his conversion to Catholicism? George Cottington, a servant of Lord Baltimore was the only one to suggest (in 1628) a direct link between the two, affirming that his conversion was under way long before it was made public.[53] As we have seen, Stock took credit for this conversion,. If this is true, Calvert must have been converted between 30 August (the date of Stock's previous letter) and 15 November 1624 (when Stock informed Propaganda), since it is unlikely that he would have delayed in passing on such an important piece of news to his new protectors in Rome.[54] The earliest rumours about Calvert's conversion began to circulate at the end of February 1625, that is, some weeks after his resignation, and it was attributed to the influence of the Jesuit Tobie Matthew.[55] Subsequently, another contemporary of Calvert's, Godfrey Goodman, claimed it was the result of the influence of the Spanish ambassador, Count Gondomar, and of Thomas Arundell, Baron Arundell of Wardour, whose daughter Anne later married Calvert's son Cecil.[56] By April 1625 Calvert was defined as "a professed papist,"[57] and from that moment on there were no doubts about his religious convictions.

Personally I am inclined to reject Cottington's statement (written some years after the events he described), in favour of historian John D. Krugler's interpretation. Krugler argues convincingly that Calvert did not resign because of his conversion to Catholicism, but inversely that it was precisely the political disappointment which caused his resignation that led him to return to the Catholicism of his childhood.[58] Stock's letter to Propaganda of 15 November 1624 both affords a precise date for Calvert's conversion (supposing it possible to date precisely a spiritual event of this nature) and gives indirect support for Krugler's interpretation. Had it been a case of cause and effect, however, Stock would have been the first to mention it and to attribute this, too, to his credit. As it is, Calvert's resignation is never mentioned by Stock, not even in letters written after the event. He obviously considered it of little relevance to Calvert's spiritual life. Indirectly, these conclusions are reinforced by various factors surrounding the choice of the name Avalon, as will be seen in the following chapter.

### CHAPTER THREE

# Sir Arthur Aston, Adventurer, Agrees to Embark for Newfoundland, 1625

Having resigned as secretary of state, George Calvert, now Lord Baltimore, immediately set about preparing for his departure for Newfoundland. In a letter to the Sacred Congregation "de Propaganda Fide" of 8 February 1625, Simon Stock was the first to give news of it. Since the English nobleman wanted "to take with him two or three religious to sow the Holy Faith in his land," Stock asked Propaganda to help him in his noble purpose because there were only three Discalced Carmelites in England at the time.[1] The departure was to take place in the spring, and some fifteen or twenty Catholics were to accompany Lord Baltimore.[2] On 15/25 March Baltimore wrote to John Coke, commissary for the Navy, demanding the restitution of his two ships, the *Jonathan* and the *Peter Bonadventure*, the latter of which was being used for cattle transportation. Requisitioned by the government when war with Spain seemed imminent, they were now needed for the journey to Newfoundland.[3] On 17/27 March George Villiers, Duke of Buckingham, replied. The two ships would be returned, he stated, but they were required to bring back to England, within ten days of their arrival in Newfoundland, a cargo-load of fish for the use of the British Navy.[4]

Although Stock had known Lord Baltimore for at least three to five months,[5] he seems to have known nothing of his friend's plans until the beginning of 1625 at the earliest.[6] It is quite possible that Lord Baltimore had simply never mentioned it before, particularly considering the political crisis he was involved in at that time, which must have made Avalon and Newfoundland seem remote, to say the least. On the other hand, Stock may have heard something of the matter, but given it no thought until the nobleman's conversion gave the colony an interest it could not have for him while Avalon was protestant.[7]

However, Stock's statement that he himself had a part in choosing the name Avalon and that he had done so because of its Catholic connotations hardly tallies with the facts reported above:

> The land of this gentleman was unknown in former times and has had no name until now, when *we* [*italics added*] have called it Avalon, [since] thus was named the land where Saint Joseph of Arimathea first preached the Faith of Our Lord Jesus Christ in Britain.[8]

Although the details of the legend varied, in Stock's time Avalon was the name given to the site of St. Joseph of Arimathea's missionary activities, where subsequently the abbey of Glastonbury, in Somerset, was built—a place still considered the cradle of English Christianity.[9] The meaning that Stock attributed to Avalon is confirmed by a work of 1665[10] and in a document belonging to the Calvert family drawn up around 1670.[11] There is no doubt that this is the correct interpretation. If, however, Stock is to be taken literally, then both his acquaintanceship with Calvert and the latter's conversion must predate 1622, when the name Avalon first began to be used publicly.[12] This seems most unlikely, since Stock would certainly have mentioned it to the Roman authorities without waiting almost two years. We must infer that, in the matter of the choice of the name Avalon, Stock ably exploited the situation in order to appear in a good light before Propaganda. Hence his expression is vague, and he cleverly uses an ambiguous plural ("we have called it Avalon"). Furthermore, as historian Raymond J. Lahey points out, the name Avalon had generically Christian, rather than primarily Catholic, connotations. Lord Baltimore could just as reasonably have chosen it before his conversion to Catholicism.[13]

Lord Baltimore's enthusiasm for Avalon was contagious, and once Stock knew of the former secretary of state's plans, he kept Propaganda constantly informed. In the first two letters in which he spoke of Avalon (8 February and 2 March 1625), even his plan for a novitiate in Saint-Omer paled in significance. Describing Lord Baltimore's colony, Stock defined it as an island some three weeks's distance from England, "three degrees nearer to the meridian than England," approximately as large as "England" without Wales and Scotland, and not known "in former times." A "most fertile" island, of a "temperate air," with "most excellent sea-ports" where "an abundance of divers sorts of vessels" docked for the fish to be found there, "beyond all manner abundant." Moreover, the island was inhabited, Stock claimed, by natives ("gentiles") and "English heretics," who had gone to live there "some three or four years since."[14] It must be remembered that Stock had known nothing of America until a few weeks before and had probably never heard of Avalon. Suddenly information, imagination, hopes, and sensations united to create in his mind a notion that he called Avalon. What, then, were the sources of his first description?

While much of the information forwarded to Propaganda was readily available to everyone (the land, climate, fishing, and distance from England), Stock apparently knew none of the many published works dealing with Newfoundland and with the various American colonies. Leaving aside works which had appeared in the sixteenth century,[15] a whole new series of books on Newfoundland had begun to appear in the early 1620s. John Mason, John Guy's successor as governor of Cuper's Cove from 1616 to 1620, published his *Briefe Discourse of the New-found-land* in Edinburgh in 1620.[16] In the same year, Captain Richard Whitbourne, governor of William Vaughan's colony at Renews from 1618 to 1620 and an important figure in Newfoundland's history, published a *Discourse and Discovery of New-Found-Land*, the second edition of which appeared in 1622, together with another of his works, *Discourse Containing a Loving Invitation*.[17] In the meantime, the letters of Edward Wynne, Lord Baltimore's first governor, had appeared in print in 1621 and 1622,[18] some also being printed in the appendix to the second edition of Whitbourne's *Discourse and Discovery*. Then in 1623 a certain T.C., still unidentified, published in Dublin a *Short Discourse of the New-Found-Land*.[19] In 1624 William Alexander, who was later to abandon his project of colonizing Newfoundland, published in London his *Encouragement to Colonies*.[20] And in the same year the Reverend Richard Eburne produced his *Plain Pathway to Plantations*.[21] None of these use Stock's image to define the size of Newfoundland, which was more commonly compared to Ireland.[22] No one identified the longitude of Newfoundland as being "three degrees nearer to the meridian than England."[23]

Stock's most probable source of information was Lord Baltimore's circle, and most likely Lord Baltimore himself.[24] A clear indication of this is Stock's mention of the "English heretics," an unequivocal reference to Wynne's colony in Ferryland, founded in 1621. Strangely, however, Stock did not realize that Avalon was only part of the island of Newfoundland, as is evident when he mentions Wynne's men as the only inhabitants other than the natives at a time when other English settlements were already active. Newfoundland, as will be seen presently, was still not considered another colony, nor was it explicitly stated that the "island" of Avalon formed part of the American continent.[25] Whether this was a result of Lord Baltimore's inaccuracy or Stock's confused ideas is not known. Supposing it to be the latter, the explanation for such elementary mistakes is to be found in Stock's sudden involvement in a whole world of which, up till that moment, he had known absolutely nothing.

Although Lord Baltimore several times expressed his intention of leaving for Newfoundland, a departure that year proved impossible. In the end, possibly on account of the flurry of events in which he found himself, he was obliged to settle for Ireland. Stock put this down to the fact that the missionaries he had requested from Propaganda had not arrived. He hoped that these would be forthcoming by the following year.[26] On 26 April/6 May 1625 Lord Baltimore was granted permission to go to Ireland with his family.[27] He left between 24 and 31 May,[28] taking with him a warm letter of recommendation from the king to his lord deputy in Ireland, Henry Cary, Viscount Falkland[29]—the same Falkland who had territorial interests in Newfoundland. According to Stock, Lord Baltimore's intention was to remain in Ireland until the following Spring.[30] In fact, Baltimore was not to leave the country other than on brief visits to England in 1626 and 1627, until his journey to Newfoundland in 1627.[31]

Prior to leaving London for good, however, Lord Baltimore managed to settle the question of a successor to his former governor. Wynne had returned some months previously,[32] and at first Lord Baltimore had thought of taking his place himself. Instead, an agreement of sorts was reached with Sir Arthur Aston. By 5/15 April 1625 Aston's permit to depart for Avalon was available.[33] Apparently Aston's condition for accepting the post as governor and spending the 1625–26 winter there was that he should first visit the island in person.[34] His departure for Ferryland was simultaneous with Lord Baltimore's for Ireland, between 24 and 31 May 1625.[35]

Until that moment Sir Arthur Aston (?–1627), father of the more famous Sir Arthur Aston (?–1649), general to Charles I, had led the life of an adventurer. Knighted on 15/25 July 1604,[36] he had obtained a licence on 23 August/2 September 1604 to "use and sell certain woods used in dyeing."[37] On 23 April/3 May 1621 he had assumed command of eight thousand English volunteers enlisted by the Polish ambassador, Osalinskie, Count Palatine of Sindomerskie, to fight against the Grand Duke Michail Fyodorovich Romanov.[38] At the request of the Russian ambassador, Isaac Sinoinwich Pogozue, on 29 March/8 April 1622, he had been ordered to return to England to receive his just punishment.[39] Imprisoned on 6/16 June 1622,[40] he was forbidden to take arms against Romanov,[41] and by 16/26 June he had already been set free.[42] Nothing more is heard of him until the Avalon assignment.[43]

Lord Baltimore and Aston obviously grew to be on excellent terms, and Stock, who seems never to have met Aston before March 1625,[44] spent considerable time in the company of Avalon's future governor. By 19 May Stock was already referring to him as "a Catholic knight and dear friend, who for many years has fought in the wars against

Turks and infidels."[45] Aston too, Stock underlined in his letter to Propaganda, shared their hope that the Congregation would favour them by
sending missionaries for the new colony.[46]

Although Lord Baltimore had decided not to go to Newfoundland
himself, the Avalon venture seemed to be taking concrete shape with
Aston's departure. Once he had founded the colony, Wynne's administration passed off uneventfully, without any undue interest being paid
to it. The relation now established between the colony and the Catholic
religion and Rome, however, gave this project an importance which
distinguished it from others of a similar kind. This, at least, was Stock's
opinion, and the idea of a Catholic colony rapidly began to replace the
far less appealing project of the novitiate in Saint-Omer, already
fraught with difficulties, in his affections.

Stock was certainly not the only one to grasp the religious implications of European expansion in America and the overseas world in
general. After a brief pause in the late sixteenth century, Protestants[47]
and Catholics[48] alike had once again and with renewed vigour set about
laying their hands on the world at large, competing for a victory on
which their very survival seemed to depend.

Richard Hakluyt was a man of the church, and for him the importance
of English expansion was in direct proportion to its capacity for extending the divine plan for the universe over the whole world.[49] Between 1620
and 1623 no fewer than three editions of Whitbourne's *Discourse and
Discovery* were published "by Authority"[50] of the Privy Council (of
which both Lord Baltimore and Falkland were members), a means of
publication which guaranteed extensive distribution throughout all the
English parishes.[51] Eburne, the author of one of the most interesting,
albeit the least known, books on the colonization of Newfoundland, was
vicar of the parish of Henstridge, in Somerset.[52] And precisely in 1625,
Samuel Purchas, also a man of the church, published his four weighty
volumes intended as a sequel to Hakluyt's works.[53]

If, then, Protestant expansion seemed to be going from strength to
strength in the early seventeenth century, as regards its amount and
quality, Catholic expansion, represented primarily by Spain and Portugal, had been in sharp decline, concerned above all with maintaining
acquired positions rather than gaining others. After his optimism of a
few years before ("we see by experience, that the losse which the [Cath-
olic] Church hath in England, and some corners of the earth, is more
than restored in *Asia & America*"),[54] Stock was beginning to understand that the situation was in fact far more serious.

The Spanish nobleman Juan Luis Arias thus expressed his concern
at Protestant expansion in the New World:

> English and Dutch heretics, instigated by the devil . . . are sowing

---

... the terrible poison of their apostasy ... before we are able to spread the divine light of the Gospel, as they do even now in that vast continent ... where lie the provinces of Florida, to advance thence into New Spain and New Mexico, the kingdom of Quivira, the Californias, and other most vast provinces. As so have they [now] colonized Virginia ... and in like manner fortified and colonized the Bermudas, sowing with great zeal and speed the infernal poison of their heresy, infesting thus those millions and millions of good people who dwell in these kingdoms. Through Virginia they can rapidly penetrate to the interior, with their ardent desire to deprive the Catholic Church of that inestimable treasure of an infinite number of souls. . . . Before the Catholic Church can arrive with that preaching of the Gospel which is our duty, they will have attracted to themselves [and] infested with the depravation of their apostasy that innumerable multitude of gentiles who dwell in those provinces, that are more vast than all of Europe.[55]

It is not certain that Stock knew of Arias's pamphlet, though it is not unlikely, considering his contacts at the Spanish Embassy. Certainly, his own gloomy forebodings had much in common with those of Arias. It was a race against time for both Protestants[56] and Catholics. At stake were the souls of multitudes of idolaters who inhabited lands still unknown. "It is of great importance to the Holy Church and to Christianity that [Avalon] be inhabited not by heretics but by Catholic Christians,"[57] he affirmed; otherwise all the inhabitants "will become heretics, to the great detriment of the Holy Church."[58] By May 1625, the danger seemed to him even more pressing: "The *English heretics have sown* their heresy in all the northern parts of America, in Virginia, Bermuda, New England, New Scotland,"[59] to which list Newfoundland was soon added.[60] All were places which were soon to be lost completely to the Catholics, just as the "most fertile and populated islands close to England,[61] that is, the islands of Man, Wight, Jersey and Guernsey had been lost in recent times.[62] In Virginia, Stock warned, the English had actually managed to establish an archbishopric,[63] and the king had issued an edict which announced the English intention "of propagating heresy in the western parts of America."[64]

The vision of the advance of Protestantism was catastrophic. At the end of May, Stock added another decisive note to his already gloomy picture. He reminded Propaganda that the danger was not only the loss of America, but also the infestation "with heresy of Japan, China, the Philippines and the East Indies, so near are they and of such easy journey and passage."[65] This, of course, is the theme, new to Stock but only too well-known to European colonists and explorers, of the search for the Northwest Passage, which would render America a bridge-head to Asia. On this point Stock would have considerably more to say in the near future.

All letters received by Propaganda were accurately catalogued. Each letter was summarized by the Congregation's clerks, then passed on to a cardinal, whose duty it was to refer it to one of the general meetings of the cardinals, the General Congregations, which took place periodically and often in the presence of the pope. Here decisions were taken on the questions raised and the requests contained in every single letter. The gist of the reply was then elaborated.[66] Stock's letters of the first five months of 1625, in which he first mentions Avalon, were received and discussed with great interest. Each one was processed within an average of forty-seven days from the date on which it was sent—a reasonably short time, all things considered.[67] If the Congregation's summaries of Stock's earlier letters had been only bureaucratic exercises, those of the letters mentioning the Avalon enterprise reveal a tone of interest which was completely new.

On 22 March 1625, when Stock's first letter concerning Avalon was discussed, Propaganda's secretary, Francesco Ingoli, pointed out the danger of the English heretics "pervert[ing] those peoples, who are gentiles."[68] Stock's letter was read out in the pope's presence and was heard "with particular interest on the part of His Holiness and the cardinals."[69] They decided to put pressure on the superiors of the Order of the Discalced Carmelites to send missionaries. Should this prove impracticable, the undertaking was still so important that regulars of another order should be dispatched. These were to be sent first to Stock, "that he might instruct them."[70] Obviously, Propaganda officials too had realized that the question of the Avalon mission went beyond the usual internal squabbles of a single religious order and required precisely the kind of co-ordinating intervention, above and beyond individual orders, which they recognized as the Congregation's chief function. Cardinal Giovanni Garcia Millini, who had reported on Stock's letter of 8 February 1625,[71] was entrusted with the matter of the Avalon mission, which charge he was to execute "with the efficiency owing to so important a negotiation."[72] However, Millini was chosen more because of his role as Protector of the Discalced Carmelites than for any particular experience of colonial matters.[73]

Propaganda immediately contacted the Discalced Carmelites. Their reply was sufficiently satisfactory for the Congregation to inform Stock as soon as 5 July 1625 of certain "labourers for Avalon," whose arrival in London was imminent, if they had not already joined Stock. Expressing "disgust" with the "great diligence with which the English sought to pervert the gentiles of those parts of North America," Propaganda advised Stock that should the new missionaries arrive too late to join the Avalon expedition, "he should not miss any extraordinary occasion that might present itself for their departure" and send them "thither to bear fruits."[74] As we shall see further on, two confrères of Stock's, Bede of the Blessed Sacrament and Elias of Jesus, did appear in London during the summer of 1625. Aston had already left for Newfoundland some weeks previously, but even more to the point, neither Bede nor Elias had the least intention of going to America; they were destined for the English mission.

How much did Propaganda officials know about the New World when they began to receive Stock's letters dealing with Avalon and America? Their knowledge of Spanish and Portuguese territories was probably reasonably good. Of the rest, of the recent struggles of the English and French to get for themselves a slice of America, they knew practically nothing. In fact, when the cardinals of Propaganda had first met to apportion the various parts of the globe, according to personal inclination or specific competency, North America was completely ignored, no one claiming or mentioning it.[75] While such ignorance seems surprising 132 years after the discovery of America, it is essential to bear in mind the far greater importance Propaganda placed on not just South America and the West Indies, but also on places like the Middle East, China, the East Indies, and the Slav countries. To those areas, then and for some two centuries after, the majority of Propaganda's attention, manpower, and general resources continued to be directed. In addition, for more than half a century the idea of expansion in America had been of little interest in Europe generally, and it was only beginning to be reconsidered in the early seventeenth century.

Almost three years after the establishment of Propaganda, however, someone realized that a major part of the world was being ignored. At this point Ingoli asked for a precise and detailed report from the Franciscan Recollet Gregorio Bolìvar, a missionary with twenty years' experience in South America with whom Propaganda was already in contact.[76] Bolìvar had never been to North America, but he sent a report rich in interesting details in reply to the request for information regarding the "position of Virginia and surrounding territory which the English Lutherans have settled" and where they had begun "to sow the faith of their pestilential sect among those poor and unsophisticated Indian barbarians." Virginia, the report affirmed, lay "between New France directly to the north ... and the territory of Florida which borders upon it from the south to the north-west, [having] in its interior ... an impressive cordillera or chain of stupendous mountains, snow-covered the whole year and of a harsh impenetrability." Virginia was defined as "very temperate" and "greatly inhabited by a barbarous people ... not very white, but rather of a brown colour," who possessed a great facility in "learning all that is taught to them."[77]

Bolìvar's report reached Propaganda at the same time as Stock's information on North America. In this way Stock's letters about America, and particularly Avalon, served a double purpose. They provided an opportunity of realizing a missionary project which, possibly because it was new and almost entirely outside the hegemony of the religious orders, seemed precisely the type of project for which the recently founded Congregation was looking. It was also the simplest and most effortless way to extend and verify their information on the New World.

This being the case, whatever was erroneous at the source (Stock) would inevitably remain so for the officials in Rome, there existing no intermediate or more sophisticated filter for the information. Thus Propaganda, like Stock, defined Avalon an island,[78] failed to identify it with Newfoundland,[79] and did not connect it geographically with America. Probably both Stock and his Roman protectors envisaged an island in the Atlantic, like Bermuda, for example, which itself had only recently been discovered.[80]

One certain fact is that Aston's departure for Newfoundland at the end of May 1625 finally concluded the organizational phase of the project and led to its realization. With Lord Baltimore's conversion and his friendship with Stock, one of the many colonial ventures had become unique because of its religious implications. In addition, there now existed in Rome an audience which was eagerly awaiting news of the colony and the settlers' impressions of that first summer.

### CHAPTER FOUR

# Simon Stock Learns About The New World, 1625

The whole of the summer of 1625 passed without further correspondence between Simon Stock and the Sacred Congregation "de Propaganda Fide."[1] George Calvert, Baron Baltimore, was in Ireland; Sir Arthur Aston, in Newfoundland, having replaced Edward Wynne as governor of Avalon. The return of "a number of those Catholics,"[2] that is, some of those who had accompanied Aston to Avalon at the end of May, was expected by October 1625. Before then it was not possible to have any information whatsoever about the outcome of the expedition and the settlers' first impressions. It was a good time for Stock to begin to document and verify his information concerning Lord Baltimore's colony. Although in September 1625 he still seemed to have read none of the works available on Newfoundland, during that summer he managed to connect Avalon with North America, possibly through private conversation. The next step had been to lay his hands on a map of America.

The map Stock consulted so avidly and from which he imbibed his first notions of America (apart from the impressions he received from those involved in the enterprise) is called "Americae Pars Borealis, Florida, Baccalaos, Canada, Corterealis," the work of the Flemish geographer, Cornelis de Jode. Published in Antwerp in 1583, it was inserted into the atlas published the same year by Cornelis's father, Gerard de Jode.[3] Although the information given was rather out of date, and some of it simply fantastical, the quality of the drawings, the many place names, and the numerous captions and explanations devoted to the Indian populations made it an attractive and easy-to-consult document. Stock never mentions it explicitly, but an analysis of the data supplied to Propaganda shows without doubt that Cornelis de Jode's map was his source.

A good portion of Stock's letter of 13 September to Propaganda, the first after the summer, is dedicated to North America and its original inhabitants, rather than to Avalon in particular. The English, Stock explains on the authority of Cornelis de Jode, "hold the best part of America," corresponding to 32° to 45° North latitude, or, on de Jode's map, to the area defined to the south by the northern border of Florida and to the north by the southern border of "Norombega." The area, Stock asserts, has an excellent climate, "equal to that of Italy and Spain" and "most rich in all things except gold and silver"—rich, that is, as Propaganda's secretary, Francesco Ingoli, inferred, "because of the fertility of the soil."[4]

One of the most interesting features of Cornelis de Jode's map is the great variety of Indian populations mentioned, either by name alone or with an explanatory note. Almost all the tribes listed belong to the Spanish zones, which occupy the largest portion of the map. From the various captions in which the Indians are described in far from flattering terms,[5] Stock is careful to choose only the completely favourable comments, which also happened to refer to the widest geographical area. Stock states in fact that the Indians

> who dwell between Florida and the Land of Bacalaos are all called Canadians, although [they are] of different nations, as the Mechelaga, the Hongueda, the Corterealis, and [are] of an excellently benign and human disposition.[6]

In this area, Stock relates, the gospel "has to this time never been preached." Nevertheless, the conversion of the natives would be relatively simple both because of their "mild disposition" and because, once converted, they in turn would become "excellent priests and religious."[7]

The rendition of Newfoundland did not escape Cornelis de Jode's considerable inaccuracy. The island is divided into two portions: the northern part is not named, while the southern is given its usual name "Ter[ra] de Bacalao." The place name "Avalon" naturally does not appear since it is of a later date than the map.[8] The map's existing data, however, together with information he had gathered over the summer, was enough to provide a general picture of the country's geography, from which Stock was finally able to connect the Land of Bacalaos with Newfoundland and, simultaneously, Newfoundland with Avalon. Of Avalon (this was the only term Stock was ever to use), he explains that lies "midway between England and Virginia,"[9] and that, once "the Faith is spread to Avalon," it will be possible "with greater ease" to extend it to Virginia, New England, New Scotland, and "amongst the Canadians."[10]

In the same letter of 13 September Stock refers to his having met a

"Catholic pilot,"[11] as he vaguely identifies him. From the wealth of particulars given later,[12] it transpires that this pilot not only contributed vastly to Stock's knowledge of America, but that he was also responsible for an important extension of the original design, namely, the "passage ... to China," which the pilot claimed to have opened himself, navigating "his ship ... along rivers from one part to the other." With such an opening, the pilot pointed out, it would be possible to journey from England to China in four months. In this way, Stock concludes, it would be possible "to have the Holy Church united," which explained the importance of the matter.[13]

Gerard de Jode's atlas could not but confirm for Stock the possibility of this passage. In fact, on the map of the world, America is depicted as being surmounted by a long, wide water-course running from between 70° and 80° North latitude into the Pacific Ocean.[14] In addition, the whole North American continent is shown as being crossed by a dense network of rivers, the St. Lawrence standing out particularly. Although they all originate in a mountain-chain in the centre of the continent, by which they are also divided, it was feasible to imagine that a passage existed between the St. Lawrence and one of the many rivers running into the "Golfo Vermeio,"[15] that is, the Gulf of California.

Stock's energies were divided that summer. On the one hand, he was busy obtaining more accurate knowledge of America and Avalon while he was waiting for more direct information from the settlers themselves. On the other, he was forced to start coming to terms with the new situation among his confrères in England. As Propaganda had announced,[16] in the summer of 1625[17] two Discalced Carmelites had arrived, Bede of the Blessed Sacrament, who replaced Eliseus of St. Michael as provincial vicar,[18] and Elias of Jesus,[19] raising the order's numbers in the country from three to five.[20] To Stock's bitter disappointment, it was immediately clear that the order had met his request only in part, since neither of them was destined for the mission in Avalon. To make matters worse, Elias had arrived without the necessary faculties (spiritual powers),[21] and he was soon quickly incapacitated by illness.[22]

Although it had been Stock himself who had sent Bede to study under the Discalced Carmelites in Brussels several years earlier,[23] his relations with the new provincial vicar were strained from the moment of his arrival. While in 1624 Bede was his junior in years and in the order, Stock had actually recommended Bede for the post as provincial vicar of the English mission.[24] But one letter from Bede had sufficed to make him change his mind.[25] Stock accused Bede of being ignorant, less than intelligent, and totally inexpert regarding the missions.[26] When Bede was eventually imprisoned by the English authorities, Stock was ready with the accusation that not only was Bede himself to blame for his imprisonment, but that his behaviour had also imperilled others of their confrères.[27] His indignation was so great that he refused to visit Bede in prison.[28] For his part, Bede was not slow to reply with violent criticism of Stock,[29] implicitly if not openly accusing him of having betrayed the order in his "great correspondence" with Propaganda.[30]

The vicious quarrel between Stock and Bede was not without repercussions for the Avalon project. Although the letters Stock sent to the order in 1625 are no longer extant, it can be presumed that he informed his superiors of his intention to plant a mission in Avalon simultaneously with his correspondence with Propaganda.[31] Bede must thus have known of the project prior to his arrival in England. In his first known letter from London, he wrote to their general, Paolo Simone di Gesù e Maria, that he was "every day . . . in greater anxiety . . . to know Your Reverence's resolve concerning the island of father brother Simon."[32] From Bede's letters it is possible to infer that the order's Roman offices, having wavered for some time (probably also as a result of pressure from Propaganda), finally decided to suggest Elias to Bede as candidate for the mission, meanwhile asking the new provincial vicar to verify Stock's enthusiastic descriptions.[33]

Bede did not trouble to hide his dislike of Stock or Stock's project, and after an initial, rather non-committal letter,[34] he set about his task energetically. He sent his superiors an ample and detailed report on North America, firmly rejecting Stock's whole proposal. At the same time he was careful to provide ammunition with which to meet the insistent requests Propaganda forwarded to the order through Cardinal Giovanni Garcia Millini.

What Bede defined as a "brief . . . report regarding the English plantations in Virginia and nearby regions" begins by stating that the first English colony was established in 1603 [sic] in Virginia, "a province bordering on the lands of Florida on its eastern side." The discovery of Bermuda followed, "made by chance on the wrecking of a ship." Having made further discoveries "towards that land which is called the Land of Labrador," the English founded New England, formerly called 'Norumbega," then "New France" by the French, and "New England and New Scotland" by the English, while the "natural populace," that is, the Indians, referred to it as "Canada." Going on to what "a pilot coming from those parts" had told him, the English had founded three colonies in New England. "[T]he first and largest possesses around 50 habitations; of the other two, one possesses some 20 same, the other some 15." While the indigenous populations were barbarous devil-worshippers, the English settlers (generally "rich knights, gentlemen and citizens" of London who hoped for "great wealth" or "country-

dwellers" to whom "great possessions" had been promised) were Protestant to a man and always had a minister with them. What was more,
the English inhabitants, who were settled there "to cultivate the land,
fish, and others for the purpose of negotiating business with the indigenous populace," lived in wretched conditions. Even the fishermen who
went there every year in March or April for the cod-fishing returned
home in September "with no merchandise of the country than some
few animal pelts." In short, "the plantations, for those who live there,
are of such miserable poverty, that I heard it said of a wrong-doer, that
rather would he suffer to be hanged here in England than go to the
plantations of the Bermudas."

Stock's colony, then, was in this area, the overall picture of which
was less than reassuring. Bede's report did not mention Newfoundland,
and he did not seem to know the name Avalon. All the English provincial vicar could say was that the "island of mister Simon" seemed to be
the one of the three New England colonies which was composed of
fifteen "habitations." He did, however, know that "amongst those that
are concerned with these plantations 2 are Catholics, knights both, and
known of mister Simon," but he added that, in any case, the only
Catholics in the colony would be "some servants of these knights."
Moreover, not only were the knights not "absolute in seigniory," having to refer back to others (which indicated that they were not autono-
mous arbiters), but it was also not even certain that they intended to go
in person to their colonies. At the time of writing, both were at some
distance from England, one in Ireland, the other heavens knew where,
and to reach them was quite impossible.

Bede assured the order that he had put Stock's project to their confrères Eliseus and Elias and had done everything to persuade the latter
to depart. They had, however, both refused, giving as a reason their
reluctance to be "1,200 leagues [away], which is the distance from here
to there," in a land governed by heretics and without the least possibility of spiritual assistance. In their opinion, the project was "a matter of
much greater difficulty than mister Simon . . . believes," and their coun-
terproposal, which Bede immediately accepted, seemed at that point
the only one possible: "[T]his is a matter for mister Simon . . . since it is
he that has started it."[35]

It is not clear whether the report, or the Avalon project in general,
was ever discussed between Bede and Stock. Bede did not even know the
name Avalon, he believed Stock's colony to be in New England, and he
was unaware of one of the most important details of the whole enterprise—that the second knight, namely Aston, whose whereabouts he
did not know, had for some time been in fact in Avalon. On his part,
Stock could certainly have used many of the details Bede gave about

North America which he did not know. Obviously, any sort of communication between Stock and his confrères was by then impossible, even supposing it ever to have been otherwise.

Bede's report was not destined to remain an internal matter for the order; from the Roman offices of the Discalced Carmelites, it soon found its way to the desks of the officials of Propaganda. Writing to Propaganda, Stock underlined with a wealth of detail the difficult state of the English mission,[36] where the superiors jeopardized the missionaries' safety and efficiency by a wilful lack of moral and material support.[37] This was all the more serious at a time when anti-Catholic persecution was tangibly increasing and a number of priests had been imprisoned.[38] Although Propaganda, through Cardinal Ottavio Bandini, had "so often"[39] written to Stock "regarding the matter of the novitiate and the Avalon mission," "nothing has been done either for the one or for the other."[40] In Propaganda's default, Stock would consider himself obliged not only to give up the Avalon project entirely, but actually to leave England.[41] In the meantime, he wished to bring to Propaganda's attention that his faculties were about to expire.[42]

To speed Stock's request for the renewal of his faculties, Propaganda promptly sent it to the competent authority, the Sacred Congregation of the Holy Office.[43] Not long afterwards, however, they were obliged to reconsider their relations with Stock, up till then essentially positive, in the light of the negative reaction of his superiors. In December 1625, Propaganda was informed by the Discalced Carmelite general that the two missionaries destined for Avalon had been imprisoned in London.[44] At the same time, the Rome officials received an extract of the report on North America that Bede had prepared for the order, entitled "Report received from the Fathers of the Discalced Carmelites who are in England regarding the mission proposed to the Sacred Congregation by Father Simon Stock, of the same Order, in the country of Virginia, which is called New England, on the entreaty of two English Catholic knights."[45] Not long afterwards, probably around February 1626, the order forwarded to Propaganda a copy of another of Bede's letters, in which the Avalon project was further discussed.[46]

The order's editing of Bede's report not only altered its sense considerably, but also managed to make it nearly incomprehensible. In the extract sent to Propaganda all place names were omitted (Virginia, Florida, Bermuda, Labrador, Norumbega, New France, New England, New Scotland, Canada), together with all co-ordinates describing them. What was left was the date colonization began, the names of the English Discalced Carmelites, some information regarding the fishing, and the reasons for the English seeking their fortunes in America. The slant of the editing was certainly deliberate, as was the fact that the only data given in the extract concerned the "island of which mister Simon spoke," and all of them, as we have seen, were negative. Two factors came into play here—the natural jealousy of a religious order having to pass on its own information to the newly founded Congregation and, more important, their intention of demonstrating, beyond a shadow of doubt, the total futility of Stock's enterprise.

What were the effects of Bede's doctored report on Propaganda officials? Until then, they had had only Stock's letters and Gregorio Bolívar's report to go by. While the new information was too vague to induce a radical change in the Propaganda officials' convictions, it certainly could not have helped to strengthen them in any way.[47]

While his order had been essentially negative in everything, Stock had something real to offer—not only an enticing missionary project, which he had managed to associate with his name (and Propaganda had actually been founded to superintend projects of this nature), but also the prospect of the American opening which Propaganda had so far been denied.[48] The Congregation was particularly interested in the possibility of a Northwest Passage. An atlas had immediately been consulted on receiving Stock's letter,[49] but it had not provided the desired confirmation. Stock had thus been asked to furnish further details of his pilot friend's voyage and to give "the names of said rivers and every particular concerning afore-mentioned voyage," since

> the maps of that part of the world show two rivers, which, in their near-opposite courses, flow into opposite seas, but the passing in vessels from one to the other appears impossible since a wide stretch of land lies between the two.[50]

Practically all the maps of the late sixteenth and early seventeenth century assert the existence of a number of rivers crossing America which originated somewhere in the centre of the continent. Propaganda's zealous official most likely consulted the Italian edition of an atlas which was enjoying great success and numerous editions in several languages, the *Theatrum Orbis Terrarum* of Abraham Ortelius.[51] One of the rivers Propaganda referred to is undoubtedly the St. Lawrence.[52] The other, almost certainly the present-day Colorado, is called the "Rio Hermoso" and "Tiguas Rio" in the map of America,[53] while on the world map it is given no name.[54] Its estuary was shown in the "Mar Vermeio,"[55] today the Gulf of California.

At the same time, two letters were prepared for the nuncio in Spain, Giulio Sacchetti, bishop of Gravina, and the nuncio in Flanders, Giovanni Francesco Guidi di Bagno, archbishop of Patras.[56] Propaganda asked them whether they knew of the famous passage's recent discovery and pointed out its importance in terms of "missions in that kingdom [China]."[57] Needless to say, the two nuncios' replies left Propaganda none the wiser.[58]

Apart from the wealth of information it gave on America, Stock's continually expanding missionary project was particularly attractive to the officials of Propaganda since it happened to coincide perfectly with their own policies. They no longer saw Avalon as one of the many American colonies, but as a base which would serve as a bridge-head for the spiritual conquest of America and in turn provide an opening towards Asia. There was also the fact that, without knowing it, Stock had touched on one of the themes most dear to Francesco Ingoli, Propaganda's secretary—what will afterwards be defined as the autochthonous clergy.[59] Stock had described the American natives as being particularly docile and so willing to be converted that they wished themselves to become good priests and missionaries.[60]

At the same time as it received the extract of Bede's report on North America in December 1625, Propaganda also had a further letter from Stock. With so many difficulties and disappointments on all sides, hope was at least forthcoming from the source itself, namely, Ferryland. Via someone returning from Newfoundland, and in October (as foreseen),[61] Stock had received a letter from Aston, possibly addressed to Stock himself.[62] "[T]his knight, our dear friend," as Stock proudly defines him, sent "marvellous reports of the island, and of the wonderful abundance of fish," and was so satisfied with everything he had seen that he had no hesitation remaining in Avalon for the winter, accepting the post of governor which Stock claimed to have procured for him.[63] Aston's opinion of the natives was equally favourable—idolaters all, but "of a benign disposition," harmless to foreigners and, in any case, very few.[64]

This apparent success of the Aston's expedition served only to render more exasperating the disinterest and apathy of the order's superiors. While Rome lost precious time, Stock argued, its Protestant enemies went from strength to strength. In Virginia, for example, they had founded a college "to infest America with their heresy."[65] The inhabitants of Avalon would soon "all ... become pernicious heretics," Stock insisted, while many of "our Catholic friends" would settle there if only there were sufficient "members of the clergy to accompany them."[66]

By now Stock was not alone in believing that a decision had to be taken about Avalon. Both Propaganda and the order's Roman offices began to consider the question in detail. Having first thought of Elias of Jesus, the order's superiors then considered Bede's proposal and came to the conclusion that Stock himself was in fact the most suitable person to come to some agreement with the two knights and leave for

Avalon. Apart from any other considerations, this was a convenient way of resolving the dissent within the English mission, removing its only rebel. Thus, on 19 February 1626, the general wrote to Stock urging him to depart. He took care to make the decision appear not his but Propaganda's.[67] In the meantime, he had managed to convince the Congregation of the soundness of the idea, and on 17 March Propaganda decided to agree.[68] Some days later, they wrote to Stock as follows: "[T]he missionaries for Avalon having been imprisoned, and there being none other or your order that speaks the language, it is necessary for yourself to arrange to depart, together with the companion the father general will provide." His patent as missionary and the relative faculties would be provided by Propaganda itself. Even if nothing else should come of Stock's mission, it would at least provide "full and accurate information of that country and of what could be done to bring those gentiles within the Holy Faith.[69] With this knowledge, Propaganda considered there would have been no difficulty in then finding priests from other orders to send on the mission.[70]

Meanwhile, while Rome discussed the matter, Lord Baltimore's colony in Ferryland was passing its first and last winter under the guidance of Aston.[71]

### CHAPTER FIVE

# The Search for the Northwest Passage, 1626

To Simon Stock, the beginning of 1626 appeared particularly difficult. After Sir Arthur Aston's letter of October 1625,[1] nothing more had been heard of the Avalon colony, while George Calvert, Baron Baltimore, was still living in Ireland. The missionaries destined for the colony still had not left, and indeed they showed no inclination to do so, either that year or the next. The whole project already seemed an illusion. What was worse, without the help of the Sacred Congregation "de Propaganda Fide," the English mission itself, under whose jurisdiction Avalon came and on which the Avalon project depended for recruiting missionaries and funds, seemed more a mission "of Wycliffe, Luther and Calvin" than of the "Sacred Holy Roman Church." The English authorities had again begun to persecute Catholics with renewed energy. Several priests had been imprisoned, including two of Stock's confrères, Bede of the Blessed Sacrament and Elias of Jesus, while Stock himself might have followed suit, "had not Our Lord blinded the police who had surrounded me to capture me." For the sake of his Roman protectors, or possibly recalling experiences in Rome, Stock compared the danger in which the English Catholics found themselves to that in which "the bandits and malefactors of Rome" lived.[2]

When his faculties finally arrived, on 22 March 1616, Stock declared them insufficient.[3] What was more, shortly afterwards Stock received the decision regarding his own departure for Avalon—and this not from Propaganda,[4] but directly from the order's general, Paolo Simone di Gesù e Maria.[5] The tone of Stock's reply is veiled but clear: "[I]n holy matters one must be realistic." It was first necessary to put the English mission on a firm footing, and only then would it be possible to think about Avalon. And for the success of the English mission, he quickly added, his presence was indispensable. Of the five Discalced

Carmelites present in England at that moment, he explained, two (Bede and Elias) were in prison and two (Eliseus of St. Michael and Edmund of St. Martin) were ill, leaving only Stock himself to maintain vital relations with his many converts, above all, those from the Canterbury area. Besides, Stock went on, to send him two thousand miles away to the island of Avalon, "a greater distance than Rome is from Persia," alone and with no possibility of receiving the sacraments, was to expose him to the risk of damnation. He would consider departing only if given "licence to observe the laws and customs of the Holy Church," that is, the necessary faculties, on the basis of a new organization of the English mission.[6] The rigidly implemented laws against Catholics made this all the more necessary.[7] He was willing to go even to Geneva, he concluded, the very cradle of Calvinism, as long as he was provided with the necessary means. But in the present situation he did not feel inclined to become the first Catholic missionary (and possibly martyr) of Avalon.[8]

Whatever the reasons for his refusal—fear of the unknown or a genuine appreciation of the needs of the English mission—Stock's pessimistic analysis of the state of English Catholicism was certainly correct. The new bishop, Richard Smith, had just been installed in England, but since he was obliged to remain in hiding, his presence was little felt. (Smith was later to create violent conflict within English Catholicism.) Relations between the various religious orders were troubled, when they were not lacking completely.[9] The position of the Discalced Carmelites was particularly unfortunate, with four of the five missionaries unable to take part in any apostolic activity. Stock was feeling isolated and vulnerable after his disagreement with his superiors, and he must inevitably have interpreted the order to leave for Newfoundland as a conspiracy on their part in which they had managed to involve Propaganda too.

Before this invitation to go in person to Avalon had arrived, Stock had been diligently collecting the more detailed information Propaganda requested concerning his friend the Catholic pilot, the Northwest Passage,[10] and his plan for "more easily planting the Holy Faith in China."[11] His letter of 7 March, the first after a silence of some three months (the result in part of new difficulties in sending and receiving correspondence),[12] is of considerable interest because of the bulk of information it contains. In it he enclosed a map of America which, although no longer in the archives of Propaganda,[13] has been identified and of which further mention will be made later.

Stock informed the officials of Propaganda in the most detailed terms of the results of his most recent meetings with the pilot. In structure and choice of detail, the pilot's account tallies exactly with the existing literature on the Northwest Passage.[14] After crossing the North American continent, passing through what he called "North Bay," and navigating in "much fresh water in the middle," the pilot had reported having reached "salt water on the other side" and having glimpsed, without being seen himself, "a ship on the other side," together with men of the same ship."[15] Supposing the passage to actually exist, the fresh water would have supplied the proof of the passage by means of a river or lake, while the salt water would have indicated the arrival at the sea "on the other side," the whole being confirmed by the presence of Europeans (obviously Spaniards) and of (Spanish) ships in a place which could only be California or its northern appendages, both at that point relatively unknown. Such was the data European explorers and navigators sought in the Indians' accounts, and such was the data which was furnished, in good faith or otherwise, as proof of the discovery of the legendary passage.

While Stock's friend clearly could not have found a passage which was not traversed until the twentieth century, the details Stock supplies of both narrator and narration give the impression of a real person, not a figment of the missionary's imagination. Speaking of him in the years 1625–28, Stock describes him as about fifty years of age, English,[16] Catholic, and with an elder brother who had died some time before 7 March 1626 (a sea-captain from whom the pilot had received his earliest information of the passage). He apparently had at least two sons, one of whom had been with him when he discovered the passage, the other, Catholic like his father, having become a priest.[17] The pilot claimed to have been to Avalon five times and offered both to take future missionaries there and to settle there himself. When Stock next met him, between January and February 1626, the pilot was in prison, from which he was released on payment of a considerable sum of money and the delivery of a promise to go no more "to those coasts."[18]

Stock was not able to obtain further information from the pilot, and thus he could not supply Propaganda with "the names of said rivers, and all particulars."[19] When Stock asked him why he had never made known his discovery, he replied that he feared for his life—someone who had already discovered the passage "had been taken, after which time no further news was had of him." In addition, the pilot added that for "infidels" to know the secret would mean the "ruin of Christianity,"[20] evidently because it would have opened the way not only to America but also Asia, a road that Protestants would have been quick to take. In fact, the pilot had good reason to be afraid, and not only because of his past prison experience, "accused of spying and of knowing above all others the secrets and passages of those seas and seacoasts."[21] Not long afterwards he was kidnapped by two Spanish secret agents, disguised as pilgrims, in Saint-Malo, where he had sought refuge from the anti-Catholic persecution in England, and was forced

---

to join the Spanish West-Indian fleet.[22] Either the pilot had been so indiscreet as to speak of his discovery with others, or Stock himself had been the unwitting cause of his abduction by transmitting the news to Rome, from where it had gone to Spain in Propaganda's letter on the subject to the nuncio, Giulio Sacchetti, bishop of Gravina.[23] The news could then have leaked out to interested ears while the nuncio was gathering information at court.

In the early months of 1626, when Stock met his friend the pilot again, he was still busy enlarging his knowledge of North America. Thanks to Aston's letter of October 1625 and to the pilot, Stock's enthusiasm was at its height. The problem now was to convince the Roman authorities of the project's viability. Hoping to gain an ally, he spoke to Jacques Bruneau, resident of the king of Spain, "a good Catholic and zealous of the honour of God."[24] At the same time, he finally began to read the literature available on America and consulted maps, which only confirmed his convictions. Whatever he found out was immediately communicated to his protectors in Rome, thus helping to broaden their own knowledge and consciousness of America.

The idea of the Northwest Passage interested Stock more and more. He wrote that although he knew no one other than the pilot to have actually used it, "many affirm the existence of a passage, and I have found it printed in some accounts."[25] The possibility of such a passage was repeatedly spoken of in the body of American literature of the late sixteenth and early seventeenth centuries and in the works on Newfoundland printed in the same period.[26] Stock's reference to "some accounts" ("alcuni relationi") is significant and might refer to the ample volumes of Richard Hakluyt and Samuel Purchas, the former having appeared at the end of the preceding century, the latter only a year before.[27] It might also refer to the many books dealing with English America, and particularly with Virginia, New England and Bermuda, which combined a general account with a selection of documents, letters and travel reports.

It is difficult to say exactly what Stock read. Even successful works enjoyed a circulation which appears extremely limited by modern standards. Whoever wanted to read them had first to find them. Moreover, any reader naturally was likely to select his information according to his own preferences or personality, with a sophistication of selection in direct proportion to his knowledge of the subject in question. Nothing had been further from Stock's cultural formation than America and the conquest of the New World. Once he entered into contact with Lord Baltimore, his interest in North America was immediately shaped by his precise purpose—to convince Rome (and himself) of the viability and desirability of a Catholic mission in the New World. It was thus necessary to demonstrate, among other things, the actual existence of the Northwest Passage, the richness of the natural resources in the new lands, the intrinsic goodness of the natives, and—as negative counterbalance—the danger of Protestant expansionism.

The absence of any specific cultural background on Stock's part had one immediate effect. Possessing no critical filter, he was unable to organize the information gained, and he limited himself to transferring piecemeal to Rome a series of facts derived from his reading and his private conversations, requiring only that they be favourable. This is obvious from the use he made of Gerard de Jode's atlas (and, as we shall see, the maps of John Speed) and from his reports of conversations with his friend the pilot. He did, of course, possess a direct source of information in the settlers in Avalon, but he had already demonstrated, at the beginning of the enterprise, a surprising obtuseness in relating Lord Baltimore's project to the context of the North American continent.

What Stock certainly did know was Humphrey Gilbert's *Discourse for a Passage to Cataia*, published in 1576,[28] although, from his reference to "some accounts,"[29] this writer is more inclined to think that it was through Hakluyt's transcription than from the original.[30] In Gilbert, Stock found confirmation of the Northwest Passage and at the same time a general ideological framework which linked America and the passage directly with Asia, the East Indies, the Moluccas, Japan, China and Cathay—the whole infused with a vaguely classical flavour which could not fail to be attractive to a priest educated by the Jesuits in Rome.[31]

However, when Stock referred to "newly printed English and Dutch maps,"[32] it was not those in the *Discourse for a Passage to Cataia* of which he was speaking. What he had in mind were the more accurate maps of Cornelis and Gerard de Jode, a thorough knowledge of which he had already revealed,[33] and those of the English geographer John Speed. It was one of Speed's maps which he sent to Rome, attached to his letter of 7 March 1626. A year later, in London, Speed published his atlas entitled *Prospect of the Most Famous Parts of the World*,[34] containing a most detailed and accurate map of North and South America,[35] together with a map of the world.[36] Both were printed in 1626, and apparently before March, since, whichever one Stock actually sent to Rome, he certainly had them both at hand when writing to Propaganda.[37]

Apart from two points which are inaccurate,[38] the information on North America (and Europe) that Stock gives in his letters of 7 March 1626, 22 April 1626, and 28 July 1628[39] tallies perfectly with that given in Speed's maps. Here America appears as a large island traversed and surrounded by water, the English possessing the area between 37° and 60° north latitude (that is, from Virginia to the known northern limit), which in Europe corresponds to Spain, France, Hungary, and Italy, while Bermuda lies at 32° north latitude. Plymouth, which is marked on both of Speed's maps, is on the same latitude as Rome.[40]

As far as the Northwest Passage is concerned, Speed marked it at around 60° north latitude, at which point there is a "Mediterranean sea,"[41] which the English navigated to longitude 270°[42] and which, in effect, is no more extensive than the distance between Gibraltar and Jerusalem. As has been noted, Stock's pilot spoke of entering the Northwest Passage through a "North Bay," which Stock took to be "that Mediterranean sea that enters America through the Straits of New Britain,"[43] obviously the straits to the north of Speed's "Newe Brittaine," namely, "Davis strait" and "Hudson strait," which lead to "Buttons bay" and "Hudsons Bay."[44] It would thus have been possible to reach the other side of the American continent, the "South Sea,"[45] Japan and China (both these last are present on Speed's world map) without crossing the equator, the temperate zone,[46] or the Tropic of Cancer, for which purpose the Azores offered a particularly convenient jumping-off point. The clearest indication that Stock used Speed's maps is the long (and occasionally inaccurate) reference to the Straits of Le Maire and Barnevelt Island.[47] This reference has nothing to do with North America and is completely unjustified. It is only to be explained by their prominence on Speed's maps of the world and America.

If, however, Stock or Propaganda hoped to get useful information on Avalon and Newfoundland from Speed, they must have been disappointed. The only data Stock obtained (which he sent on to Propaganda only two years later) regarded Newfoundland's cartographical position, "at latitude 54 and longitude 330, near to northern America"[48]—information that corresponds with both Speed's maps. None of the place names Speed gives bear any reference to Avalon or Lord Baltimore's colony, although they are relatively numerous considering the map's scale.[49] From the information gathered from his friend the pilot, his reading of Gilbert, Hakluyt and de Jode, Stock must by then have been convinced (and probably was already convinced in the summer of 1625, as I have suggested) that Avalon formed part of Newfoundland, or at least that they were one and the same thing. The explicit mention to Propaganda in another letter six weeks later[50] was then almost redundant. Speed's maps, however, provided no confirmation whatsoever.

In this letter of 22 April 1626, Stock still refers to Speed's maps, but he updates his description on the strength of new data. For the first time since his letter of 13 September 1625,[51] he speaks of the Indians. In the temperate zone where the English have settled, he writes:

---

the infidels are more benign, humane, ingenious, valorous, nimble and more able to endure than those of other parts, of comely stature and of good proportions. When born they are all white, but since they use no art to protect themselves from the sun and colour themselves to appear more terrible in warfare, they become brown.[52]

Not only had some of them been in England, but one had actually taken part in the Bohemian wars. So positive was Stock's opinion of the indigenous population that he felt moved to add that "[t]hey lack only the Holy Faith to become like Italians"[53]—a comment which must have been most gratifying to the vanity of the Roman cardinals.

While Stock gave extra information and Cornelis de Jode's influence was still apparent ("benign, humane"), his main source could only have been Captain John Smith, a person of considerable importance in Virginia and New England. His *Generall Historie of Virginia, New-England, and the Summer Isles*[54] appeared in 1624 and met with great success; indeed, its very title would have guaranteed its interest in Stock's eyes.[55] Smith's description was repeated in Purchas,[56] who also quoted passages from John Guy and Richard Whitbourne which on a first reading recall Stock's words.[57] In fact, however, many of Stock's details are to be found in neither Guy nor Whitbourne, and both spoke of ochre-coloured Indians, not brown ("bruni" in Stock, "browne" in Smith). If this is not sufficient to mark out Smith as Stock's source, the missionary's words concerning Plymouth dispel any remaining doubt. Plymouth is present on both of Speed's maps, but Stock had paid no particular attention to it. Plymouth now becomes "a town on hills like those of Rome," with a "fortress" where "three years ago"[58] there were two "ministers or preachers," and others had since gone "to infest those peoples with heresy."[59] The last chapter of Smith's book, which is concerned with "The Present estate of New-Plimoth," contains all the information Stock gives.[60]

It is interesting to note that this appendix on Plymouth did not appear in Purchas's selection, further proof that Stock did not know *Purchas His Pilgrimes* as yet. This gives rise to two important considerations. First, from a negative slant, the fact that he did not know Purchas excludes the possibility of his using the various maps printed in *Purchas His Pilgrimes,* not only the numerous but relatively uninteresting maps of Josse de Hondt,[61] but also the far more important ones of New Scotland by William Alexander[62] and of North America by Henry Briggs.[63] Similarly, he could not be familiar with the various accounts of the Northwest passage which Purchas gives, above all that of Briggs with its relative map,[64] or, which would have interested him even more, those of Guy, Whitbourne and Wynne on Newfoundland.[65]

Second, his reading of Smith's book in its entirety, with the maps of Virginia, Bermuda and New England, constituted Stock's most detailed and accurate body of information on English America to date. Stock's horizons had thus been extended from Avalon to Newfoundland and the whole of North America, but his information was still not up to date with the most recent literature.

On 4 May 1626 Propaganda wrote with obvious satisfaction how "welcome" Stock's letter of 7 March had been. It had provided them with new information on "that newly discovered passage in North America which would ensure easy and rapid crossing from the Mediterranean Sea to that other sea named South Sea." At the same time Propaganda regretted that the information was incomplete, "since he [the Catholic pilot] did not see fit to reveal in entirety the new passage." Propaganda's summary of Stock's letter reveals the care with which they had noted down the new information, having first checked it diligently on the "new map compiled by the English" which Stock had enclosed. Stock was to persevere with the pilot, Propaganda wrote, so that he "bestir himself at least in the service of God and those of his labourers that may be sent to those parts, to reveal all that he knows of this passage." As regards Avalon, Propaganda merely repeated that it was necessary for Stock to go in person, "the better to know the country." On his return, or on his writing to them from Newfoundland (Propaganda was obviously hinting that a longer stay would not be a bad idea), they could then send out the recruited missionaries—Capuchins or Franciscan Recollets, if no Discalced Carmelites were available.[66]

This reference to other orders is particularly interesting. In the first place, it again[67] reveals Propaganda's intention of operating on a large scale, involving other orders as the need arose and taking for granted Stock's acquiescence in the project, in spite (or possibly because) of its not being directly connected with his order. Secondly, the exclusion of the Jesuits in favour of the Capuchins and the Recollets indicates that contacts existed with these orders and that they were considered satisfactory.[68]

On 18 December 1626, upon receiving Stock's letter of 22 April, Propaganda appeared even more interested. While obviously not imagining that Stock had extended his reading (Smith had been added to the de Jode, Hakluyt and Speed), they now decided to give "per extentum" his "curious account . . . of those countries described in the map of America which he [had] sent to the Sacred Congregation,"[69] instead of summarizing the salient points as they had done formerly. Neither Stock's familiar reports of the Northwest Passage nor his detailed description of Plymouth seem to explain this change in attitude. What particularly interested them in Stock's letter was the information given on the American Indians, too substantial and compact (indicative of a single source) to summarize easily.

Whether Propaganda, like Stock, had by now managed to connect Avalon with Newfoundland is difficult to say. Speed's map was of no help on this point, and so far Stock had sent no other, nor had he ever specifically connected the two in his letters (the co-ordinates of the islands were sent some time later).[70] More than Avalon, however, it was the Northwest Passage that particularly intrigued them at this moment, and the precise position of Avalon was not important, as long as "missions in the whole of northern America would be viable from that island."[71]

The general outlines of the Avalon project were gradually becoming clearer, both for Stock and for Propaganda. What was needed now was news from the settlers in Ferryland. Nothing had been heard from them since October 1625, and that news was already out of date since it referred to the previous summer. Both in Rome and in London people were anxious to know how Aston and his men had passed their first winter in Newfoundland.

### CHAPTER SIX

# Lord Baltimore's Pleasant Summer in Avalon, 1627

After a long silence lasting almost eight months, probably as much the result of the "troubles and persecution"[1] in England as of postal difficulties,[2] on 12 February 1627 Simon Stock wrote once more to the Sacred Congregation "de Propaganda Fide." As he did not hesitate to point out, he had been asking Propaganda's help regarding the Avalon mission for two years now, and still nothing had been done.[3] His disillusionment was obvious, as was the fact that the many frustrations had greatly cooled his initial enthusiasm. While the letters of 1625 and 1626 had been almost exclusively taken up with matters in America, the two of 1627[4] relegated the Avalon mission to second place and were more concerned with the ever-deteriorating state of affairs in England.

Richard Smith, bishop of Chalcedon, had arrived in England at the end of April 1625[5] as the country's ordinary, that is, the person responsible for the English ecclesiastical hierarchy. The first two years of his appointment were relatively uneventful. In 1627, however, he had claimed the same prerogative as a bishop resident in a Catholic country. In compliance with the dictates of the Council of Trent, he had obliged the regulars to ask his permission before hearing confession, remodelled the episcopal chapter, set up a church tribunal, and ordered visits in private houses. His authoritarian behaviour had already incensed the English Catholic nobles and some of the regulars, above all, the Jesuits and Benedictines.[6] Following an appeal to Rome, a partial condemnation of Smith's actions had arrived on 16 December.[7]

Smith had resided for some time at Turvey, in Bedfordshire, in a house belonging to Anthony Browne, Viscount Montague,[8] who was related to the Roper family.[9] Stock's close relations with the Ropers certainly aided his acquaintanceship with Smith, and when the dispute arose between the bishop and the regulars, Stock took the former's part.

Meanwhile, Stock's own dispute with his superiors was coming to a head. He had no intention of abandoning the English mission (possibly making a veiled allusion to the attempt to exile him in Avalon). As he had always told them, he "could not be content except in this mission."[10] His superiors' attitude, together with their "incompetent management," Stock asserted accusingly, were "a far greater impediment to the fruitful conversion of souls" than was the anti-Catholic persecution itself.[11] For such reasons, Stock asked Propaganda if he could be released from obedience to his superiors and come within the jurisdiction of Bishop Smith like a simple secular.[12]

What had been happening to Sir Arthur Aston and his men in the meantime? After they left for Newfoundland at the end of May 1625 and sent favourable reports in October of the same year, no more had been heard of them. Unfortunately, information is almost completely lacking from which to attempt a reconstruction of the events. Once again, Stock himself is the only source. On 12 February 1627, he somewhat laconically informed Propaganda that "those Christians from Avalon have come here and in the spring intend to return to Avalon."[13] But who had returned? When? And why?

There is little difficulty in fixing the date of their return between 30 June 1626 and 12 February 1627, most probably, following sailing practice, in October 1626.[14] Those "Christians" Stock spoke of must be the survivors from among the fifteen or twenty Catholics who had accompanied Aston,[15] and Aston himself had returned with them. Apparently, the colony had not been abandoned, however, and it had been left (all the Catholics having returned) in the hands of some Protestant subordinate.

The reasons for their return are more difficult to establish. Aston spent the summer of 1625 and the winter of 1625–26 in Ferryland. Then at some point during the summer of 1626, he had decided to come back. Reasons that can almost certainly be excluded are that he refused to spend another winter there or that he intended to leave the colony for good. Both Stock[16] and George Calvert, Baron Baltimore,[17] implied the contrary. Once back in England, however, something—a disagreement with Lord Baltimore, perhaps, or simply a better offer—made him change his mind. That decision proved fatal to him.[18] Aston died on 29 October/8 November of the same year while taking part in the siege of the Île de Ré, opposite La Rochelle, in the service of George Villiers, Duke of Buckingham.[19]

Lord Baltimore was in England from February 1627 onwards,[20] but at least up until 7/17 April,[21] he showed no intention of taking Aston's place himself. The two must have been in contact immediately after the governor's return. While it is impossible to know when the signs of discord began, the definitive break between them must have been in April or May.[22] Lord Baltimore, however, had early begun to have doubts concerning the state of the colony, and at the end of May, in a letter to his friend Thomas Wentworth, later Earl of Strafforde, he expressed his concern clearly, at the same time revealing his intention of going himself to Newfoundland:

> being bound for a long Journey to a Place which I have had a long Desire to visit, and have now the Opportunity and Leave to do it: It is *Newfoundland* I mean, which it imports me more than in Curiosity only to see; for, I must either go and settle it in a better Order than it is, or else give it over, and lose all the Charges I have been at hitherto for other Men to build their Fortunes upon. And I had rather be esteemed a Fool by some for the Hazard of one Month's journey, than to prove myself one certainly for six Years by past, if the Business be now lost for the want of a little Pains and Care.[23]

Lord Baltimore assured his friend that, on a ship of 300 tons, possessing twenty-four pieces of artillery, with two or three more ships as escort, he would be safe from the danger of French pirates. They were to leave within three or four days, and the return was fixed for the end of September.[24]

On 1/10 June 1627, a few days after this letter to Wentworth, Lord Baltimore left England, arriving in Ferryland on 23 July/2 August.[25] Unfortunately, as in the case of Aston's stay in Newfoundland, there is an almost total dearth of information regarding Lord Baltimore's first American journey. Stock, usually so accurate, mentioned neither his departure for Avalon nor his return to England.[26] The only reasonable hypothesis is that he did not return before 10 October 1627[27] and possibly not before 2/12 November.[28] The only definite clue is the permission granted Lord Baltimore and his family to go to Ireland, which bears the date 31 December 1627/10 January 1628.[29] Obviously, things had gone well in Ferryland, so much so that Lord Baltimore decided to settle in Avalon for good and to return the following summer with the majority of his family.

On one particular of his first stay in Newfoundland the sources are relatively eloquent, namely, the fact of his being accompanied by two secular priests, Thomas Longville and Anthony Pole. The presence of the two missionaries marked, in the Revered John Southcote's words, the beginning of the "first mission into New found land."[30] Stock himself gave notice of their departure, albeit with a slight delay, and once again revealed that he was extremely well-informed. One of the two, he related, was to stay in Ferryland for the winter, along with the twenty or so Catholics who lived in the colony, while the other would return to England earlier, "in the hope of further help in the spring."[31] Pole, in fact, returned to England on 13/23 September 1629,[32] while

Longville came back with Lord Baltimore within the year.[33]

Up until that time both Longville and Pole had led relatively hectic lives—and indeed they carried on doing so afterwards. Born Protestant, Longville was converted to Catholicism and studied first in Saint-Omer, then (like Stock) at the Venerable English College in Rome, from which he was expelled. After his summer in Avalon, he distinguished himself above all for his anti-Jesuit zeal, taking part, for example, in the arrest of the Jesuit Henry Morse.[34] Pole too (who at that point called himself Anthony Smith) was born of Protestant parents; he had studied at Saint-Omer and Valladolid. He became a Jesuit, was subsequently expelled from the order, and in 1626 was imprisoned for religious reasons. Like Longville, Pole devoted the rest of his ecclesiastical career to antagonizing and arguing with his former confrères.[35] A fair guess would be that both, and especially Pole, saw the Newfoundland mission as an escape route from the trouble they had landed themselves in in England.

In giving the news of their departure, Stock was not slow to point out his own share in the matter, asserting that he himself had "procured" it, "not wishing to miss the chance," in lieu of missionaries from Rome.[36] It is, of course, impossible to know how much truth there is in this statement, and it seems just as likely that Southcote was behind their departure.[37] Both the two seculars' personal histories and their joining the Avalon mission suggest that Lord Baltimore had not yet taken a clear stand in the quarrel between Bishop Smith and the regulars (in particular, the Jesuits),[38] though he was subsequently to do so. On the other hand, the quarrel was still in its early stages, and he had been in Ireland for much of it.

Stock's role in the whole affair is far from clear. How is it that, informed in such detail of Longville and Pole's departure, he nowhere mentioned that Lord Baltimore took part in that year's expedition to Newfoundland? With whom did Stock use his influence to procure the departure of the two seculars, if not with Lord Baltimore? Once again, the information available does not permit an adequate answer. One can only suppose that Lord Baltimore's absence from London from 1625 to 1627 had weakened the intensity of a relationship which had been flourishing two years earlier, even though it had never reached the degree of familiarity evident in Stock's relations with Aston, for example, or his friend the Catholic pilot.

Stock's two letters of 1627 took almost three months to reach the officials of Propaganda in Rome.[39] In the meantime, they had been facing the delicate problem of the mission in England, and their energies were now directed towards it rather than to Avalon. English Catholics were contending with the double dangers of internal dissent and external persecution, and their situation was far from enviable. As the

Congregation's secretary, Francesco Ingoli, noted on the occasion of a letter from Stock,[40] Propaganda was for the most part on the bishop's side, while the Holy Office favoured the regulars.[41] The fact that Stock and Ingoli were in agreement on the English question certainly helped to further Stock's cause with Propaganda, even though normal caution prevented Ingoli from meeting all Stock's requests. Concerning his relations with his superiors, for example, while Stock might have every reason to complain, still, Propaganda explained, "this Sacred Congregation does not of habit violate the wishes of the Superiors of religious orders, since this very violating of their will, creates much difficulty in negotiations."[42] As to Stock's request that he come under the jurisdiction of Bishop Smith, it was not to be thought of "since it is not meet that a dutiful regular shirk obedience to his Superiors."[43] Though their firmness is obvious, so is their desire to avoid a break with Stock, which would cost them a first-hand account of the situation in Avalon and in England.

Propaganda was, in fact, careful to emphasize that the possible failure of the American mission would be the result of Stock's refusal to go in person to Avalon:

> The Sacred Congregation has been unable to determine any course of action concerning the mission in Avalon, there lacking any person to send thither. Since you yourself do not deem fit to accept the task, the Congregation cannot know whom to send, unless your reverend self may not suggest some suitable subject, of your own or of another order.[44]

However, except for this matter, Stock's recent good news had been received with satisfaction ("most welcome"). Longville and Pole's departure was seen as a chance to obtain, at last, the long-awaited "full account of the island."[45] The Avalon news must have given someone the idea of reviewing the Newfoundland file again, since it was only now noticed that the map Stock had sent some time before[46] had been lost. Stock was thus asked to send a second copy forthwith.[47]

Sixteen twenty-seven was a decisive year in the history of the Avalon colony. Aston had returned to England, and his place had been taken by Lord Baltimore, who found it so satisfactory that he wished to settle there permanently. Furthermore, after all Stock's urgent pleading, two Catholic priests had finally arrived in Newfoundland to establish the first Catholic mission in the island. Yet all this information Stock mentioned and Propaganda received very summarily. The problems of English Catholicism now obviously took precedence over the Avalon project, which was gradually being relegated to second place at the very time when events and circumstances were finally proving favourable.

---

### CHAPTER SEVEN

# Lord Baltimore Decides to Settle in Avalon for Good, 1628

George Calvert, Baron Baltimore, quickly showed his satisfaction with his stay in Ferryland. No sooner had he come back to England than he set about making preparations for his permanent return to Newfoundland. He immediately informed the king, Charles I, who promptly wrote to his lord deputy in Ireland, Henry Cary, Viscount Falkland (19/29 January 1627/1628) informing him that, since Lord Baltimore wished to supervise the colony personally, he had given him leave to depart. He was to be allowed, the king specified, to depart from whichever Irish port he chose and to take with him whatever he saw fit.[1] A short time later, Lord Baltimore wrote from Bristol to John Harrison in London to obtain money to finance the expedition.[2]

Shortly before leaving, Lord Baltimore wrote a long letter to his friend Thomas Wentworth from Cloghammon, his Irish residence. Its tone marks it as a letter of farewell. With their mutual friend Francis Cottington, Wentworth was named executor and warrantor for the marriage of his son Cecil, who would retain his hereditary rights only if he married within the year and with the consent of both warrantors. Then, after reminding his friend of his promise to visit him in Newfoundland, "though you never meane to performe it," Lord Baltimore took leave of him for ever: "God send us a happy meeting in heaven and in earth yf it please him."[3]

Lord Baltimore left for his colony around May 1628,[4] arriving in Ferryland towards the end of June. He took with him his second wife Joane, all his children (except Cecil, his heir), his two sons-in-law, Sir Robert Talbot and William Peaseley, some forty Catholics,[5] and a Catholic priest by the name of Hacket.[6] (Possibly, as we shall see, more than one priest was of the party.)

After the many letters of 1625 and 1626, at the beginning of Stock's acquaintanceship with the Sacred Congregation "de Propaganda

Fide" when his enthusiasm for the Avalon project was at its height, there followed a lull in the correspondence. Internal dissidence among English Catholics and disagreements with his order had certainly had their part in lowering his morale. Even more decisive was his disillusionment with Propaganda's unkept promises. He wrote two letters in 1627 and two more in 1628—these last following almost one after the other.[7] A whole winter thus went by with no news from Stock.

Although the two letters of 1628 were for the most part concerned with problems in England, Stock did not fail to report on the developments within the Avalon colony. It may be that the interest with which Propaganda had replied to his letter of 10 October 1627[8] had led him once more again to hope for some concrete help from that quarter. Possibly the departure of the two secular priests, Thomas Longville and Anthony Pole, the year before and Lord Baltimore's recent departure may have seemed signs of activity at last.

Stock's source was probably no longer Lord Baltimore, now so remote both in spirit and in space, although whoever it was was certainly well informed. Stock knew that Lord Baltimore had sailed and laconically described him as "he of whom I did write when I first wrote to Your Most Illustrious Worships of this mission." He repeated that the two missionaries who left for Avalon in 1627 were seculars and stated that although no one from his order was able to go , "others" had accompanied Lord Baltimore, together with some "of my spiritual children."[9] He would have news of the expedition, he went on, in October, when some of its members were expected back.[10] By "spiritual children," he simply meant that some of the forty Catholics who went with Lord Baltimore,[11] belonged to the London-Canterbury area where he was active and that he personally had persuaded them to go.[12] Of the "others" Stock wrote about, one of whom was to go to Rome "to carry reports and request assistance of the Holy Church"[13] once the mission in Avalon was well established, we know almost nothing. We do not even know whether they were priests or not. We know that a secular priest, Hacket (probably a pseudonym),[14] went with Lord Baltimore, to replace Longville and join forces with Pole. But Stock's use of "others" ("altri" is both a pronoun and adjective in Italian) as a pronoun makes it impossible to be sure whether Stock meant "other seculars"—he could have meant simply "other Catholics."[15]

Enclosed with the two letters of 27 June and 28 July 1628 were the three maps which Propaganda had asked for when they discovered they had lost the copy of John Speed's map which Stock had previously sent.[16] Unfortunately, none of these three maps, which have all disappeared from the archives of Propaganda, can be identified with the certainty with which it was possible to identify those of Cornelis de Jode and Speed, since Stock's comments about them are so vague. Of the two maps sent with the letter of 27 June, Stock says only that one was printed in 1624, the other in the latter being "darker" ("più negra") than the former.[17] At first, because Stock speaks of sending Propaganda "the map that you desire,"[18] it is easy to assume that it was an additional copy of the map he had already sent, that is, one of Speed's.

Further details about the maps come from the summary of Stock's letters prepared by one of the clerks of Propaganda, and some marginal notes in the hand of the secretary of the Congregation, Francesco Ingoli. The maps were "of America" and revealed "a recently discovered northern archipelago, through which it is believed possible to reach the Indies quickly." This archipelago did not exist, Ingoli added, "in the old maps."[19] It is difficult to say which "archipelago" is meant. With a little imagination, some maps could give the impression of a group of islands either around Newfoundland[20] or in what is now Hudson Bay.[21] Since the archipelago in question was then of recent discovery, the second hypothesis is more probable. If by "old maps" Ingoli meant the atlas of Abraham Ortelius,[22] none of the above-mentioned groups of islands appear there.[23]

Only two points are certain. First, the maps are not Speed's, both of which are clearly dated 1626. Thus the map Stock sent to the Congregation was not the same as that sent two years previously. Second, in neither of the two is the publishing date visible, since this would have rendered redundant Stock's information that the 1625 map was "darker" than the other—the dates would have distinguished them quite clearly.

The 1624 map is almost certainly none of those John Smith published in his *Generall Historie of Virginia*, with which we know Stock was familiar.[24] The only likely candidate at the present stage of research is the map of New Scotland which William Alexander inserted in his *Encouragement to Colonies*.[25] But only the date and the fact that if Stock did by chance know the map its importance would not have escaped him support this hypothesis. Against it is that it is certainly not a map "of America." In addition, no Northwest Passage or archipelago are visible.[26]

The 1625 map was probably Briggs's "North part of America." Although the map was probably drawn in 1622—the date of the publication of Briggs's "Treatise of the North-west passage"—it was not published until 1625 when it appeared in *Purchas His Pilgrimes*. It is without question a map of America. It places a number of islands in Hudson Bay which could give the idea of an archipelago. There are frequent references to the Northwest Passage in the captions.[27]

As for Stock's third map, which was enclosed with his letter of 28 July 1628,[28] a well-founded hypothesis can be advanced. It is unlikely to be one of the maps he had already sent the previous month.[29] More probably it was a copy of the Speed map which Propaganda had explicitly asked for.[30] This identification can be confirmed by the fact that all the information in Stock's letter seems without exception to be taken from Speed,[31] which was easily accessible to Stock and which he had probably consulted once more to refresh his own and Propaganda's ideas about America.

While Propaganda still duly summarized the new information Stock gave about Avalon, there is no proof that the Congregation paid any great attention to events in America. They would appreciate a complete report on the island and, above all, on the Northwest Passage. In the meantime, they reminded him to "report at length on all he may be told by the missionaries of same isle"[32] and to give all details regarding the "capacity of those peoples and of all that may be done there in order that our Holy Faith be propagated."[33] Stock was also urged to obtain "every particular of the navigation of that [Mediterranean] sea"[34] when his friend the Catholic pilot returned to England. (Stock had already told them of his abduction.)[35]

Like Stock, Propaganda now devoted their attention almost exclusively to problems in England. In the quarrel between Bishop Richard Smith and the regulars, Stock's position was more than clear; the regulars had been so many years without a bishop ("in such liberty that they did as they pleased, and many much more than they should have") that they no longer accepted the bishop's jurisdiction. In Stock's opinion there was only one solution: to put both monasteries and missions back in the hands of the bishops "as in the primitive Church." As far as he was concerned (obviously referring to his request to be transferred within the jurisdiction of the bishop), whether he lived "in obedience to bishops or generals" was of no importance to him, as long as the laws and customs of the church were observed. Comparing the situation in England to that in Avalon, Stock could not resist the temptation to state that "[s]uch is the wretchedness of human nature, that it is easier to plant a new church and faith where they have not existed [hitherto], than to curtail liberty once granted."[36]

The picture Stock painted was not, however, completely negative. The Protestants, too, had their problems, and the quarrel between the king and the Puritans, "an ungovernable people and as sworn enemies of the king as of the supreme pontiffs," had reconciled Charles I to the Catholic church, thanks chiefly to the good offices of the ambassador of Savoy, the *abate* Alessandro Cesare Scaglia.[37] However, since Scaglia was about to leave the kingdom, it would be a good move, Stock suggested, to replace him with another ambassador from a neutral state such as Tuscany or Savoy who could carry on the task of bringing the king over to the Catholic side.[38]

As has already been noted, Ingoli and Stock were in total harmony on English matters. The missionary was thus duly thanked and invited to continue to inform Propaganda of the "progress" between the regulars and Bishop Smith "and at the same time how the king is disposed towards our Holy Faith."[39] The Congregation, Stock was assured, "puts great faith in your letters, and receives them most willingly."[40]

Ironically, just when Lord Baltimore's definitive departure for Newfoundland seemed to assure the inevitable success of the Avalon colony and mission, both Propaganda and Stock (who could now consider himself somewhat an expert on American affairs) began to show a certain detachment from the new enterprise. No one, however, could have imagined that Lord Baltimore's decision was soon to lead to the most disastrous experience of his life.

### CHAPTER EIGHT

# The Tragic Ending of an Adventure, 1629–30

From the time he set foot in Newfoundland at the beginning of the summer of 1628, George Calvert, Baron Baltimore, had precious little time in which to organize and consolidate the position of his colony. Only a few weeks after his arrival, he was writing, with an obvious note of bitterness: "I came to builde, and sett, and sowe, but I am falne to fighting with frenchmen who have here disquieted mee and many other of his Maiesties Subiects fishing in this Land."[1]

That year the French pirates who overran Newfoundland under the command of Captain Raymond de La Ralde[2] were particularly active, and, raid for raid, returned the forays made by the English on the French settlements of the St. Lawrence. Lord Baltimore's first worries were thus of a military nature, to assure the safe defence of his colony. Although Lord Baltimore was no soldier, he managed to get the better of the French, notwithstanding his having to deal with "La fleur de la Jeunesse de Normandye."[3] At Cape Broyle he captured no fewer than sixty-seven Frenchmen, and only a few days later at Trepassey, he gained possession of six ships from Bayonne and one from Saint-Jean-de-Luz.[4]

Six of the French ships taken were sent to England with Lord Baltimore's future son-in-law, William Peaseley, bearer of two letters for King Charles I and George Villiers, Duke of Buckingham.[5] Without His Majesty's special protection, Lord Baltimore urged, survival would be difficult in that "remote wilde part of the worlde."[6] He would need two warships, at least until the winter, to protect the English fishermen, who could be asked to defray the expenses of the protection.[7]

Some time passed before Lord Baltimore's request was discussed. Initially, on 13/23 December 1629, the Privy Council decreed that the *Esperance*, part of the summer's booty, would be assigned to Lord Baltimore for twelve months.[8] But when Peaseley asked that the *Esper-*

*ance* be exchanged for the *Saint-Claude*,[9] confiscated from the French because of its dealings with the Spanish,[10] a further three months were required before the ship was finally assigned to Leonard Calvert, one of Lord Baltimore's sons, on 3/13 March 1628/1629.[11] At the same time, the division of the booty between Lord Baltimore and the owners of the other ships which took part in the raids of the summer of 1628 was not without difficulties.[12]

If the slowness of English bureaucracy did not help Lord Baltimore, he had now to deal with an even worse enemy than the French pirates— the winter. To Ferryland, defined by one of its travel-seasoned visitors as "the coldest harbour of the Land, where those furious Windes and Icy Mountaynes doe play, and beate the greatest part of the Yeare,"[13] came the cold of the "intolerable"[14] winter that lasted from October to May and froze land and sea for most of that period.[15] With the cold came the inevitable illnesses,[16] turning Lord Baltimore's house into a hospital.[17] Of the one hundred settlers, as many as fifty fell sick at a time, Lord Baltimore being no exception; ten of them died.[18]

Food was scarce, and Lord Baltimore had forwarded a request to London asking for supplies, "in regard of the scarsetie of corne there [in Newfoundland], and of the greate plentie therof in this kingdome." On 25 February 1628/7 March 1629, his request was granted by the Privy Council, on condition that taxes were paid in advance and a guarantee given that the grain really was for use in Newfoundland.[19] On 20/30 April the supplies finally left Studland Bay for Ferryland on the *Saint-Claude*, the *Scythe of Poole* and other ships, under the command of Leonard Calvert. They reached their destination on 3/13 June. The unloading of the grain and loading of the fish went on speedily and without mishap, supervised by Lord Baltimore's loyal agent, Thomas Walker, and the convoy was soon on its way back to England.[20]

As if the cold, illness, and hunger were not sufficient, Lord Baltimore was also involved in violent quarrels of a religious nature. Little is known of religious practice in Ferryland, other than that the Catholic priests "Hacket and Smith [that is, Anthony Pole] evry sunday say Masse and doe use all other the ceremonies of the church of Rome in as ample manner as tis used in Spayne,"[21] while under Lord Baltimore's tolerant roof, "the heretics do as they please."[22] What emerged from these brief but evidently tendentious notes was a regime of religious tolerance disapproved of by both parties.

Of Hacket's and Pole's likely objections there remains no record. The person who caused a public uproar was the Reverend Erasmus Stourton, chaplain to Christopher Villiers, Earl of Anglesey and brother to the Duke of Buckingham. He attacked Lord Baltimore so violently that the latter took the first available opportunity to expel him from the colony and dispatch him back to England. Naturally, once back home Stourton lost no time in testifying against Lord Baltimore,[23] accusing him not only of openly allowing the profession of Catholicism in his colony, but of actually having baptized by force the son of a Protestant settler, a certain William Poole.[24] It is not clear what weight Stourton's accusations carried, although the Anglican minister certainly used every possible means, perhaps including his familiarity with the Villiers family, to take his revenge. For his part, Lord Baltimore did very little to defend himself against the accusations of "that knave Stourton,"[25] as he privately referred to him, putting up an unspirited and unconvincing defence in a letter to the king written in the summer of the following year.[26]

In the summer of 1629, Lord Baltimore made the decision to put a definitive end to the terrible experience of Avalon, "this wofull country," where "crosses and miseryes is my portion," as he put it in a letter of the end of August 1629 to his friend Francis Cottington. "It is not to be expressed wth my pen what wee have endured." Indeed, "[o]verwhelmed wth troubles and cares," he was obliged to write "but short and confusedly."[27] His health, too, had suffered, and he no longer felt up to the enormous difficulties involved.[28] Around August he sent back to England all his sons and daughters[29] and approximately ten settlers.[30] Of his family, only his wife Joane stayed on.

Tried as he was by his experience of Newfoundland's winter, Lord Baltimore's energy for colonial adventure was in no way abated. He intended to end his days, not in England, but in Virginia, and hoped the king would allot him a fair-sized piece of land, with the same privileges James I had conferred in Avalon. On it he intended to grow tobacco.[31] His wife and some forty of the settlers were to accompany him.[32]

Of Lord Baltimore's hardships, his quarrel with Stourton, and his decision to transfer his colony to Virginia, Simon Stock knew nothing at least until the end of 1630, when he met Lord Baltimore in person in London.[33] Once again, it is thanks to him that an important detail of the history of Avalon is known. Stock's letters to the Sacred Congregation "de Propaganda Fide" spoke of the departure, around Easter 1629,[34] of two Jesuits, probably Alexander Baker and Lawrence Rigby.[35] It can be safely assumed that they left for Ferryland from Studland Bay on 20/30 April in the company of Leonard Calvert.[36] They returned to England, according to Stock, around Christmas of the same year.[37]

This time Stock did not attempt to take any of the credit for recruiting the two missionaries, probably realizing the difficulty of such a claim since the Jesuits depended directly and exclusively on their own order. He merely remarked that "[b]eing one only [Stock], and without help," he "could not hope for missionaries from the [Discalced Carmelite] order for such an end."[38] It is not known how or when Lord Baltimore had got in touch with the Jesuits of the English province. As we have seen, however, his good friend Tobie Matthew was a Jesuit, and on Lord Baltimore's return to England from Virginia, he decided to side with the regulars against Bishop Richard Smith.[39] We also know that the first missionaries in Maryland were Jesuits.[40] Going back for a moment to the question mentioned earlier,[41] it is possible that the cooling of relations between Lord Baltimore and Stock was owing to their taking opposite sides on the issue which was dividing the English Catholic community.

Towards the end of August or at the beginning of September 1629,[42] Lord Baltimore left Ferryland and sailed for Jamestown, Virginia, in the company of his wife Joane and some forty settlers,[43] including all the Catholics who had not gone back to England[44] and probably the two Jesuits.[45] Lord Baltimore declared that he wished to leave Newfoundland to the fishermen.[46] Two or three women stayed behind with about thirty Protestants,[47] among whom was a certain Hoyle, who was to take care of Lord Baltimore's business and general concerns.[48] Lord Baltimore's difficulties were not at an end. The acting governor of Virginia, Dr. John Pott, refused him a residence permit on the grounds that he was unwilling to take the requisite oath.[49] Baltimore therefore had no option but to set off for England, where he landed around Christmas 1629.[50]

Shortly after Baltimore departed for Virginia, a letter arrived from Charles I in which the king warmly advised him to desist from his colonial adventures since "men of yor condition and breeding are fitter for other imployments, than the framing of new plantations, which commonly have rugged & laborious beginnings, and require much greater meanes, in managing them, than usually the power of One private subiect can reach unto." If he were to return to England,"you shall bee sure to enioye both the libertie of a subiect, and such respects from Us, as yor former services and late indeauors die justly deserve."[51] But even this strongly expressed opinion of the king was insufficient to deter Lord Baltimore, and about February 1630, he once more wrote to the secretary of state for foreign affairs, Dudley Carleton, Viscount Dorchester, asking him to concede an estate in Virginia[52] and to lend him once again the *Saint-Claude*, at the same time begging him to intercede with the governor of Virginia for his wife Joane's return to England.[53]

That Stock was gradually becoming less and less interested in the affairs of Avalon is evident in the very few lines he devoted to the subject in 1629 and 1630.[54] Only at Propaganda's express request [55] did he pass on his news of the Jesuits Baker and Rigby.[56] He took that opportunity to mention that he had met Lord Baltimore, who "is sorry to be back and says that it is his intention to return thither once more."[57] Either Baltimore and Stock continued to speak at crosspurposes (Stock's early obtuseness in grasping that the Avalon colony was in Newfoundland should not be forgotten), or Stock was by then so spiritually remote from the whole idea of an American mission that he had confused Lord Baltimore's desire to go to Virginia with a wish to return to Avalon.

The whole American question, however—Avalon, his relationship with Lord Baltimore, Sir Arthur Aston, and the Catholic pilot, his requests to Propaganda, and all the pieces of information he had assembled—had inevitably raised in Stock a certain interest in the New World, an interest in which he was not alone, to judge from the development of events at that time. In the spring of 1629 the Reverend Francis Higginson had taken some four hundred settlers to New England. The following year John Winthrop, the first governor of the colony of Massachusetts Bay, left England on 29 March/8 April 1630 with almost three hundred settlers, more following about a month later.[58] In the meantime, Higginson's brief treatise, *New-England Plantation*,[59] had arrived in England towards the end of November 1629 in manuscript form. Once printed, the first edition (1630) met with so much success that two more had to be printed within the same year.[60] It was not, therefore, incidental that on 28 April 1630, Stock wrote to Propaganda about the mass exodus of the Puritans for New England:

> Great numbers of the Puritan sect have gone from here to live in the northern part of America, 4,000 thousand [*sic*] or more, and they will infest those infidels with their heresy, who, as I have heard tell from those coming from those parts, are desirous to be Christians, and they are innumerable peoples and near to Europe.[61]

No comment followed, no hope of Rome's intervention, no suggestion of action to counterbalance the extension of the Puritan heresy throughout the New World. Stock was disappointed and disillusioned and more than ever convinced that his gloomy prophecies of a few years before were all coming true. He was convinced that the lands of America, with all their "innumerable" indigenous populations, were now easy prey for the English heretics.

After this time Stock no longer concerned himself with Avalon or matters in America, all future references to which are purely incidental. But prior to concluding his unfortunate experience, Stock submitted a new project to Propaganda, which, despite its ingenuousness, contained elements which are worthy of note. His description of the project is as follows:

Since this part of the world is now for the most part at peace, and the English, French and Scots have colonies in those parts of America, if it would please His Holiness to establish in this part of America a colony of Italians, with a bishop, and humble religious accustomed to withstanding hardship and privation to plant the Holy Faith in that part of the world, which is as big as Europe and near and opposite Europe and in no part converted, this would be a deed of great honour to the Holy Church, and in time very useful, and it is the most expedient way of converting them.[62]

What is most astonishing is not so much the utter impracticality of Stock's project as its extraordinary likeness to another project which was to be submitted to Propaganda sixteen years later by another missionary, the Capuchin Pacifique de Provins, who, like Stock, was eager and zealous and also at perpetual loggerheads with his superiors.[63] If the pope—the project went on—is a sovereign as absolute as other European sovereigns (and certainly with greater right), why seek the help and collaboration of others when it is possible to expand and colonize autonomously with Italian settlements depending directly on the Holy See?[64] Needless to say, neither project was taken at all seriously by Propaganda.[65] Within a temporal vision whose only limit *ad quem* is eternity, the whole strength of missionary expansion lies precisely in its being above and beyond national interests while using secular channels prepared by others in different parts of the world. It was this that both Stock and Pacifique were unable to understand, tied, like all common mortals, to the biological limits of their own brief existence.

When Stock ceased to be interested in Avalon, Propaganda ceased to be interested in Stock. It was by then perfectly clear that the English Discalced Carmelite mission would play no significant part in the affairs of America, and Stock's disillusioned disinterest was the most eloquent proof. But Propaganda, while formed of individuals, was not an individual. It might make a mistake, but it would never give up. If the English opening was shut to Propaganda, new ways would have to be found, new schemes devised, old relationships renewed, new solutions envisaged.

Stock's news of the Puritan mass exodus was a salutary warning. Something had to be done, and straight away. A letter was despatched to Fabio de Lagonissa, archbishop of Conza, nuncio in Brussels, and as such responsible for English affairs, asking for his advice on how to counteract the expansion of English Protestantism. One idea, Propaganda suggested, would have been to seek the help of Rome's natural allies, the French Catholics, using French missionaries[66] as had been done with the Capuchin project some years previously.[67] Rome then lost no time in acting. The nuncio's answer having arrived,[68] they decided to speak with the procurator general of the Capuchins, Francesco de Genova. He in turn was to approach the Grey Eminence, Joseph de Paris, prefect of the order's missions, urging him to establish a mission in New England.[69] The idea turned out to be welcome, and within a short time the Capuchin mission in Acadia was a reality.[70]

When Stock was informed of Propaganda's collaboration with the Capuchins,[71] he put up a show of enthusiasm[72] although in fact Avalon and America were no longer of any interest to him. He had expended much time and energy on the project to no avail. It could now be left to others younger and more energetic than himself while he returned mentally to the England he had refused to leave, its religious disputes, quarrels with his superiors, and all the risks of persecution.

### CHAPTER NINE

# Conclusion

Simon Stock's interest in North America finally waned just as the great Puritan emigration, whose beginnings he had witnessed with consternation, took a firm and lasting hold. The America Stock abandoned in 1630 was already very different from the America he had stumbled across in 1625, and it was to change still more in the two decades to follow. While thousands of English settlers occupied the coasts of America, the French, who settled along the shores of the St. Lawrence, steadily established themselves in the continent's interior. In the second half of the seventeenth century, the Atlantic Ocean was to become more European than the Mediterranean Sea itself.

Prospects in Newfoundland failed to live up to the high expectations raised in the sixteenth and early seventeenth centuries, and it played no part in the impressive and often dramatic development of the rest of North America. The fruitless ventures of the 1620s later appear as the high spot in the history of European interest in the island. After George Calvert, Baron Baltimore abandoned Newfoundland in 1630, little was heard of it. None of the previously founded colonies prospered. Some scattered settlers made a living fishing, and their descendants were later involved, like everybody else, in the Anglo-French conflict which raged over the whole of North America. Newfoundland's isolated position, however, at least meant that its inhabitants were left unscathed by the tragic events to which the richer American colonies were subjected.

Lord Baltimore's dream of founding a colony in America did not fade with his return to England. Two years after leaving Newfoundland he obtained for himself and his heirs the concession of a vast stretch of land to the north of the Potomac River, the future state of Maryland. He died, however, on 15/25 April 1632, before his rights to the concession could be officially proclaimed, and it was his son Cecil who inherited the lands along with his father's title. His brother Leonard was sent as governor in 1634.

Although the Calvert family had never formally renounced its rights to Avalon (where Cecil had sent Captain William Hill in 1634), they were contested by a London-based group headed by Sir David Kirke, who had conquered Quebec in 1629. By the end of 1637, he had managed to procure joint-ownership of the whole island. The dispute of the two families lasted for years and was only decided in the Calverts' favour after the restoration of the monarchy with Charles II.

When Stock again met Lord Baltimore in London at the end of 1630, America and Avalon were no longer of interest to him, and his failure to grasp that Lord Baltimore's sights were now set on Virginia, and not Avalon, is significant. Three years later, in 1633, he was still making the same mistake. Speaking of the imminent departure of a number of Jesuits for Maryland, he stated that they had "taken over that mission of Avalon,"[1] as if Maryland and Avalon were one and the same place. By 1636, however, while claiming ignorance about the state of events in the colony, he at least clearly knew where it was situated: "Of that mission of Avalon little news reached me, although it yet progresses. The site is now changed, being towards Virginia."[2]

While Stock's relationship with the Sacred Congregation "de Propaganda Fide" was not born out of a common interest in Avalon and America, this mutual interest certainly cemented it as the subject matter of the intensive 1625–30 correspondence shows. The correspondence fell off abruptly after 1630, and Stock, who had set great hopes on the officials of Propaganda, now wrote less and less frequently,[3] although his letters to the Congregation continued until a few years before his death, which took place in Canterbury in 1652 (his last letter to Propaganda is of 1649). After 1630 he reverted to his original interests, those which had concerned him before his meeting with Lord Baltimore— the novitiate, the proper establishment of the English mission, and the zeal and success of other religious orders. When Stock praised the Jesuits' success in the Avalon/Maryland mission[4] (a success that only served to show up all the more clearly the failure of the Discalced Carmelites), he mentioned it in the context of rivalry between the orders in England, not America. Thwarted and frustrated by his superiors, Stock repeatedly asked to be allowed to leave the order. Even this request was refused, and Stock was to die at the age of seventy-six in the habit of a Discalced Carmelite, all his dreams and projects unrealized, in America as in England.

Stock's life of frustration was only momentarily interrupted by his vision of America, but the five years between 1625 and 1630 were without doubt as important for him personally as they are interesting to the historian. He converted Lord Baltimore, convinced him to impose a specifically Catholic stamp on his colony in America, took care of Avalon's spiritual welfare, and dispatched there a number of Catholic settlers, possibly even missionaries. Moreover, while he never set foot there himself, Stock painstakingly built up an image of America out of nothing, following a rather singular intellectual itinerary. To his less than systematic reading of books and avid consultation of atlases and maps, he brought a mass of details from his personal acquaintance with the protagonists—hence the many details concerning Avalon not available elsewhere. Much is known of what adventurers, sea captains, settlers, and pioneers knew or imagined about America. Little remains of the knowledge and impressions of people like Stock, who glimpsed the New World but refused to make it their promised land.

As stated in the Introduction, however, Stock's role as Propaganda's "American" agent was also public. He received information, filtered it, and transmitted it to Rome, thus directly shaping and influencing the Congregation's awareness and knowledge of America. In the first decade of its existence, Propaganda had access to only three sources of information—Gregorio Bolìvar, Bede of the Blessed Sacrament, and Simon Stock. Of the three, only Stock played a part which was in any way formative and organic. Censured and manipulated by the superiors of the order, Bede's report was so mutilated as to render it incomprehensible. The main defect of Bolìvar's was its blandly descriptive nature and the absence of specific requests or queries that needed to be examined and acted upon. As an essentially bureaucratic organization, Propaganda was more used to working in response to externally received *stimuli* that put its administrative machine to work, and Bolìvar's report was lost in the welter of requests arriving daily from all parts of the world which required immediate and specific answers. Stock's letters differed precisely because of the catalogue of requests, questions, doubts, and advice they contained, which put Propaganda under continual pressure to compare, evaluate, and decide. Paradoxically, it is their very lack of description which made these letters so interesting to the officials in Rome. Slowly, but constantly, Stock's information and ideas came to form part of Propaganda's mental frame of reference.

After its first decade of activity, Propaganda could consider itself relatively well-informed about what was happening on the other side of the Atlantic Ocean. The bulk of its awareness came not simply from the arithmetical sum of all the information that had gradually been collected, but rather was the result of an (often fortuitous) elaboration of data acquired in various ways, either on Propaganda's own initiative (as in the case of Bolìvar) or, more frequently, thanks to unsought *stimuli* from external sources (as in Stock's case). Given this wealth of information, Propaganda was well-equipped to decide on a basic policy and approach to the North American question by the beginning of the 1630s. The strategy its officials so laboriously pondered and evolved in these early years was the result of a shrewd and clear-headed mediation between the solicitations of individuals (Bolìvar, Bede, and Stock), and the (often contrasting) necessity of maintaining good relations with the other organs of the Holy See, not least the religious orders—a compromise which they attempted to formulate within an ampler and more complex world strategy. In the years to follow, for the whole of the seventeenth and eighteenth centuries, although relations between Propaganda and North America were to become more complex and considerably less casual, the basic guidelines of their American policy laid down in this first decade remained essentially unchanged.

# Part Two

## The Letters of
## Simon Stock

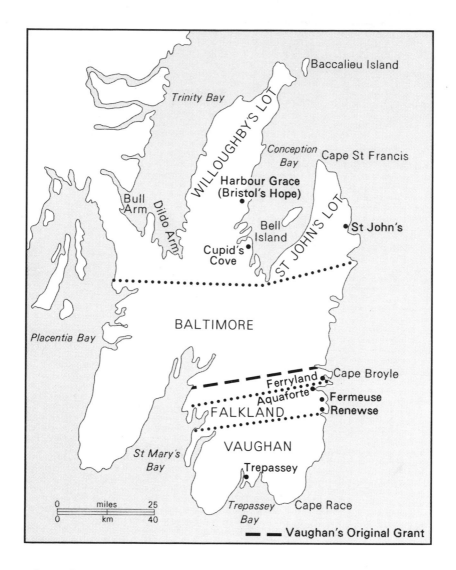

*The Avalon Peninsula, early seventeenth century. Source: Gillian T. Cell,*
English Enterprise in Newfoundland 1577–1660. *University of Toronto Press,*
*1969, facing p. 82.*

# *Introductory Note*

Part Two of this book gives all the extant letters of Simon Stock, plus a series of documents enclosed with the letters—a total of ninety-five items in all. Here and elsewhere, I have used the term "letter" to refer both to the letters proper and to the enclosures. Seventy-three of these were found in the archives of the Sacred Congregation "de Propaganda Fide" in Rome in various volumes of the *SOCG* series. Twenty belong to the General Archives of the Order of the Discalced Carmelites in Rome, in a series entitled *Litterae, Stock*. One was found in the Vatican Secret Archives in the series *Segreteria di Stato, Francia*, and one in the Westminster Diocesan Archives in London. (These last two were unavailable when the Italian edition of this book was printed. I have therefore numbered them 31a and 37a). Very few of these letters have been known or published before.

I have arranged Stock's letters in chronological order. While they are almost all clearly dated in Stock's hand, the enclosed documents rarely are. The date I have given them is usually that of the letter to which they were originally attached. Seventeenth-century England used the Julian (Old Style) Calendar, which was ten days behind the Gregorian (New Style) Calendar. The latter was introduced in 1582 by Gregory XIII, but it was only put into use in Protestant countries in the second half of the eighteenth century (in England, in 1752). English Catholics often employed the New Style Calendar prior to 1752, following the dictates of Rome. Thus, it is often impossible to establish with certainty which system is being used. With the exceptions of letters 75 and 76, however, Stock always uses the Gregorian Calendar (see also n5).

The data that follow each letter-heading give the archival series (*SOCG* in the Propaganda archives and *Litterae, Stock* in the archives of the order), volume, folios, blanks, type of document, language, any enclosure, and any extant copy of the same document. At the head of the text of each letter, I have indicated whether the complete text or a summary is given.

It is impossible to know whether the present letters are all that Stock wrote to Propaganda and the order. Although no significant gap is evident from their content, some letters appear to have been lost. One letter (letter 67) addressed to Propaganda is now in the archives of the order. So far as the years 1624-31, of special importance for the present book, are concerned, the correspondence between Stock and Propaganda seems complete with the exceptions of a letter that should fall between letters 39 and 40 which the Congregation never received and all the maps.

Some of the letters have been summarized. Those which deal, directly or indirectly, with Avalon and North America are reproduced in their entirety. The only exceptions are letters 23, 25, 45 and 79, in which the references to Avalon are too cursory to justify the transcription of the whole letter. In the case of complete transcriptions, I have given in addition to Stock's text all the notes made on it by the officials in Rome. Generally Stock wrote only on the *recto* of the first folio, leaving blank the *verso* and the *recto* and *verso* of the second folio. The *verso* of the second folio was then used by Propaganda for notes and comments. At their most complete, these include a summary of the letter itself, the minutes of the General Congregation in which the letter was discussed, with its progressive number and date (the fair copy of the minutes is now in the *Acta* series), and the draft of the Congregation's reply (the definitive version of which was successively registered in the *Lettere* series). Some of these elements are frequently missing. The order's clerks, on the other hand, were content with a summary of the letter of no more than ten lines.

Because letters were dispatched by courier with other items and the address appeared on only one piece, Stock's addressees cannot always be identified. We know for certain that he wrote to Paolo Simone di Gesù e Maria, the order's general (letters 4-6, 32, 68, 70-4, 77-8); to Propaganda as a body (letters 26, 56, 61, 65, 76, 92-3); to Francesco Ingoli, the secretary of Propaganda (letters 62, 79, 86); to Giovanni Francesco Guidi di Bagno, archbishop of Patras, nuncio in Flanders (letters 7, 9, 31a); to Cardinal Ottavio Bandini, member of Propaganda (letter 13); to the Congregation of Regulars (letter 60); to his confrère Bede of the Blessed Sacrament (letter 8); to the definitor general, Angelo (letter 1); to Bernardino Spada, archbishop of Tamiathis, nuncio in France (letter 31a); and to the procurator general of the order, Giovanni Maria di San Giuseppe (letter 69). In all these cases, the name of the addressee is clearly stated on the letter itself. In all the others, it remains a question of conjecture, since the original address is missing. Similarly, the register containing copies of Propaganda's replies to Stock (the *Lettere* series) only states the name of the Congregation official who signed the letters in very rare cases (and none of those pertain to Stock).

As regards the addressees of those of Stock's letters preserved in the archives of Propaganda, I believe we may presume: that all the letters with plural headings ("My Most Illustrious and Reverend Honoured Lords," for example) are to be taken as letters to Propaganda as a body; that all the letters with single headings, up to and including letter 33, are to be read as addressed to Bandini, who died in 1629; and that the letters with single headings from letter 62 onwards were addressed to Ingoli, to whom Stock wrote for the first time, we know, in letter 62.

Of the Propaganda officials to make notes on Stock's letters (no more than three separate people), only Ingoli can be identified with certainty. His comments are to be found on almost all the letters (with the exception of letters 21, 35-6, 43, 47, 54, 57, 61, 65, 75-6, 79, 82-3, 85-7)—an indication not only of the enormous workload he took upon himself as secretary, but also of his particular interest in Stock. In fact, and unknown to Stock, Ingoli's notes clearly demonstrate that he, and not Bandini, was behind all Propaganda's correspondence and that it was he who drafted most of the minutes of the General Congregations and the replies to Stock. A word concerning Ingoli's language—his mixture of Italian and Latin, with words of both languages often alternating within the same sentence, and the enormous quantity of abbreviations used are obviously a form of learned officialese, the language of a man fluent in both languages who had too much to do and too little time to do it.

As far as we know, Propaganda wrote twice to Stock on its own initiative, on 6 December 1625 (*Lettere*, vol. 4, f. 201v) and on 7 September 1630 (ibid., vol. 10, f. 138rv). Almost all his letters from 1624 to 1631 were carefully examined, discussed and answered. From 1632 onwards, while his letters were still discussed, they were rarely answered, or if they were, the answer was not registered in the *Lettere* series). As I maintain elsewhere in this book, this is far from a matter of chance; while in the 1624-31 period Stock's letters speak chiefly of Avalon and North America, the subject is seldom mentioned after 1631 and the importance of his comments was commensurately lessened.

Stock's letters have here been translated into English. Stock wrote them in Italian and Latin—ecclesiastical, elementary Latin, the Latin of his time; spaniolate Italian, often incorrect, but almost always clear. Since Stock had studied in Italy and frequented the Spanish embassy circles in London, he was probably equally fluent in Italian and Spanish. His handwriting is relatively clear, and few words are illegible. The very few alterations I have made to the text of Stock's letters, normally the addition of a word to make the meaning clearer, appear between square brackets. These have also been used in places in which the sheet was torn or worn away and a word or part of one is consequently missing.

Only when I consider them particularly significant have I included words that were subsequently deleted or altered by Stock. I have modernized the punctuation and the use of lower case and capital letters which Stock, following the custom of his time, uses with no uniformity, thus creating some confusion for the present-day reader. Indentation is a problem. I have respected Stock's for place and date and then given my own in accordance with present-day criteria of legibility and clarity.

Some words which Stock and the Roman officials use repeatedly require explanation. "Our Lord" means both God and the pope. "Labourers" means missionaries or priests generally. "Religion" often means religious order. People frequently referred to include the bishop of Chalcedon, Richard Smith; the pope, Urban VIII; the order's general, Paolo Simone di Gesù e Maria; and the king of England, James I up to 1625, and afterwards Charles I.

Stock's letters are by no means an open book. The references are obscure, and people's names and place-names are few and far between. As a result, there are many footnotes, and Parts One and Two are to be considered complementary.

# List of Stock's
# Letters

An asterisk (*) means a letter is transcribed in full.

| | | |
|---|---|---|
| 91 | *27. | To [Propaganda], 5 December 1625 |
| 93 | *28. | To [O. Bandini], 15 December 1625 |
| 94 | *29. | To [Propaganda], 7 March 1626 |
| 98 | *30. | To [O. Bandini], 2 April 1625 |
| 99 | *31. | To [Propaganda], 22 April 1626 |
| 101 | 31a. | To G.F. Guidi di Bagno, 22 April 1626 |
| 101 | *32. | To Paolo Simone di Gesù e Maria, 22 April 1626 |
| 103 | 33. | To [O. Bandini], 30 June 1626 |
| 103 | *34. | To [Propaganda], 30 June 1626 |
| 105 | 35. | To [Propaganda], [30 June 1626] |
| 105 | *36. | To [Propaganda], 12 February 1627 |
| 106 | *37. | To [Propaganda], 10 October 1627 |
| 108 | 37a. | To [Propaganda], 10 October 1627 |
| 108 | *38. | To [Propaganda], 27 June 1628 |
| 112 | *39. | To [Propaganda], 28 July 1628 |
| 114 | *40. | To [Propaganda], 2 July 1629 |
| 116 | *41. | To [Propaganda], 9 August 1629 |
| 118 | 42. | To [Propaganda], 1 November 1629 |
| 118 | 43. | To [Propaganda], [1 November 1629] |
| 118 | 44. | To [Propaganda], 8 January 1630 |
| 119 | 45. | To [Propaganda], 1 March 1630 |
| 119 | *46. | To [Propaganda], 28 April 1630 |
| 120 | 47. | To [Propaganda], 30 April 1630 |
| 121 | 48. | To [Propaganda], 25 July 1630 |
| 121 | 49. | To [Propaganda], 16 September 1630 |
| 121 | *50. | To [Propaganda], 1 January 1631 |
| 123 | 51. | To [Propaganda], 4 February 1631 |
| 124 | 52. | To [Propaganda], 5 March 1631 |
| 124 | 53. | To [Propaganda], 6 April 1631 |
| 124 | 54. | To [Propaganda], [6 April 1631] |
| 125 | 55. | To [Propaganda], 27 April 1631 |
| 125 | 56. | To [Propaganda], [27 April 1631] |
| 125. | *57. | To [Propaganda], 25 June 1631 |
| 127 | 58. | To [Propaganda], 1 November 1631 |
| 127 | 59. | To [Propaganda], 7 December 1631 |
| 127 | 60. | To the Sacred Congregation of Bishops and Regulars, [7 December 1631] |
| 128 | 61. | To Propaganda, [7 December 1631] |
| 128 | 62. | To F. Ingoli, 7 December 1631 |
| 129 | 63. | To [Propaganda], 24 December 1631 |
| 129 | 64. | To [Propaganda], 28 January 1632 |
| 129 | 65. | To Propaganda, [7 December 1631] |
| 130 | 66. | To F. Ingoli, 24 March 1632 |
| 130 | 67. | To [Propaganda], 24 March 1632 |

---

| | | |
|---|---|---|
| 130 | *68. | To Paolo Simone di Gesù e Maria, 25 July 1633 |
| 131 | 69. | To Giovanni Maria di San Giuseppe, 2 November 1633 |
| 132 | *70. | To Paolo Simone di Gesù e Maria, 3 November 1633 |
| 133 | 71. | To Paolo Simone di Gesù e Maria, 3 January 1634 |
| 133 | 72. | To Paolo Simone di Gesù e Maria, [15 May 1634] |
| 133 | 73. | To Paolo Simone di Gesù e Maria, [2 August] 1634 |
| 133 | 74. | To Paolo Simone di Gesù e Maria, 2 November 1634 |
| 133 | 75. | To [F. Ingoli], 14/24 December [1634] |
| 134 | 76. | To Propaganda, 14/24 December 1634 |
| 134 | 77. | To Paolo Simone di Gesù e Maria, 7 February 1635 |
| 134 | 78. | To Paolo Simone di Gesù e Maria, 13 April [1635] |
| 135 | 79. | To F. Ingoli, 15 October 1636 |
| 135 | 80. | To [F. Ingoli], 15 April 1637 |
| 135 | 81. | To [Propaganda], 2 June 1637 |
| 136 | 82. | To [Propaganda], 23 January 1638 |
| 136 | 83. | To [Propaganda], [1638] |
| 136 | 84. | To [Propaganda], [1638] |
| 137 | 85. | To [Propaganda], 23 June 1638 |
| 137 | 86. | To F. Ingoli, 23 June 1638 |
| 137 | 87. | To [F. Ingoli], 8 April 1639 |
| 137 | 88. | To [Propaganda], 22 February 1641 |
| 138 | 89. | To [Propaganda], [22 February 1641] |
| 138 | 90. | To [Paolo Simone di Gesù e Maria], [after 21 April 1641] |
| 138 | 91. | To [F. Ingoli], 19 June 1649 |
| 139 | 92. | To Propaganda, 19 June 1649 |
| 139 | 93. | To Propaganda, 28 June 1649 |

# *Letters*

1. SIMON STOCK TO ANGELO, OCD, DEFINITOR GENERAL, IN ROME, LONDON, 8 NOVEMBER 1622

*Litterae, Stock*, 271.g.2, ff. [1rv–2rv]. Autograph letter signed. Italian, Latin. Summary.

On his return to England from Flanders[1] he found the mission in some disorder. In compliance with the addressee's request, he describes the state of the English mission, listing the factors which in his opinion necessitate the founding of a novitiate, a visit from the superiors, full electoral rights, and the sending of a procurator to the general chapter.[2]

2. [SIMON STOCK] TO [THE GENERAL CHAPTER OF THE DISCALCED CARMELITES, IN ROME], [LONDON, MARCH 1623]

*SOCG*, vol. 347, ff. 337rv–40rv. B: f. 340r. Autograph memorandum unsigned. Latin, Italian. Enclosed with letter 3. Summary

In seven points the "Rationes ob quas patres carmelitae anglicanae missionis novitiatum pro natione anglorum requirunt." There follow, in ten points, the "Rationes ob quas desiramus quod missio anglicana et dicta domus novitiatus sint immediate sub Praeposito Generali et Definitorio Generali."

3. SIMON STOCK TO [GIOVANNI FRANCESCO GUIDI DI BAGNO, ARCHBISHOP OF PATRAS, NUNCIO IN FLANDERS, IN BRUSSELS],[3] [LONDON], 10 NOVEMBER 1623

*SOCG*, vol. 347, ff. 333rv, 334rv. B: f. 344r. Autograph letter signed. Italian, Latin. Enclosure: letter 2. Summary.

He wishes to found a novitiate for English Discalced Carmelites. An English nobleman[4] has offered to finance the project. Enclosed is the letter to this effect which was sent to the general chapter of the order, which rejected the project. A serious incident occurred the previous Sunday when a Jesuit was celebrating mass with a confrère and ninety-three faithful.[5]

4. SIMON STOCK TO PAOLO SIMONE DI GESÚ E MARIA, OCD, GENERAL, IN ROME, LONDON, [9 MAY 1624]
*Litterae, Stock*, 271.g.11, ff. [1rv–2rv]. B: f. [2r]. Autograph letter signed. Italian, Latin. Summary.

Since the addressee is to go to France, it is hoped that he will take this opportunity to visit the English mission, to assess for himself the need for the novitiate which a certain gentleman[6] has offered to finance. A superior for the English mission is imperative. Should his request not be met, he will ask to move to another order.

5. SIMON STOCK TO PAOLO SIMONE DI GESÚ E MARIA, OCD, GENERAL, [IN ROME], LONDON, 12 JULY 1624
*Litterae, Stock*, 271.g.4, ff. [1rv–2rv]. Autograph letter signed. Italian, Latin. Summary.

He asks the general to visit the English mission himself or send a substitute, to assess the need for a novitiate for the English Discalced Carmelites. Should this novitiate not materialize, he would ask to leave the order. Bede of the Blessed Sacrament could be sent out from Brussels to England with the appropriate authority to act as superior.[7] His two confrères[8] are ill and live in constant danger of imprisonment. Millini writes that he is negotiating with the addressee and that both of them are to approach the pope.[9]

6. SIMON STOCK TO PAOLO SIMONE DI GESÚ E MARIA, OCD, GENERAL, [IN ROME], [LONDON, 25 JULY] 1624
*Litterae, Stock*, 271.g.5, ff. [1rv–2rv]. Autograph letter signed. Latin. Summary.

Citing the dictates of the Council of Trent, he states his requests for visits, houses for the English Discalced Carmelites, full electoral

rights, and the founding of a novitiate, all of which other orders operating in England already possess.

7.   SIMON STOCK TO GIOVANNI FRANCESCO GUIDI DI BAGNO, ARCH-
BISHOP OF PATRAS, NUNCIO IN FLANDERS, [IN BRUSSELS], [LONDON], 26
JULY 1624
*SOCG*, vol. 347, ff. 358rv, 369rv. B: f. 369r. Autograph letter signed.
Italian, Latin. Summary.

For some eight years or more[10] his request for the founding of a
novitiate for the English has met with no success. As in his preceding
letter,[11] he asks the addressee's help. This would be particularly
timely in view of the visit of the general of the order to Brussels.[12]

8.   SIMON STOCK TO BEDE OF THE BLESSED SACRAMENT, OCD, IN
BRUSSELS, [LONDON], 23 AUGUST 1624
*Litterae, Stock*, 271.g.6, f. [1rv]. Autograph letter signed. Italian.
Summary.

He has duly received the addressee's letter and agrees that Bede
should not have the care of the English mission. Being almost sixty
years of age,[13] he is unable to go to Flanders, as his superiors would
like, because of the dangers accruing to the journey. His two confrères[14] are weak and in poor health and not destined to live long.

9.   SIMON STOCK TO GIOVANNI FRANCESCO GUIDI DI BAGNO, ARCH-
BISHOP OF PATRAS, NUNCIO IN FLANDERS, [IN BRUSSELS], LONDON, 23
AUGUST 1624
*Litterae, Stock*, 271.g.7, ff. [1rv–2rv]. B: ff. [1v–2r]. Autograph letter
signed. Italian. Summary.

As requested by Diego de La Fuente, who is in Brussels,[15] he sends
his reasons for requesting a novitiate for the English. He fears that a
previous letter to that effect may have gone astray.[16] The gentleman
who has offered to finance the novitiate is at that moment in Flanders.[17] He himself refuses to go to Flanders, as ordered by the general,
because of the dangers accruing to the journey. Asks the addressee to
speak personally to the general who is in Brussels or will be shortly.[18]

10.   SIMON STOCK TO [CARDINAL OTTAVIO BANDINI, MEMBER OF PROPAGANDA, IN ROME],[19] LONDON, 30 AUGUST 1624

SOCG, vol. 347, ff. 349rv, 356rv. B: ff. 349v, 356r. Autograph letter signed. Italian. Summary.

He expresses his satisfaction that Propaganda is considering the matter of the novitiate, as Diego de La Fuente informed him when passing through England on his way to Spain.[20]

Possibly discussed by Propaganda on 4 October 1624, in General Congregation no. 23. Answered by Propaganda on 12 October 1624 (*Lettere*, vol. 3, f. 176r).


11.   SIMON STOCK TO [PAOLO SIMONE DI GESÚ E MARIA, OCD, GENERAL, IN ROME], LONDON, 6 SEPTEMBER 1624

*Litterae, Stock*, 271.g.8, f. [11v]. Autograph letter signed. Latin. Summary.

He expresses his hopes that the addressee will visit the English mission personally. He is unable to go to Flanders, as requested by the general in his letter to Eliseus of St. Michael,[21] because of the dangers of the journey. Repeats the need for an English novitiate.


12.   SIMON STOCK TO [CARDINAL OTTAVIO BANDINI, MEMBER OF PROPAGANDA, IN ROME], LONDON, 15 NOVEMBER 1624

SOCG, vol. 347, ff. 294rv-5rv. Autograph letter signed. Italian, Latin. Summary.

He has received the addressee's letter.[22] Repeats that a novitiate is needed for the English Discalced Carmelites and states that the person who offered to finance the project "is known by the name of mister *Brune*." He gives the complete text of the report made by Bernard de Saint-Joseph on his recent visit to the English mission,[23] which is dated, London, 21 September 1624. "I have gained for Our Lord, by His Grace, two councillors of the King's Privy Council, the most intelligent and sufficient men that are of the Royal Council. And not since the time of the Queen Mary, which is now some sixty years, has any other councillor been gained but these two. And most religious men are they, and live beneath our government."[24] On Diego de La Fuente's departure, he became confessor to Count Gondomar[25] and Don Carlos[26] successively and is at present confessor to the Spanish agent.[27]

Discussed by Propaganda on 22 March 1625, in General Congregation no. 33, item no. 18 (*Acta*, vol. 3, f. 208v). Answered by Propaganda on 26 March 1625 (*Lettere*, vol. 4, ff. 52v–3r).

13.   SIMON STOCK TO CARDINAL OTTAVIO BANDINI, MEMBER OF PROPAGANDA, IN ROME, LONDON, 20 DECEMBER 1624
*SOCG*, vol. 347, ff. 292rv, 297rv. B: ff. 292v, 297r. Autograph letter signed. Italian. Summary.

Letter of recommendation of the bearer of the present letter,[28] who has offered to finance the novitiate for the English Discalced Carmelites to be founded in Saint-Omer.

Discussed and answered as in letter 12.

14.   SIMON STOCK TO [PROPAGANDA, IN ROME], LONDON, 8 FEBRUARY 1625
*SOCG*, vol. 347, ff. 291rv, 298rv. B: 298r. Autograph letter signed. Italian. Complete text.

[291r] My Most Illustrious and Reverend Honoured Lords,

Among those others whom I have here converted to Our Holy Faith there is a lord[29] of a land some three weeks' distance by sea from Great Britain, where our Holy Faith has never been preached.[30] And in the spring this gentleman means to return to his land[31] with his servants (some of whom I have converted) and desires to take with him two or three religious to sow the Holy Faith in his land. Here we are no more than three, and our two companions are ill.[32] For this reason I conceived the idea of writing most humbly to Your Most Illustrious and Revered Worships to beg your help in this holy undertaking. The land of this gentleman was unknown in former times[33] and has had no name until now, when we have called it Avalon, [since] thus was named that land where Saint Joseph of Arimathea first preached the Faith of Our Lord Jesus Christ in Britain.[34] It lies three degrees nearer to the meridian than England[35] and is a most fertile land, of a temperate air, with an abundance of divers sorts of vessels, and most abundant fish, and most excellent sea-ports.[36] The inhabitants are gentiles and English heretics who went to live there some three or four years since.[37] And it would now be an easy matter to plant there our Holy Faith since the principals are converted. And if the Holy Church offer no assistance at this time, all will become heretics, to the great detriment of the Holy Church. In like manner I have planted our Holy Faith in different parts of England where formerly no Catholic existed, but one person alone cannot continue the conversion, nor keep them converted, since it is impossible for one person to attend to so many things and so many different places. For ten years I have laboured[38] to obtain licence to found a novitiate for the English as other religious orders [291r/v] and all that are sent fruitfully on their missions possess, and I have been unable to obtain it. If we had had a novitiate for the English, there would now have been thirty or forty good priests to work here, to the great benefit of the Church and the salvation of an infinite number of souls, where now we are not able to increase in numbers. And being allowed no house for this mission, those of this mission are unable to be as one body, nor can they live in common, nor beg alms for the mission. And since they do not permit us to have any say in matters, as have the members of other orders, we are not permitted to share in government. After much entreaty I obtained a visitor here.[39] He came, he saw all that was amiss, but he cannot obtain remedy. For this I do most humbly beg Your Most Illustrious and Reverend Worships to take this mission under your protection and to give licence to use all the necessary means that it may bear fruit in conformity with the laws and customs of the Holy Church so that we may be in the condition of all other religious here, who proceed fruitfully and with no other labour. The mission will be most useful to the Holy Church. And lastly do I kiss the garments of your Most Illustrious Worships, and most humbly beg your holy benedictions.

From London, in England, 8 February 1625.

Your Most Illustrious and Reverend Worships' most humble servant,

      frà Simone Stock

[Following on, in Ingoli's handwriting] [298v] London, 8 February 1625. Father Simon Stoch, Discalced Carmelite. Announces his having converted a gentleman of a land three weeks' journey from London, three degrees nearer to the meridian, and with no name, having been only recently discovered. He has similarly converted some of his servants. And since this gentleman must return to his land in spring and desires to take two or three religious, he asks that these be sent, he himself being alone, and the land excellent and of a temperate air, where English heretics go who will pervert those peoples, who are gentiles. He has converted many others in England and in places where there was not even one Catholic. He speaks once more of the novitiate for the English, that labourers may be supplied[40] for such places as have need.

Die 22 martii 1625.[41] That His Lord Cardinal Millini[42] has spoken in the Congregation held before Our Lord of your letter which mentions the new island Avalon, as you have called it, and that it was attended to most carefully by His Holiness and by the Lord Cardinals, who, in agreement with you, have determined to form a mission of priests from your order, should the general have such as would be suitable, and otherwise of some other order. These are to be sent to you first for instructions, and are then to go to this island to help those peoples. The matter of the novitiate was similarly dealt with in the same Congregation, but no decision could be taken since certain information was lacking, and the nuncio in Flanders[43] has been written to for it. That you would be informed when the decision had been reached.[44]

Discussed and answered as in letter 12.


15. SIMON STOCK TO [PROPAGANDA, IN ROME], LONDON, 2 MARCH 1625
*SOCG*, vol. 347, ff. 311rv, 316rv. B: ff. 311v, 316v. Autograph letter signed. Italian. Complete text.

[316r] Most Illustrious and Reverend Honoured Lords,
    The Avalon matter progresses. Fifteen or twenty more Catholics are to accompany the first that I converted to found the Church of Our Lord there. Avalon is an island as large as England, if Wales and Scotland be excluded,[45] most fertile and stocked with fish beyond all manner abundant, with good sea-ports. It is of great importance to the Holy Church and to Christianity that it be inhabited not by heretics but by Catholic Christians. For this reason I fervently hope that two priests may be sent to accompany them this spring with sufficient authority to found and continue in this Avalon mission. In Canterbury I have begun to found a Church of Living Peter, and in other places I have gained many [souls], and always (notwithstanding the persecution that is universal) gain more and more souls for the Holy Church.[46] But yet it will be impossible to continue thus without licence to found a novitiate of the English and without licence to observe the laws and customs of the Holy Church and the rule and constitution of the order. Without a novitiate for the English, help of any kind is impossible, and without obedience there can be no government, and we shall slacken and lose force. For this reason I have offered these matters for the consideration of Your Most Illustrious

and Reverend Worships, most humbly begging their assistance. And lastly do I kiss your garments, and most humbly beg Your Most Illustrious Worships' holy benedictions.

London, in England, 2 March 1625.

Your Most Illustrious and Reverend Worships' most humble servant,

frà Simone Stock

[Following on, in Ingoli's handwriting] [311r] London, 2 March 1625. Father Simon Stoch, Discalced Carmelite. First. That fifteen or twenty more Catholics are to go to the newly discovered island of Avalon to found a church there. 2. Aforementioned island is as large as the rest of England with Scotland and Wales excluded; it possesses good seaports and most abundant fish. 3. He hopes that the Congregation will send priests. 4. In Canterbury he has set about the founding of a Catholic Church, and in other places is gaining souls notwithstanding the persecution. 5. Without an English novitiate and without a strict observance of the rule, no help will be forthcoming anywhere, and things will slacken.

Lecta die 2 maii 1625.[47] That the Sacred Congregation has instructed His Lordship Cardinal Millini, as protector of your religion, to provide labourers for the new mission to be established on the island of Avalon, in accordance with the opinion of Your Reverence, which was most welcomed by Our Lord for its importance. This same cardinal will already have executed the order with the efficiency owing to so important a negotiation. As regards the novitiate for the English, no reply from the nuncio in Flanders[48] is yet forthcoming, and no decision had thus been taken.[49]

Discussed by Propaganda on 2 May 1625, in General Congregation no. 35, item no. 13 (*Acta*, vol. 3, f. 218v). Answered by Propaganda on 7 May 1625 (*Lettere*, vol. 4, ff. 75v-6r).

16. SIMON STOCK TO [CARDINAL OTTAVIO BANDINI, MEMBER OF PROPAGANDA, IN ROME], LONDON, 10 MAY 1625
*SOCG*, vol. 347, ff. 225rv, 236rv. B: f. 236r. Autograph letter signed. Italian. Complete text.

[225r] Most Illustrious and Reverend Honoured Lord,

I have received a letter from Your Most Illustrious Worship,[50] and great was my consolation to note the zeal of Your Most Illustrious

Worship and that of the other holy cardinals. And I shall always be most ready to do all that you command.

For the whole of the spring the wind is favourable for embarking for Avalon, and many ships depart from here, but none after May. And for this reason it is clear from Your Most Illustrious Worship's letters that the priests cannot arrive in time. However, a Catholic knight and dear friend, who for many years has fought in the wars against Turks and infidels, is resolved to go thither in May with two faithful servants, and all the help I can give them is to teach them acts of contrition and pray that Our Lord may assist them.[51]

The Avalon gentleman, of whom I have already written,[52] is to remain in Ireland until the coming spring, and it is his hope that you will not fail to provide him with two or three priests to accompany him. It is unfortunate that I do not have religious to send in his company to keep him and his men in that zeal which he so eminently possesses, to the admiration of all here.

I remain for the most part in London, but I go when time permits to Canterbury, the archbishopric of this kingdom, forty-seven miles distant from London.[53] And there too I have won over the principal citizens (excepting the pseudo-archbishop),[54] along with many others. And when they were all united in one place, I was able to give assistance to all, but the persecution is so great now that they are obliged to flee in all directions. [Canterbury] is the most heretical city in this kingdom, and before my practising there, no Catholics existed. For this reason the pseudo-archbishop called it his virginal city, being pure [and] reformed of all papistry. And now, seeing Catholics in nearly all the streets, he has brought great persecution against us, and so dispersed are they that I am powerless to assist them. In this, as in all else, I am without help.

The *English heretics have sown* their heresy in all the northern parts of America, in Virginia, Ber[225r/v]muda, New England, New Scotland.[55] And there are many most fertile islands close to England that in times past were Catholic and in which no Catholic is now to be found, such as the Isle of Man, of Wight, of Jersey and of Guernsey.[56] And I find from experience that no priests are better suited to convert nations than ours [Discalced Carmelites], for their eminent demonstration of exemplary lives and the austerity in which they live. Not eating meat has been of great edification here. And if it were to please His Holiness and all the holy cardinals of Propaganda Fide to grant licence for the founding of a novitiate for the English, as other missionaries here have, and to allow us full electoral rights, as all the other religious orders have, they would find that much fruit would grow on this vine. But without a novitiate for the English we are unable to increase in number; and having no electoral right, we can have no share in governing; and without these two can there be no mission. And with this I kiss the garments of Your Most Illustrious Worship, most humbly begging your holy benediction.

London, 10 May 1625.

Your Most Illustrious and Reverend Worships' most humble servant, ·

frà Simone Stoch

[Following on, in Ingoli's handwriting] [236v] London, 10 May 1625. Brother Simon Stoch, Discalced Carmelite. 1. The priests that the father general speaks of sending cannot arrive in time, since it is only possible to embark for Avalon in the spring.[57] 2. A knight, however, with two of his servants, intends to go this May, and to these has he taught the little he is able, so that they may help that people.[58] 3. The gentleman of that island of whom he wrote is to remain in Ireland until the following spring, to then take with him the priests that are to arrive, since he had none to send him. 4. He goes when possible to the city of Canterbury, which was formerly totally heretical, to such an extent that the pseudo-bishop called it virginal; now there are many Catholics there, although dispersed on account of this pseudo-bishop's persecution. 5. The English heretics have sown their heresy in almost all northern parts of America—in Virginia, Bermuda, New England, and New Scotland. 6. Near to England are there most fertile isles, all of which were once Catholic, viz., of Man, Wight, Jersey and Guernsey; now all are heretical and to convert them the Discalced fathers would be most suitable, since their not eating meat is greatly esteemed; and thus the novitiate of which he has so often written is mandatory.[59]

Die 27 junii 1625. Congregatio 38.[60] Acknowledge the receipt of the two letters written on 10 and 24 May last.[61] And that the news given of the great diligence with which the English pervert the gentiles of the northern part of America was heard with disgust, and that particular consideration will be given to what you write concerning the providing of Catholic labourers for that province. News of your work in Canterbury was most welcome to the Congregation, which exhorts you to attend to the needs of that mission whenever you are able. The labourers for Avalon may already have arrived.[62] Do not fail to take up any occasion that might present itself for their departure, that they may go thither and bear fruit. No decision has yet been made regarding your novitiate, since the nuncio in Flanders,[63] who had been approached on certain points, was now in France on other matters and unable to attend to the question.[64]

Discussed by Propaganda on 27 June 1625, in General Congregation no. 38, item no. 27 (*Acta*, vol. 3, f. 240rv). Answered by Propaganda on 5 July 1625 (*Lettere*, vol. 4, ff. 106v-7r).

17.   SIMON STOCK TO [PROPAGANDA, IN ROME], LONDON, 24 MAY 1625
*SOCG*, vol. 347, ff. 226rv, 235rv. B: f. 235r. Autograph letter signed. Italian, Latin. Complete text.

[226r] Most Illustrious and Reverend Honoured Lords,

In the spring the wind is always favourable for embarking for Avalon, and some two thousand ships will leave from different parts,[65] but not after May. And as no hope exists that priests will be sent in time for this year, the gentleman principally concerned[66] will retire to Ireland. Another Catholic knight, our dear friend,[67] will now leave for Avalon with two faithful servants, in the hope that priests will be sent this coming year, as promised. In the meantime I have made acts of contrition available to him. To the great shame of the Catholic Church, the heretical English ministers have sown their heresy in many western parts of America, such as New England, New Scotland, Virginia, Bermuda, and Newfoundland,[68] and in all these lands there is not a single Catholic. And in Virginia they have created a pseudo-archbishop with an income of 5,600 scudi per annum.[69] And moreover there exist many most fertile and populated islands close to England, such as Jersey, Guernsey, Wight, Man, etc.,[70] where there is now not one Catholic, and in past times they were all Catholic.

Ten years have I laboured[71] to procure licence from the order's superiors to found a novitiate for English Discalced Carmelites, which, had it been granted, would now supply sufficient and worthy priests to send in all these various parts of the world, to the benefit of millions of souls, where now (being without permission to receive novices or to found a novitiate has the other orders have), we die out leaving no successors, and those whom we have gained with great labour and danger are lost for lack of assistance.

Most humbly do I supplicate your Most Illustrious Worships to consider that, with no monastery for the mission, we are unable to be as one body, or to live together, or to beg alms; since quicquid monacus acquirit, monasterio acquirit (caput In principio de probationibus).[72] And not having full electoral rights in accordance with the rule and constitutions of the order, as have the religious of other orders, we are unable to work canonically or observe religious discipline. And [226r/v] for these reasons I most humbly beg Your Most

Illustrious Worships to obtain the benediction of His Holiness for the establishment of a novitiate for English Discalced Carmelites and to observe the canons and customs of the Holy Church and the rule and constitutions of the order as far as this should be possible. And this mission will bear much fruit for the Holy Church. And lastly do I kiss the garments of Your Most Illustrious Worships, and most humbly beg your holy benedictions.

London, 24 May 1625.

Your Most Illustrious and Reverend Worships' most humble servant,

      frà Simone Stoch

[Following on, in Ingoli's handwriting] [235v] London, 24 May 1625. Brother Simon Stoch, Discalced Carmelite. Warns of the progress being made by English heretics in northern America, with the establishment of a pseudo-bishop with 5,600 scudi per annum at his disposal. With a reminder that some missions must be undertaken in those parts.

Missio informetur.

Die 21 julii 1625.[73]

Discussed by Propaganda on 21 July 1625, in General Congregation no. 39, item no. 25 (*Acta*, vol. 3, f. 245rv). Answered by Propaganda on 26 July 1625 (*Lettere*, vol. 4, f. 115r).

18.  SIMON STOCK TO [PROPAGANDA, IN ROME], LONDON, 31 MAY 1625
*SOCG*, vol. 347, ff. 227rv, 234rv. B: ff. 227v, 234r. Autograph letter signed. Italian. Complete text.

[227r] My Most Illustrious and Reverend Honoured Lords,

After that [letter] that I have written to Your Most Illustrious Lordships one week ago,[74] His Majesty of Great Britain has in a public edict announced his intention of propagating heresy in the western parts of America,[75] of which I wrote in my last [letter]. For this reason it is of absolute importance that the Holy Roman Church establish missions in all those lands which the English hold in America, such as Virginia, Bermuda, New England, New Scotland, Newfoundland, etc.,[76] since they will thus infest with heresy not only America, but also Japan, China, the Philippines and the East Indies, so near are they and of such easy journey and passage, as I wrote in my last [letter].[77]

As Your Most Illustrious Worships have failed to send religious for the Avalon mission, of those that thought to go some have departed without regulars or seculars, some have gone to Ireland, while the others are dispersed here and there, though yet with the hopes of departing this coming year.[78] In the meantime we can found a novitiate for English Discalced Carmelites as the other orders possess. As there can be no river without a spring nor tree without roots, in like manner there can be no mission without a novitiate for that mission. Money with which to purchase the site and to found it is ready; all that is lacking is the benediction of His Holiness to begin it. Persecution has increased since the death of King James,[79] and every day the monetary fine is increased.[80] May Our Lord grant the Christians patience to bear it. And lastly do I kiss the garments of Your Most Illustrious Worships, and most humbly beg their holy benedictions.

London, the last day of May 1625.

Your Most Illustrious and Reverend Worships' most humble servant,

frà Simon Stocho

[Following on, in Ingoli's handwriting] [234v] London, the last day of May 1625. Brother Simon Stoch, Discalced Carmelite. Firstly. That the new king of England has issued an edict for the propagation of heresy in northern America, namely in Virginia, Bermuda, New England and New Scotland. It is necessary to establish a Catholic mission in those parts, since the English will otherwise infest Japan, the Philippines, China and the East Indies, owing to the easy passage from America to those parts. 2. That the money to found the novitiate is ready, and only licence from His Holiness is now awaited. 3. That after the death of King James anti-Catholic persecution increased and is still increasing.

Die 21 julii 1625.[81] That your letters regarding the English etc. have been referred etc., and they were most welcome to the His Holiness and the Sacred Congregation, which will seek to act on his advice and according to the needs of the countries concerned to the best of its ability. The nuncio of Flanders[82] not yet having returned from Paris, no decision can be made about the novitiate.[83]

Discussed and answered as in letter 17.

19. SIMON STOCK TO [PROPAGANDA, IN ROME], LONDON, 13 SEPTEMBER 1625

*SOCG*, vol. 347, ff. 253rv, 266rv. B: f. 266r. Autograph letter signed.

Italian, Latin. Enclosures: letters 20-2. Complete text.

[235r] My Most Illustrious and Reverend Honoured Lords,

Still nothing has been done for the Avalon mission nor for that principal gentleman[84] who has requested some religious from His Holiness. Two of our confrères have come from Flanders,[85] but neither of them possess faculties or ability for such a mission , and the ships had already gone[86] before their arrival. In October I expect the return of a number of those Catholics who left for Avalon in the spring, and at that time I shall write to Your Most Illustrious Worships at greater length.

The English heretics hold the best part of America, did they know how to govern it, since it is most rich in all things except gold and silver, and the inhabitants more civilized and benign than are the other Americans,[87] and the climate equal to that of Italy and Spain, videlicet a gradu 32 as far as 45, and where the Gospel has to this time never been preached. And the geographers write thus of the natives and infidels of that part of America: qui inter Floridam et terram Bacalaos habitant, omnes uno nomine Canadenses appellantur, sed diversae nationes populorum, Mechelaga, Hongueda, Corterealis, prae caeteris benigni et humani.[88] And coverting them will present no great difficulty since they are of such a mild disposition; nor will it be necessary to send great numbers of seculars or regulars from Europe to convert them since the converts themselves will be excellent priests and religious. And the matter is of great importance for the passage from there to China and to have the Holy Church united. When once the passage is clear, it will be possible to go from England to China in four months, as I have been informed by a Catholic pilot who has traversed it with his ship, navigating along rivers from one part to the other.[89]

Avalon lies midway between England and Virginia,[90] and when the Faith is spread to Avalon, with greater ease may we extend it to Virginia, New England, New Scotland and amongst the Canadians.[91] But without licence to use the necessary means to bear fruit, we shall be unable to bear fruit, in this mission or any other, and shall be obliged to abandon them, as indeed we are resolved. And in truth it is a matter of dishonour to the Holy Church that religious are sent among infidels and persecutors without faculties or the means to live and bear fruit.

[235r/v] I enclose for Your Worships a proclamation of the king of Great Britain banishing all priests and and [sic] religious from his kingdom. I enclose the original with the Spanish translation.[92] And lastly do I kiss the garments of Your Most Illustrious and Reverend Worships, [and] most humbly beg your holy benedictions.

---

London, 13 September 1625.

Your Most Illustrious and Reverend Worships' most humble servant,

     frà Simone Stoch

[Following on, in Ingoli's handwriting] [266v] London, 13 September 1625. Brother Simon Stoch. 1. That the two religious have arrived from Flanders, etc., ut in sequentibus litteris.[93] 2. Reports on some of the peoples of northern America who dwell between 32 and 45 degrees in the region of the Arctic Pole and who are called Canadians, affirming that they are most civilized and benign and could be converted with ease, and very rich because of the fertility of the soil. 3. Avalon lies almost midway between England and these peoples and those of Virginia, New England and New Scotland. And by gaining this with the introduction of the Catholic Faith, it will similarly be of no great difficulty to gain the aforementioned peoples, and with few priests, since the country will itself provide able subjects. But nothing will be done and the mission of Avalon will be abandoned if a college or novitiate for the English is not established because there is no other way to have subjects. 4. He has spoken with a Catholic pilot who be means of the rivers of northern America has passed from one end to the other[94] and who has informed him that by opening this route that he himself has taken, it is possible to reach China from England in four months, a most important point as regards the undertaking of missionary activities in China. 5. Sends the proclamation issued by the English king against the Catholics, in English and Spanish.

Die XI novembris 1625.[95] Acknowledge the receipt of the letters sent[96] and thank him for his diligence in the service of God and the Holy Church. And that he give more details of the route which he has been informed exists which would permit travelling from England to China in four months along the rivers of northern America, since the maps of that part of the world show two rivers which, in their near-opposite courses, flow into opposite seas, but passing in vessels from one to the other appears impossible since a wide stretch of land lies between the two.[97] To try also to furnish the names of said rivers and every other particular. He is to be provided with faculties, which will be sent to him on their being sent by the Holy Office. The nuncio in Flanders being now returned from France,[98] he will be requested by letter to give the Congregation his opinion concerning the matter of the novitiate.[99]

To the nuncio of Spain and the nuncio of Flanders. Write to them[100] according to number 4, with the order to seek to verify this in their stations. To the nuncio of Flanders add that his opinion is awaited concerning the novitiate for the English that the Discalced

Carmelite Simon Stoch wishes to found in Saint-Omer, at the expense of a certain English gentleman,[101] in conformity with the letters written on . . .[102]

Discussed by Propaganda on 11 November 1625, in General Congregation no. 46, item no. 24 (*Acta*, vol. 3, f. 284rv). Answered by Propaganda on 15 November 1625 (*Lettere*, vol. 4, ff. 190v–1r).


20.   [SIMON STOCK] TO [PROPAGANDA, IN ROME], [LONDON, 24 AUGUST 1625]
*SOCG*, vol. 347, ff. 211rv, 218rv. B: ff. 211v, 218r. Translation into Latin of letter 21. Enclosed with letter 19. Summary
    Translation into Latin of Charles I's proclamation of 14/24 August 1625.

Discussed and answered as in letter 19.


21.   [SIMON STOCK], TO [PROPAGANDA, IN ROME], LONDON, 14/24 AUGUST 1625
*SOCG*, vol. 347, ff. 212rv–13rv. B: ff. 212r, 213v. Printed matter. Translation into Italian: letter 20. Translation into Spanish: letter 22. Enclosed with letter 19. Summary.
    Proclamation entitled "A Proclamation for recalling His Maiesties Subiects from the seminaries beyond the Seas, and putting the Lawes against Iesuites and Popish Priests in execution," dated 14/24 August 1625.

Discussed and answered as in letter 19.


22.   [SIMON STOCK] TO [PROPAGANDA, IN ROME], [LONDON, 24 AUGUST 1625]
*SOCG*, vol. 347, ff. 215rv–16rv. Translation into Spanish of letter 21. Enclosed with letter 19. Summary.
    Translation into Spanish of Charles I's proclamation of 14/24 August 1625.

Discussed and answered as in letter 19.

23. SIMON STOCK TO [CARDINAL OTTAVIO BANDINI, MEMBER OF PROPAGANDA, IN ROME], CHELSEA,[103] 14 SEPTEMBER 1625

*SOCG*, vol. 347, ff. 251rv, 267rv. B: ff. 251v, 267r. Autograph letter signed. Italian. Summary.

He has received the addressee's letters written on 5 and 16 July.[104] Two confrères[105] have arrived, but lack faculties. His own faculties, granted for seven years, are about to expire.[106]

In Ingoli's summary, among other matters, it is stated: "Two religious have arrived sent by his general from Flanders, but without the faculties necessary to proceed to Avalon."[107]

Discussed and answered as in letter 19.

24. SIMON STOCK TO [PROPAGANDA, IN ROME], CHELSEA, 20 OCTOBER 1625

*SOCG*, vol. 101, ff. 27rv, 34rv. B: ff. 27v, 34r. Autograph letter signed. Italian, Latin. Enclosure: letter 25. Complete text.

[27r] [Note in Ingoli's handwriting] Avalon and the novitiate for the English.

[Following on, in Stock's handwriting] My Most Illustrious and Reverend Honoured Worships,

The island[108] of which I have written to Your Most Illustrious Worships is so pleasing to this knight, our dear friend, who went thither in spring, that he is established there, and I have procured him the governorship of the same island.[109] And he sends marvellous reports of the island and of the wonderful abundance of fish. The natives are few and of a benign disposition, intending no harm to foreigners, though idolaters all.[110] I fervently hope that Your Most Illustrious Worships will not fail to send missionaries for this mission as you have promised.[111]

Two of our confrères have come here, the one to go to the new mission, but he is infirm and unsuitable, the other to act as superior, although without experience or sufficient learning.[112] And if Your Most Illustrious Worships fail to take this our English mission under your protection, I shall be forced to abandon it. I have given the reasons in the letter enclosed herein. And with this I kiss the garments of Your Most Illustrious Worships, humbly begging their holy benedictions.

Chelsea, 30 octobris 1625.

Your Most Illustrious and Reverend Worships' most humble servant,

fra Simone Stoch

---

[Following on, a note in Ingoli's handwriting] [34v] Die 6 februarii 1626, congregatio 51.[113]

[Following on, the summary of the letter, in a third hand] Chelsea, 30 October 1625. Brother Simon Stoch. That his friend the knight is gone as governor to the isle of Avalon and writes of the great abundance of fish; and that the inhabitants are of an excellent nature, although idolaters. Asks that the promised labourers be sent. Two of his confrères have arrived there, one for the Avalon mission, who is infirm and unsuitable, the other sent as superior, but who possesses neither experience nor learning. That the mission of England is untenable for the reasons given in the enclosed sheet.

[Following on, in Ingoli's handwriting] Ad Illustrissimum Millinum,[114] pro sequenti coram Sanctissimo.

*Number 5.* Referente Illustrissimo Cardinale Millino difficultates quas patres carmelitani discalceati Angliae circa missionem ad novam insulam Avvaloniae faciendam proponebant, Sacra Congregatio iussit committi Generali dicti ordinis, ut missionarios quos ad eam insulam iam destinavit illuc cum duobus nobilibus anglis,[115] qui eos secum suis sumptibus ducere volunt, omnino mittat, quia saltem per illos gentium regionem illam incolentium relatio habebit, et fortasse etiam Dei auxilio, qui id quod humano iudicio impossibile videtur facillimum reddere solet, viam operariis suis aperiet ad convertendos non solum indigenas infideles, sed etiam haereticos qui colonias ibi constituerunt.[116]

Discussed by Propaganda on 6 February 1626, in General Congregation no. 52, item no. 5 (*Acta*, vol. 4, ff. 14v–15r).


25.   [SIMON STOCK] TO [PROPAGANDA, IN ROME], [CHELSEA, 30 OCTOBER 1625]
*SOCG*, vol. 101, ff. 28rv, 33rv. B: f. 33r. Autograph memorandum unsigned. Italian, Latin. Enclosed with letter 24. Summary.

In five points, a memorandum listing "The reasons for which the Discalced Carmelites of the English mission are unable to work fruitfully in the mission of England or in that of the new island."[117]

Discussed as in letter 24.


26.   SIMON STOCK TO PROPAGANDA, [IN ROME], LONDON, 2 DECEMBER 1625

———

*SOCG*, vol. 347, ff. 219rv–24rv. B: 219v, 224r. Autograph letter and memorandum signed. Latin, Italian. Enclosed with letter 27. Summary.

A letter on the subject of the state of religion in England followed by a memorandum, in twelve points, containing suggestions on how the English mission could be organized entitled "Modus missiones in Angliam et in terras infidelium recte faciendi. . . ."

27.   SIMON STOCK TO [PROPAGANDA, IN ROME], LONDON, 5 DECEMBER 1625

*SOCG*, vol. 101, ff. 29rv, 32rv. B: ff. 29v, 32r. Autograph letter signed. Italian. Enclosure: letter 26. Complete text.

[29r] Most Illustrious and Reverend Honoured Worships,[118]

I herein enclose the means to bear fruit in the mission, humbly submitting it and myself to Your Most Illustrious Worship's mandates.

Here there is great persecution. Many priests have been seized and thrown into prison,[119] and the king has commanded by public edict that all anti-Catholic laws be executed with greater vigour even than the laws themselves command, without giving cause or reason other than the zeal of propagating Protestantism.[120]

In Virginia the English heretics have founded a college to infest America with their heresy.[121]

Most humbly do I beg Your Most Illustrious Worships to remember the Avalon mission, for if the Faith be not planted there at this time, all will become pernicious heretics, to the great detriment of the Holy Church. Many of our Catholic friends would go to live there if there were sufficient members of the clergy to accompany them. From the beginning I have explained to Your Most Illustrious Worships that no suitable father exists here, and Your Most Illustrious Worships, in your letter of 16 March,[122] promised to send missionaries to this end. But to this end one only has been sent, and he infirm and without sufficient faculties,[123] since he is dependent upon the English ordinary,[124] while Avalon is at least two thousand miles away from England.[125]

As I have worked at this new mission at the request of Your Most Illustrious Worships, I hope that you will not fail to help me proceed with it, to the honour of the Holy Church and the benefit of an infinite number of souls. And with this I kiss the garments [of] Your Most Illustrious Worships, and most humbly beg your holy benedictions.

London, 5 December 1625.

Your Most Illustrious and Reverend Worships' most humble servant,
          frà Simone Stoch

[Following on, in Ingoli's handwriting] [32v] Die 17 martii 1626, congregatio 53.[126]

London, 5 December 1625. Brother Simon Stoch. 1. Sends a means of conducting the missions in England, and in partibus infidelium (vide hanc in libro relationi 1626).[127] Gives an account of the serious persecution in England and of the imprisonment of many priests, without specifying a cause, but only for the zeal of propagating the Protestant religion. 3. In Virginia the English have founded a college to infest America. 4. Repeats the request for good missionaries for Avalon, that it not be infested, since those sent thither are unsuitable and have faculties only for England.

The general says that the two aforementioned missionaries are imprisoned in London.[128]

Ad Illustrissimum Dominum Cardinalem Millini.[129]

Most Reverend Father, the Lord Cardinal Millini has reported Your Reverence's letters at the congregation of Propaganda Fide together with the means you suggest should be adopted for conducting the missions.[130] In reply Their Most Illustrious Lordships affirm that, the missionaries who were sent for Avalon having been imprisoned, and there being none other of your order who speaks the language and is suitable, it is necessary for you to arrange to depart yourself, together with the companion the father general will provide; [and] that the necessary patents and faculties will be sent from here. And your journey, should it bear no other fruit, will at least provide full and accurate information of that country and of what could be done to bring those gentiles to our Holy Faith. Since with this knowledge it will not then be difficult to find suitable subjects for the mission in other orders. But let Your Reverence prepare himself for this journey, since from your zeal and charity great conversions of those peoples are hoped for. As regards the means of conducting missions, the Sacred Congregation first[131] sends thanks for the labour involved in the giving of these excellent memoranda, which will be applied as the need presents itself. And with this I wish for Your Reverence all God's blessings.[132]

Discussed by Propaganda on 17 March 1626, in General Congregation no. 53, item no. 6 (*Acta*, vol. 4, f. 30r). Answered by Propaganda on 21 March 1626 (*Lettere*, vol. 5, f. 51r).

28.   SIMON STOCK TO [CARDINAL OTTAVIO BANDINI, MEMBER OF
PROPAGANDA, IN ROME], LONDON, 15 DECEMBER 1625
*SOCG*, vol. 101, ff. 30rv–1rv. B: ff. 30v–1r. Autograph letter signed.
Italian. Complete text.

[30r] My Most Illustrious and Reverend Honoured Lord,

Great is my sense of obligation to Your Most Illustrious Lordship
for the charity shown me in writing so often regarding the matter of
the novitiate and the Avalon mission, although until this time nothing has been done either for the one or for the other. For this I must
humbly beg Your Lordship to labour in these matters that we may
obtain licence to found a novitiate and have missionaries for Avalon,
and Our Lord will repay your labours in this life and the next.

Persecution is great here. Many priests have already been seized
and thrown into prison, and they have seized a number of my letters
to the Sacred Congregation de Propaganda Fide.[133] And if by good
grace Your Most Illustrious Lordship, or others, have written to me,
those letters too have been seized. And it is no longer possible to send
or receive letters through that channel because of the war between
Spain and England.[134] For this reason, should it please Your Most
Illustrious Lordship or the Sacred Congregation de Propaganda Fide
to communicate anything to me, it will be necessary to send the letters
through the ambassador of France in Rome,[135] or through the nuncio
of Our Lord who is in Paris,[136] that they thus may be forwarded safely
to the French ambassador here.[137]

Most humbly do I beg Your Most Illustrious Lordship to consider
the justice of our requests. They are: 1. *faculties like those of other
religious sent hither*. 2. licence to *found* a novitiate for the English in
order to have missionaries. 3. *full electoral rights* as the other confrères of the order have, without which we are unable to proceed
canonically or have good government. 4. *the confirmation* of certain
constitutions, the better to proceed in the mission, and this I ask not
for myself but for the Holy *Church that loses* honour with these illusory missions that possess neither foundation nor means to bear fruit.
And with this I kiss the garments of Your Most Illustrious Lordship
and most humbly beg his holy benediction.

London, 15 decembris 1625.

Your Most Illustrious Lordship's most humble servant,

    frà Simone Stoch

[Following on, in Ingoli's handwriting] [31v] London, 15 December
1625. Brother Simon Stoch, Discalced Carmelite. Adds to the letters of
the 14th[138] that his letters written to the Congregation have been inter-
cepted and requests the faculties which other missionaries in England

possess, licence to found the novitiate for the English, and that the missionaries be granted full electoral rights.

Die 3 martii 1626, congregatio 52.[139]

Possibly discussed by Propaganda on 3 March 1626, in General Congregation no. 52.

29.   SIMON STOCK TO [PROPAGANDA, IN ROME], LONDON, 7 MARCH 1626

*SOCG*, vol. 101, ff. 17rv–18rv. Autograph letter signed. Italian. Complete text.

[17r] My Most Illustrious and Reverend Honoured Worships,

Your Most Illustrious Worships' letter of 15 November[140] only reached me on 3 March. Regarding the matter of more easily planting the Holy Faith in China, as I have received no reply, I have communicated it to Mister Bruneau, His Catholic Majesty's resident, who, as a good Catholic and zealous of the honour of God, will advance it as far as is possible, I believe.[141] It is a negotiation of no slight difficulty or expense, particularly since this is the beginning.

This pilot (of whom Your Most Illustrious Worships wish information)[142] was brought up to that trade with his elder brother. And he had often heard from his elder brother, now dead, that there was a passage in those parts, and thus he was desirous of trying it out. And having decided to turn to trafficking, he procured a captain and a number of soldiers to go on his own ship. Passing through the midst of those peoples, the captain, who was more valorous than wise, wanted to leave the ship and sack a settlement of the infidels, and he was killed with all his people. The pilot, once rid of them, went on with his sailors and one of his sons. And he went on and on, until, having passed through much fresh water in the middle, he reached salt water on the other side, and he pressed on through the salt water until not only he but also his sailors glimpsed a ship on the other side. And thus, the better to hide his intent, he left the ship and, walking a little way on land, saw not only the ship but also the men of the same ship, and at this point he returned.

I have given credence to this pilot since I have found him a good Catholic, with one of his sons a religious. And he paid greatly for his curiosity, having been accused of spying and of knowing above all others the secrets and passages of those seas and sea-coasts. He was imprisoned and freed upon payment of a great sum of money, the obligation of another [and the promise] not to return ever to those

---

coasts. And of this I am certain, having visited him in prison, and there was no reason for him to tell lies to me. And I have found him a most able man, over fifty years of age, and I have asked him many things concerning the peoples of northern America and about the plantations of the English, and I have found all that he told me to be true.

I have asked him why he has never made known this secret passage, and he replied that it would be the ruin of Christianity if it were to be known to the infidels, and that he would [risk?] his life since he knew one who had discovered a similar secret who had been taken, after which time no further news was had of him.[143]

And as to the probability, many affirm the existence of a passage, and I have found it printed in some accounts. But I have met with no other who [17r/v] I have met with no other who [*sic*] has passed along it other than this pilot. And on the newly printed English and Dutch maps it appears probable, since northern America is not terra firma, as commonly depicted, but islands and land divided by waters and seas, as almost all expert pilots affirm, and as Your Most Illustrious Worships may in part verify on the enclosed map.

And as Your Most Illustrious Worships may see from this map, the English have possession of the best part of America, not for the wealth of gold mines or silver or pearls, but for the excellence of the soil and of the men, who, as I have written elsewhere, are prae caeteris benigni et humani, for the temperate air and climate, corresponding to Italy, France, Spain, Bohemia and the most noble parts of Europe, between 37 and 60 degrees towards the island of Bermuda that lies at 32 degrees.[144] And it is a great shame that no missionaries are sent to such well-disposed people, where few missionaries would bear much fruit, because the inhabitants of those parts will in a few years make excellent missionaries and priests and religious, with no need of supplement from Italy or any other part.

I desired to further the new mission of which I have written on other occasions,[145] since from there it would be convenient to extend missions through the entire northern part of America. But since Your Most Illustrious Worships have failed to send missionaries as promised, and now another spring has come with nothing done, I have lost hope, and we shall lost both the occasion and those souls there. And if Your Most Illustrious Worships do not take our English mission under your protection and ensure that it proceeds in a manner befitting Catholics, all will come to nothing. Since to proceed in a mission without jurisdiction or faculties, and observance of the laws and customs of the Holy Church, is to proceed in the manner of Luther and Calvin, and not of the Sacred Holy Roman Church.

The pilot does not live in England because of the persecution, but he has offered to go and settle in the land of Avalon (whither he has been five times), and to transport there missionaries from one part to the other. But lacking missionaries, all has come to nothing. It is a matter of no wonder if the sea passages are not to be easily found, although that the passage exists is secretly known, also because of the ebbing and flowing of the sea and the currents, since until the time of Henry VII, king of England, the English were unaware of a passage to Rus[17v/18r]sia, which is now a most common thing. And for many years no other passage was known to the South of Pacific Sea, except for the Straits of Megalanes, but three or four years ago the Dutch discovered another much easier to pass through, which they call Mayres Straites, near an island which is named the isle of Barnevelt. And thus this pilot did not pass through those rivers which Your Most Illustrious Worships observe in the old maps[146] but entered through another, which he calls North Bay, and I am unable to imagine which passage it may be, unless it be that Mediterranean sea that enters America through the Straits on New Britain and passes through America, in the same manner as the Mediterranean Sea in Europe, as you may see from the enclosed map of America.[147]

In England persecution is rife. Two of our fathers have been seized and thrown into prison,[148] with many others, and I would have been taken, had not Our Lord blinded the police who had surrounded me to capture me. We live in peril equal to that in which the bandits and malefactors of Rome live. And though it is of little account to suffer and die for love of Our Lord and of the Holy Faith, [yet] to die with so little fruit gives great pain, and I am forced to see so many souls dying eternally and am unable to help them.

My faculties are not yet arrived.[149] And lastly I kiss the garments of Your Most Illustrious and Reverend Worships, and most humbly beg their holy benedictions.

London, 7 March 1626.

Your Most Illustrious and Reverend Worships' most humble servant,

frà Simone Stoch

[Following on, in Ingoli's handwriting] [18v] Die 4 maii 1626, congregatio 56.[150]

[Following on, the summary of the letter, in a third hand] London, 7 March 1626. Brother Simon Stoch, Discalced Carmelite. First. Has spoken once again with the pilot, for further information regarding the route which makes it possible to travel from England to the Indies in four months, and although he did not wish to name the passage through northern America, for fear of suffering the same fate as another who, for having revealed another secret passage, was thrown into prison, and nothing further was heard of him, yet some light was thrown on the situation from the generalities of his discourse. Namely, that northern America is not terra firma, as shown in the old maps, but has a mediterranean sea that makes it into an island, as is clear in the new map compiled by the English that he encloses. And, this being the case, it is easy to see that the South Seas may comfortably be reached from the isle of Terzera, one of the Azores, three days' distance from ·Spain. That he believed the pilot, since on all matters regarding northern America he replied truthfully to all his questions. 2. He laments that no decision has been reached concerning the Avalon mission, notwithstanding two years of negotiations,[151] since missions in the whole of northern America would be viable from that island, and since the population of those parts is docile and humane because they inhabit the temperate zone, between 37 and 60 degrees, corresponding to Italy, France, Spain and Germany. Thus some energy should be devoted to this mission, since the pilot has offered to take the missionaries to Avalon. 3. Reports of the passage to Russia discovered by the English and that of the Dutch by means of which the South Sea may be reached swiftly without passing through the Straits of Magaglianes. 4 and last. Reports on the grave persecution in England, where the priests live in great peril, like the bandits in Rome, and many have been imprisoned.

[Following on, in Ingoli's handwriting] Die 4 maii 1626, congregatio 56.

That his letter to the Sacred Congregation was most welcome for the news it contained regarding the pilot, being more extensive, [152] if not yet complete, since he did not see fit to reveal in entirety the new passage discovered in northern America which would ensure easy and rapid crossing through the new Mediterranean Sea to the other sea named South [Sea]. Your Reverence must prevail upon the said pilot so that he bestir himself at least in the service of God and those of His labourers who may be sent to those parts to reveal all that he knows of the said passage. You will now have received the Sacred Congregation's letter regarding Avalon,[153] in which they advance their wish that you go thither, the better to know the country, their Most Illustrious Worships placing great trust in your zeal and manifest compassion for the loss of so many, confident that on your return, or on receiving news from those parts, subjects for the mission may be abundantly supplied, if not from your own order, which is somewhat deficient in numbers, at least from others, namely Capuchins or Recollets,[154] should you see them fit.[155]

Discussed by Propaganda on 4 May 1626, in General Congregation no. 56, item no. 28 (*Acta*, vol. 4, ff. 55v-6r). Answered by Propaganda on 9 May 1626 (*Lettere*, vol. 5, ff. 92v-3r).

---

30. SIMON STOCK TO [CARDINAL OTTAVIO BANDINI, MEMBER OF PROPAGANDA, IN ROME], LONDON, 2 APRIL 1626
*SOCG*, vol. 101, ff. 15rv, 20rv. B: ff. 15v, 20r. Autograph letter signed. Italian, Latin. Complete text.

[15r] My Most Illustrious and Reverend Honoured Lord,

Your Most Illustrious Worship' letter of 6 December [156] arrived on 22 March together with my faculties, which are insufficient in these times of persecution and for the lands of the infidels.

1. They last only for seven years; thus once taken a missionary may be all his life in prison without faculties.

2. They are granted with relation to the licence of bishops or vicars apostolic, who are not to be found here, being all in hiding, the police seeking out priests with the same diligence with which malefactors and murderers are sought in Rome, since they are held and esteemed as traitors, and [with them] all who give them shelter.[157]

3. The faculty to consecrate portable altars has not been granted. There are no public altars here, and the police and heretics daily break and profance our secret altars. Moreover the faculties granted do not allow the saying of mass.

4. There has been granted no faculty communicandi aliis facultatem legendi libros hereticorum. Many souls are to be gained with this faculty, which confirms them in the Faith by demonstrating the falsity and corruption which abounds in their own books.

All those laws brought out against the Catholics (excepto presente martyrio) are enforced with great severity. And if His Holiness does not grant faculties to assist them in this time, they will be lost. All other regulars and secular possess the usual faculties. Only ours are limited. Most humbly do I beg Your Most Illustrious Worship to put this to the pious consideration of His Holiness. Your Most Illustrious Worship writes nothing regarding the novitiate. As the Sacred Congregation has failed to send missionaries, nothing has been done for Avalon. Nor can we bear fruit in the mission without licence being granted to apply the means. All will be insubstantial, useless ado, and foliage without fruit. And lastly do I kiss the garments of Your Most Illustrious Worship, most humbly begging your holy benediction.

London, 2 April 1626.

Your Most Illustrious and Reverend Worship's most humble servant,
frà Simone Stoch

[Following on, the summary of the letter in the hand of an official of Propaganda] London, 2 April 1626. Brother Simon Stoch. That he has received his faculties, which are insufficient in these times of persecution against Catholics for four reasons which he briefly outlines. And if Our Lord deny the faculties he requests, those Christians will be lost for lack of aid in such dire persecution.

[Following on, in Ingoli's handwriting] Die 18 Decembris 1626, congregatio 68.[158]

Discussed by Propaganda on 18 December 1626, in General Congregation no. 68, item no. 5 (*Acta*, vol. 4, f. 157r).

31.   SIMON STOCK TO [PROPAGANDA, IN ROME], LONDON, 22 APRIL 1626
*SOCG*, vol. 101, ff. 16rv, 19rv. B: f. 19r. Autograph letter signed. Italian. Enclosed with letter 31a. Complete text.

[16r] My Most Illustrious and Reverend Honoured Lords,

I have sent to Your Most Illustrious Worships the map of America,[159] on which you may verify the probability of a passage through the northern part of America to Japan and China, without going past the equinoctial line or the Tropic of Cancer or the temperate zone, which will be of great benefit to the Holy Church and an easy journey.

Your Worships may also see that English heretics possess the greater part of northern America, which corresponds to Italy, Spain, Hungary, and France and in the temperate zone,[160] where the infidels are more benign, humane, ingenious, valorous, nimble and more able to endure than those of other parts, of comely stature and of good proportions. When born they are all white, but since they use no art to protect themselves from the sun and colour themselves to appear more terrible in warfare, they become brown. Both men and women from that land have been here in England, and they are like those of Europe, and one of them has taken part in the recent Bohemian wars. They lack only the Holy Faith to become like Italians.[161]

Among the other settlements of the English heretics in northern America, and on the same line [and] distance from the pole and on the same latitude as Rome, they have built a town on hills like those of Rome and a fortress where three years ago there where two ministers or preachers, and more will since have gone to infest those peoples with heresy. On this map this town is called Plymouth.[162] Your Most Illustrious Worships may find it by observing the latitude of Rome and 320 [degrees] of longitude.[163]

You may likewise see that island of which I have written formerly and the excellence of its position for beginning the conversion of that

part of the world, which is as large as Europe and on a parallel with
Europe. However no missions have ever existed there, except those of
heretics.[164]

Our father general has informed me that Your Most Illustrious
Worships have asked that I be sent alone to that island.[165] If Your Most
Illustrious Worships may grant or procure me licence to establish this
English mission as an initial step, so that it can afterwards help [16r/
v] and supply the new mission with missionaries and all necessities,
most willingly shall I go thither. Nowhere can there be greater persecution than here, nor difficulty in bearing fruitful, unless it be in
Geneva, and there too will I go, if the necessary means to bear fruit
can be afforded me. But in holy matters one must be realistic, and by
this lack of circumspection I would only make the conversion of infidels more difficult than it is, and the apostolic mission odious,
because of the ill-success attendant on the lack of foundations or
means. The religious of other orders here: 1. Have novitiates and col-
leges for the English, and by these means have missionaries in abundance and temporal means that permit them to live as befits their
state. 2. They possess experienced, learned, and able superiors to help
the missionaries in all that is necessary. 3. Full electoral rights, by
which means they are well governed. 4. Sufficient faculties. And if
they, notwithstanding all this, find difficulty in converting the infidels,
how much more should we encounter, who are lacking in all the
above.

Here we are no more than five in all, of whom two are in prison,
and two infirm, while I sustain the mission.[166] And as I have converted
many, they will be lost if left alone amid persecution. And in like
manner may I be lost, journeying 2,000 miles alone with no possibility of meeting with the benefits of the sacraments. And without the
faculty to consecrate a portable altar, it would be impossible to say
mass.

I put myself once more in the hands of Your Most Illustrious
Worships, that they do with me what they will, and send me where
they will, only that it be with licence to observe the laws and customs
of the Holy Church and with the means necessary to bear fruit among
the heathen and to save my soul. And lastly do I kiss the garments of
Your Most Illustrious Worships, most humbly begging your holy
benedictions.

London, 22 April 1626.

Your Most Illustrious and Reverend Worships' most humble
servant,

frà Simone Stoch

[Following on, in the hand of an official of Propaganda] [19v] London, 22 April *1626*. Brother Simon Stoch. Furnishes a curious account, to be read per extentum, of those countries described in the map of America which he has sent to the Sacred Congregation, which, should it resolve to send him to those parts, must first establish the English mission, so that he afterwards will have the help it affords and that he will need in such remote lands. All the more so as there are only five fathers there, two of whom are [in] prison, while two more are infirm. Nor have they novitiates, nor temporal goods, nor suitable superiors, nor other faculties as have other orders that are there who find difficulty in converting the infidels notwithstanding all their manifold advantages.

[Following on, in Ingoli's handwriting] Die 18 Decembris 1626, congregatio 68. [167]

Discussed as in letter 30.

31a. SIMON STOCK TO BERNARDINO SPADA, ARCHBISHOP OF TAMIA-
THIS, NUNCIO IN FRANCE, LONDON, 22 APRIL 1626
Vatican Secret Archives, *Segreteria di Stato, Francia*, vol. 396, ff. 378rv-9rv. B: ff. 378v-9r. Autograph letter signed. Italian. Enclosure: letter 31. Summary.

He is grateful to the addressee for his offer to forward his letters to Propaganda and asks that the enclosed letter be forwarded.

32. SIMON STOCK TO PAOLO SIMONE DI GESÚ E MARIA, OCD,
GENERAL, [IN ROME], [LONDON], 22 APRIL 1626
*Litterae, Stock*, 271.g.9, ff. [1rv-2rv]. B: f. [2rv]. Autograph letter signed. Italian, Latin. Complete text.

[1r] Jesus Maria Joseph.
My Most Reverend and Honoured Father,
Pax Christi. I have received Your Reverence's letter of 19 February,[168] and in reply beg Your Reverence not to take ill what I write, since all is written in charity and affection, both for your honour and the honour of the Holy Church and the religion itself. If the fathers are in prison,[169] only Your Reverence is to blame. To send a novice as missionary superior, who is without sufficient experience or learning to govern his own self,[170] you must marvel, not that those two fathers are in prison, but rather that we all are not. Caecus si caeco ducatum praestet ambo in foveam cadunt. I see that they have sufficient

[money], but all the money given to the order is spent by them. And such is the help we are given. Nor do I esteem it a fault in them, [since] live they must, but [the fault is rather of] the lack of obedience.

That the cardinals[171] had requested Your Reverence that only one person be sent to that land I did not know before;[172] had I known, I would have prevented it and sought other means.[173] I submit to the pious consideration of Your Reverence whether it be a mark of wise obedience to send one of the confrères alone a greater distance than Rome is from Persia without sufficient faculties, and without the possibility either there or on the way thither [to] find the help of the sacraments. And Your Reverence is obliged to recognize what is seemly. If an angel from Heaven should preach inopportunely, nos talem consuetudinem non habemus neque Ecclesia Dei. More persecution than exists here could nowhere be found, but here there are other priests, there none.

Before concerning myself with this new mission, the cardinals of the Sacred Congregation promised me that religious of other orders should be sent were Your Reverence unable to provide suitable ones.[174] And only a short time ago they wrote that I should be provided with all that was necessary for the mission.[175] Thus I have written to them complaining of all that is lacking and of this unsatisfactory obedience.[176] And at such time as Your Reverence see fit to grant licence to establish this mission in England in such a manner that, once established, it is able to help the new mission and supply it with missionaries and all that is necessary to plant the Holy Faith in that land, where it has never been preached, then shall I go thither most willingly. But in holy matters one must be realistic. [1r/v] I was sent hither to convert souls, and Our Lord, unthinking, has placed me above these. And being aware of my own poor strength, and of the difficulty in sustaining it, and [of] the opposition which always exists in holy matters, I have placed it in the hands of the Sacred Congregation de Propaganda Fide to do with it what they will. When I am provided with all that a similar mission requires, as, by the grace of Our Lord and the orations of Your Reverences, they have recently assured me I shall be,[177] I hope that we shall not be found wanting. But without this I can do no more. And if some other order wishes to take it upon themselves, I will offer them all assistance if licence be given me, and most certain am I that they will depart with the foundation to bear fruit.

If I were blindly to defend Your Reverence's dealings in this mission, it would be the heresy of Wycliffe, Luther and Calvin, who sent their disciples on missions without jurisdiction or faculties, and with no obligation to observe the laws of the Catholic Church. It was sufficient for them to follow their individual conscience and personal judgment. And nor were the religious allowed goods or property, etc.

It is my hope that Your Reverence will not take this ill. As a good Christian and man of religion you will be friend to true virtue within the Catholic Church, without mistaking the way or indulging in vain and illusory imaginings. And it is my opinion that this proceeds from the lack of experience. And if I have spoken too plainly to Your Reverence, I beg Your Reverence to pardon me. I write not to offend, but to save my soul from error and [*illegible*] Deus de proximo suo. Et sicut laudabile est et discretum reverentiam et honorem praebere prioribus, ita rectitudinis et Dei timoris, si quae in iis sunt quae correctione egeant, nulla dissimulatione postponere (caput sicut 2.9.7.). And with this I kiss Your Reverence's feet, most humbly begging your holy benediction.

22 April 1626.
Your Reverence's humble servant,
    frà Simone Stoch

33.    SIMON STOCK TO [CARDINAL OTTAVIO BANDINI, MEMBER OF PROPAGANDA, IN ROME], LONDON, 30 JUNE 1626
*SOCG*, vol. 101, ff. 21rv, 26rv. B: ff. 21v, 26r. Autograph letter signed. Italian. Summary.

He has received his faculties, but deems them insufficient.[178] Has converted many heretics, particularly in Canterbury.

Discussed as in letter 30.

34.    SIMON STOCK TO [PROPAGANDA, IN ROME], LONDON, 30 JUNE 1626
*SOCG*, vol. 101, ff. 22rv, 25rv. B: ff. 22v, 25r. Autograph letter signed. Italian. Enclosure: letter 35. Complete text.

[22r] My Most Illustrious and Reverend Honoured Worships,

Nothing has been done for the Avalon mission. I shall go there most willingly if Your Most Illustrious Worships will first grant me licence to establish the mission in England in such a way that it can then assist me in supplying the Avalon mission with missionaries and all that will be required there. But I shall be unable to proceed should Your Most Illustrious Worships refuse me licence to use the means necessary for planting the Holy Catholic Faith that the Holy Church has always used and that the religious of other orders use. All that we can do above all others is add greater poverty, penitence, and silent prayer. But as to the way and the means, these must be the same, or all will be heresy.

I presume that Your Most Illustrious Worships wish to know something concerning the condition of the Church of England in these times of persecution. And I shall enclose it as it is depicted in the public laws drawn against the Catholics, all of which, excepting martyrdom, are executed. And from these laws Your Most Illustrious Worships may see how necessary it is to proceed with prudence and caution here, since the slightest deviation may be the ruin of the Catholics, and religious are frequently lost. From here I have sent apostates of the five orders. And indeed no mission whatever would be better than one without form or foundation. For this reason I most humbly beg Your Most Illustrious Worships to take the mission under your protection and to order our superiors to follow in the footsteps of the Holy Church, as do the Jesuit fathers, the Benedictine fathers, the fathers of St. Francis, and all those who live here fruitfully. If even in a Catholic land, and in times of peace, it be necessary for the religious to have monasteries, full electoral rights, and sufficient faculties, [how] much more [necessary must it be] here, in times of war and in the land of the infidels. And most humbly do I get Your Most Illustrious Worships to put an end to this matter. And finally I kiss your garments, and most humbly beg your holy benedictions.

London, last day of June 1626.

Your Most Illustrious and Reverend Worships' most humble servant,

   frà Simone Stoch

[Following on, in the hand of an official of Propaganda] [25v] London, last day of June 1626. Brother Simon Stoch. First. That he will proceed most willingly to the mission in Avalon, having once satisfactorily established that in England, which is mandatory for the sustaining of the other. For this reason he begs that his superiors be commanded to assist him as do those of other orders, who there possess monasteries, full electoral rights, and sufficient faculties for the conversion of the infidels. 2. Sends some laws at present executed (with the exception of martyrdom) against the Christians.

[Following on, in Ingoli's handwriting] Die 18 decembris 1626, congregatio 68.[179]

Discussed as in letter 30.

35. [SIMON STOCK] TO [PROPAGANDA, IN ROME], [LONDON, 30 JUNE 1626]
*SOCG*, vol. 101, ff. 23rv–4rv. Autograph memorandum unsigned. Latin, Italian. Enclosed with letter 34. Summary.

A list of twenty-three anti-Catholic laws in force under Elizabeth I and James I, in a memorandum entitled "Persecutio anglicana ex haereticorum publicis legibus collecta, quae omnes excepto martyrio hoc tempore summo cum vigore mandantur."

Discussed as in letter 30.

36. SIMON STOCK TO [PROPAGANDA, IN ROME], LONDON, 12 FEBRU-ARY 1627
*SOCG*, vol. 129, ff. 347rv, 352rv. B: ff. 347v, 352r. Autograph letter signed. Italian. Complete text.

[347r] My Most Illustrious and Reverend Honoured Lords,

For more than two years now[180] I have humbly begged the assistance of Your Most Illustrious Worships for the mission in Avalon and this in England, and nothing has so far been done either for the one or for the other. Thus those Christians from Avalon have come here and in the spring intend to return to Avalon.[181] I still retain those already converted here, albeit with great difficulty because of the persecution and the lack of obedience and incompetent management of the superiors of the order, which is a far greater impediment to the fruitful conversion of souls for Our Lord than the persecution itself, denying me the licence to use the necessary means which the Holy Church has always used, depriving me of help, and afflicting me with inopportune orders. And for fourteen or fifteen years now I have been thus oppressed,[182] and while under obedience to the order there is no hope of improvement. For this reason I most humbly beg the Sacred Congregation to grant me licence to live under obedience to the Most Illustrious bishop of Chalcedon, vicar apostolic of England, which would be a great favour to me. And with his licence and advice, I shall more easily be able to do anything to aid my poor afflicted homeland. I am sending this letter through the ambassador of the Grand Duke of Tuscany to His Majesty here,[183] and should it please Your Most Illustrious Worships to instruct me in any thing, the ambassador of the same duke in Rome[184] will forward it safely here. And lastly I kiss the garments of Your Most Illustrious Worships, humbly begging their holy benedictions.

London, 12 February 1627.
Your Most Illustrious and Reverend Worships' most humble servant,
frà Simone Stoch

[Following on, in the hand of an official of Propaganda] [352v] London, 12 February 1627. Brother Simon Stoch, Discalced Carmelite. Speaks once more of the mission on the island of Avalon, some Christians being come thence with intent to return there in the spring. Matters within his mission in England are unable to proceed with satisfaction, less because of the persecution than of the opposition of his superiors, who deny him the licence to use the apposite means, depriving him of help and afflicting him with inopportune mandates. He thus asks to be placed under obedience to the bishop of Chalcedon, convinced that he will in this way be more fruitful in the conversion of souls. The answer is to be entrusted to Signor Moracello Sacchetti.

[Following on, in the hand of a second official of Propaganda] Die 12 julii 1627, congregatio 77.[185] Turn over.[186] Concerning the novitiate for the English, which Your Reverence has been demanding for so many years, it has been impossible to reach the decision Your Reverence so desires, since your superiors deem the enterprise beyond the resources of the order; and this Congregation does not of custom violate the wishes of the superiors of religious orders, finding that going against their will creates much difficulty in negotiations.[187] Concerning the Avalon mission, no course of action has been determined, there lacking any person to send thither; since you yourself, as the person most greatly informed on the subject, do not deem fit to accept the task, we cannot know whom to send, unless Your Reverence may suggest some suitable subjects of your own or of another order.[188]

Discussed by Propaganda on 17 July 1627, in General Congregation no. 77, item no. 12 (*Acta*, vol. 4, ff. 242rv–8rv). Answered by Propaganda on 17 July 1627 (*Lettere*, vol. 6, f. 94r).


37.   SIMON STOCK TO [ PROPAGANDA, IN ROME], LONDON, 10 OCTOBER 1627
*SOCG*, vol. 102, ff. 12rv, 17rv. B: ff. 12v, 17r. Autograph letter signed. Italian. Another copy: letter 37a. Complete text.

[12r] My Most Illustrious and Reverend Honoured Lords,
The troubles and persecution here have for a long time[189] rendered impossible writing to Your Most Illustrious Worships.

No religious having been sent for the new mission of which I have so often written to Your Most Illustrious Worships and not wishing to miss the chance, I have procured two secular priests to go thither, one to remain with the Catholics there, who are approximately twenty, the other to return here in the hope of further help in the spring.[190]

I continue to sustain those already converted here, albeit with great difficulty, receiving from the order all the impediments they can offer me and no help at all. For this do I most humbly beg Your Most Illustrious Worships to give me leave to live in obedience to the Most Illustrious bishop of Chalcedon, that without these impediments and with his counsel, leave and help, I may do some good in this mission. And the order has no cause to lament, since they do not consider me worthy of aid or participation in their affairs, not to share in those common privileges with other religious. They knew before I was made priest that I could not be content except in this mission, since this was my vocation, and I stated this most clearly, and it was their wish that I enter the order to work as missionary here. If they now see this as an error or if they regret having received me in that manner, it was not my wish to deceive them. I have now served the order some fifteen years,[191] [and] all the English they have, who are entirely English, I have sent to the order, hoping that their intention was to establish a formal mission in England. Both human and divine law obliging me to wish for the conversion of my homeland to Our Lord, my one desire is to be allowed to live in obedience to the Most Illustrious bishop of Chalcedon and to found a monastery under his jurisdiction and that of his successors, where Our Lord will give me grace and favour to do this. And this being to the benefit of the Holy Church, it is my hope that the Holy Church will not deny me. With this I kiss the garments of Your Most Illustrious Worships, and most humbly beg your holy benedictions.

London, 10 October 1627.

Your Most Illustrious and Reverend Worships's most humble servant,

      frà Simone Stoch

[Following on, in the hand of an official of Propaganda] [17v] London, 10 October 1627. Brother Simon Stoch. That because of the difficulty of the times, he has been unable to write; having had no answer concerning that mission of which he wrote so long ago, he has sent thither two religious; that since he is greatly impeded in that mission by his superiors, he asks that he may be exempted from same and desires to live under the jurisdiction of the bishop of Chalcedon and to found thither a monastery to assist the homeland.

[Following on, in the hand of a second official of Propaganda] Respondeatur.

[Following on, in Ingoli's handwriting] Die 19 januarii 1628, congregatio 86.[192] That the news of the religious destined for Avalon was most welcome, and a full report of the island would be similarly welcome; this His Reverence should procure from those same religious, to then send it to the Sacred Congregation together with another map like that already sent, which has been lost.[193] As to the desire expressed to live under the jurisdiction of the bishop of Chalcedon, since it is not meet that a dutiful priest shirk obedience to his superiors although,[194] he is to persevere in his vocation and look to do all that is in his power to assist the souls in those countries that have such need of labourers.[195]

Discussed by Propaganda on 19 January 1628, in General Congregation no. 86, item no. 35 (*Acta*, vol. 6, f. 7r). Answered by Propaganda on 28 January 1628 (*Lettere*, vol. 7, f. 9rv).

37a. SIMON STOCK TO [PROPAGANDA, IN ROME], LONDON, 10 OCTOBER 1627

Westminster Diocesan Archives, *A*, vol. 20, no. 138, pp. 503-4. Copy in another hand unsigned. Italian. Original version: letter 37.

Text as in letter 37, without Propaganda's notes and comments.

38. SIMON STOCK TO [PROPAGANDA, IN ROME], LONDON, 27 JUNE 1628

*SOCG*, vol. 102, ff. 13rv-16rv. B: ff. 13v, 15r, 16r. Autograph letter signed. Italian, Latin. Complete text.

[13r] My Most Illustrious and Reverend Honoured Worships,

I enclose for your Illustrious Worships the map that you desire, and of two sorts: the one printed in the year 1624, the other in the year 1628, which is darker.[196]

I had not written to inform Your Most Illustrious Lordships that I was sending religious to the new mission[197] since I had none to send, except those two who went last year who were secular priests.[198] And others went the same year, and with them he of whom I did write when I first wrote to Your Most Illustrious Worships of this mission, and others of my spiritual children, and I have advised them, once the mission there is established a little, to send someone to Rome to carry reports and request assistance of the Holy Church, and this they will

do; and at such time as they shall return here, and times be less difficult, I shall write at length.[199]

Here seculars and regulars are in total discord. As they have been
for so many years without a bishop and in such liberty that they did
as they pleased, and many much more than they should have, the
name of bishop and subordination is far from welcome to them. And
in the end Your Most Illustrious Worships and the Holy Church will
find no better way to quieten this discord and to conduct missions
than to found monasteries and organize missions of religious under
the jurisdiction of bishops, as in the primitive Church, and to begin
these missions as you wish them to be continued and established.
Such is the wretchedness of human nature, that it is easier to plant a
new church and faith where they have not existed [hitherto], than to
curtail liberty once granted.

As to myself, it is a matter of indifference whether I live in obedience to bishops or generals. All I desire is the observance of the rule
to which I am professed and of the laws and customs of the Holy
Church, all things so far denied; such as to have a house, full electoral
rights, chapters, exhortations, communities, the receiving of novices,
etc., things possessed by all other religious and orders, [which] the
rule and the the [*sic*] laws of the Holy Church declare a necessity to
religious life. And if it should please Your Most Illustrious Worships
to procure this much for the mission from my superiors, I shall be
most glad and most grateful to Your Most Illustrious Worships. And
finally I kiss the garments of Your Most Illustrious Worships and most
humbly beg your holy benedictions.

London, 27 June 16[28].

Your Most Illustrious and Reverend Worships' most humble
servant,

   frà Simone Stoch

[Following on, in the hand of an official of Propaganda] [16v] London, 27 June 1628. Brother Simon Stoch. Encloses two maps of America, printed in 1624 and 25,[200] and tells of labourers sent to the new
mission in Avalon, one of whom is ordered to collect as much information as possible and afterwards come to Rome to inform the Sacred
Congregation and to take back thither some assistance. That all the
ruin and discord that is among the religious is owing to their not
being under the jurisdiction of the ordinary, in the absence of whom
they have lived for so many years that they now do as they please.
That the best way is to found monasteries and missions of religious
under the jurisdiction of bishops as in the primitive Church. As to his
own person, he states that he is indifferent whether he live under bishops or under regulars, but greatly desires the observance of the rule to

which he has pledged himself, principally the right to a house, full electoral rights, chapters, communities, and to train novices, all of which is denied him. And should he be able to obtain this from his superiors, he would live contentedly, and therefore supplicates the Sacred Congregation to this end.

[Following on, in Ingoli's handwriting] Number 20.[201] Referente Illustrissimo Domino Cardinale Barbarino[202] literas fratris Simonis Stoch, carmelitani discalceati, quod duas mappas Americae novas Sacrae Congregationi misit, eidemque significavit in Anglia esse necessarium ut omnes regulares subsint Episcopo Chalcedonensi, Sacra Congregatio iussit praefato fratri gratias agi de mappis et de admonitionibus circa regulares.[203]

[Following on, in the hand of a second official of Propaganda] [14r] Summary of a letter from brother Simon Stoch, London, 27 June 1628.

Encloses two maps of America printed in 1624 and 1625, and tells of labourers sent to the new Avalon mission,[A] one of whom is ordered to collect as much information as possible and afterwards come to Rome to inform the Sacred Congregation and to take back thither some assistance. 2. That all the ruin and discord among the religious[B] is owing to their not being under the jurisdiction of the ordinary, in absence of which they have lived for so many years that they now do as they please; that the best way is to found monasteries and missions of religious under the jurisdiction of bishops as in the primitive Church. 3. As to his own person, he states that he is indifferent whether he live under bishops or under regulars, but greatly desires the observance of the rule to which he has pledged himself, and principally the right to a house, full electoral rights, chapters, communities, and to train novices, all of which is denied him. And should he be able to obtain this from his superiors, he wold live contentedly, and therefore supplicates the Sacred Congregation to this end.

[Following on, in Ingoli's handwriting] In these maps there exists a recently discovered northern archipelago, through which it is believed possible to reach the Indies quickly. And this archipelago does not exist in the old maps.[204]

[Following on, still in Ingoli's handwriting, the footnotes to the foregoing A and B indicators] A. This Avalon is a newly discovered island mid-way between England and Virginia.

B. It is known, from those who have great experience and knowledge of the missions, that the exemption of regulars within it is the cause of some scandal. Because it is observed that in great and rich places there exist abundance of regulars, while poorer places are left to their own devices. It has been noted that in the mountains of Scotland, where all are poor [14r/v] and where no Catholic priests nor heretic preachers ever set foot, there being nothing other than a little barley, have been found people become like gentiles and men of seventy still unbaptized. Thus is the account given by the four missionaries sent to those parts by the Sacred Congregation with a sum of sixty scudi per head to answer to Our Lord, then a cardinal.[205]

The regulars in England had become accustomed to the freedom granted them by the archpriest, and this notwithstanding, they were always in conflict.[206] Now they are unable to suffer the authority of the bishop. Your Most Illustrious Worship, as protector of that kingdom,[207] should take measures against the present discord and schism, since losses are incurred, not gains. And recall that maxim given by Aristotle in the Metaphysics: Entia nullum male gubernari, unus ergo princeps. The which was never more true than in missions, which require a director to dispose of the labourers in those places where there is most need, not to leave the poor to die without the sacraments.

The same error, [*illegible*] greater, may be seen in Scotland, where the regulars not only choose the richer areas and abandon the poor, but act according to their own will, there existing no superior there, and there is no way to tell what they are doing. I consider it the duty of my office to bring this to Your Most Illustrious Worship's notice with all due reverence. The remedy must be left to Your Worship, who possesses both the authority and the protection.

In the Holy Office, reason of Catholic state had it that the regulars were to be supported because of the reasons discussed in the Council of Trent at the time of Pius IV.[208] But this is the case in such churches as are already established with regulars who live conventually, but not of the missions, where experience has amply shown the need of a director [14v/15r] for friars living in liberty far from monasteries or their superiors, these latter for the most part being in Flanders or England and unable to proffer remedy. Let me add that in the absence of any director many apostate and vicious friars go to England, and no one is there to expel them or deal with them in any way. We have the most recent example of father Brown of the Minims,[209] who is there without authority or obedience, and the harm he does cannot be told in a few words.

[Following on, further notes in Ingoli's handwriting] [15v] To the Most Illustrious Secretary, Cardinal Barberini, Protector. For the next [congregation] before Our Lord. May it please Your Most Illustrious Worship to read and attend to these writings, which are of some importance.

Letter from father Simon Stoch, Discalced Carmelite, with Ingoli's notes.

Die 24 novembris 1628, congregatio *100*.[210]

Discussed by Propaganda on 24 November 1628, in General Congregation no. 100, item no. 22 (*Acta*, vol. 6, f. 168rv). Answered by Propaganda on 2 December 1628 (*Lettere*, vol. 7, f. 163rv).

39.  SIMON STOCK TO [PROPAGANDA, IN ROME], LONDON, 28 JULY 1628
*SOCG*, vol. 131, ff. 342rv. B: ff. 342v, 345r. Autograph letter signed. Italian, Latin. Complete text.

[342r] My Most Illustrious and Reverend Honoured Lords,

Many days past I sent that map which Your Most Illustrious Worships wished to see, and since it is not unusual for letters to become lost in these times of war, I considered it my duty to send this other enclosed.[211]

That island[212] of which I have written lies at latitude 54 and longitude 330, near to northern America and [is] of great convenience both for trade and for conducting missions in all the northern parts of America, which are full of peoples that never have heard the news of the Holy Gospel and which are near to Europe.

Concerning that pilot of the passage to China, as he was going to live in St. Malo in France, there came there two Spaniards, dressed as pilgrims, and took him back to Spain with them. The last news I had of him was that he was alive and travelling with His Catholic Majesty's fleet of the West Indies.[213]

The mouth of that Mediterranean Sea of which I have written[214] lies at latitude 60. And many English have navigated this sea to longitude 270, which is *60* degrees inland, as far inland as the longitude of the Mediterranean Sea of Europe from the Straits of Gibraltar to Jerusalem. Whether it is possible to navigate yet further, this is not yet known.[215]

Of the new mission[216] nothing new may be known until October, when some [settlers] are expected back, and at such a time I shall send Your Most Illustrious Worships a more detailed account.

Never was time riper for the Holy Catholic Church to win the affections of the king of Great Britain, who now sees by experience that his Puritans are an ungovernable people and as sworn enemies of the king as of the supreme pontiffs.[217] The Lord Ambassador of Savoy[218] has performed many good offices with the king, but is now to depart and no ambassador will then be left for these negotiations. It would be of great benefit both to the Holy Church and to His Majesty if an ambassador from a neutral state, such as Lorraine or Savoy, could be prevailed on to come hither by Your Most Illustrious Worships and continue this office of negotiation. And lastly do I kiss the

garments of Your Most Illustrious Worships, and most humbly beg
your holy benedictions.

28 July 1628, from London.

Your Most Illustrious and Reverend Worships' most humble
servant,

[frà Simone Stoch]

[Following on, a note in Ingoli's handwriting] [345v] Sequenti coram
Sanctissimo.

[Following on, in the hand of an official of Propaganda] London,
28 July 1628. Brother Simon Stoch. First. That the island of which he
wrote lies at 54 degrees latitude and 330 longitude, near to northern
America, and is convenient both for trade and for missions in those
northern parts where the Holy Gospel has never arrived. 2. That the
mouth of the Mediterranean Sea of which he has also written is at *60*
degrees latitude, and many English have navigated as far as 270 longitude, which is some 60 degrees inland, just as the Mediterranean Sea
in Europe is from the Straits of Gibraltar to Jerusalem, and it can be
navigated further into lands unknown.[219] 3. That the pilot of the ship
of which he spoke is alive and travels with His Catholic Majesty's
fleet. 4. Of the new mission he can know nothing until October. 5.
That the time would now be ripe to win over the king of England,
since he has realized that the Puritans are an ungovernable people
and the enemy of the king as they are of the pontiffs. It would thus be
advantageous to send thither a neutral ambassador, such as that of
Lorraine or Savoy, to continue these dealings with His Majesty,
already begun by the ambassador of Savoy who is about to depart.

[Following on, in Ingoli's handwriting] Numero *31*, die 12
januarii 1629, congregatio 103.[220] Per Illustrissimum Cardinalem Bar-
barinum.[221]

Relatis litteris fratris Simon Stoch, carmelitani discalceati, quibus significabat longitudinem et latitudinem novae insulae Avaloniae
et Maris Mediteranei in America septemtrionali nuper reperti, et com-
monebat Sacram Congregationem nunc esse tempus opportunum
procurandi conversionem Regis Angliae mediante aliquo ex oratori-
bus catholicorum principum in eam insulam mittendis, quia Rex
puritanos haereticos ut sibi et coronae parum fidos odie vel etiam
timet, Sacra Congregatio mandavit commendari diligentiam dicti fratris, eique gratias agi de admonitione, ciuis suo tempore eam habebit
rationem, quam magnitudo negotii requirit.[222]

The father to be written to ut supra, with a reminder to pass on
any news forthcoming from the missionaries of the island of Avalon.
That he should seek to know of the pilot, on the latter's return to
England, all particulars concerning the navigation of this American

Mediterranean Sea and pass on the information. At the same time he is to write about the progress of the bishop of Chalcedon and the other missionaries, and in particular of the regulars and of how the king is disposed towards the Catholics and our Holy Faith.[223]

Discussed by Propaganda on 12 January 1629, in General Congregation no. 103, item no. 31 (*Acta*, vol. 6, f. 198v). Answered by Propaganda on 20 January 1629 (*Lettere*, vol. 8, ff. 15v–16r).

40.   SIMON STOCK TO [PROPAGANDA, IN ROME], LONDON, 2 JULY 1629
*SOCG*, vol. 131, ff. 341rv, 346 rv. B: f. 346r. Autograph letter signed. Italian, Latin. Complete text.

[341r] My Most Illustrious and Reverend Honoured Lords,

There lacking missionaries for the new mission, two fathers of the Society of Jesus have gone there.[224] Thus Your Most Illustrious Worships will receive through them a full account of what is being done or may be done there. Being one only, and without help, it is impossible to attend to so many matters, and I could not hope for missionaries from the order for such an end.[225]

Persecution, however, here goes on apace, principally against Monsignor the bishop of Chalcedon, who is unable to fulfil the duty of his office or to govern the secular clergy. And should Your Most Illustrious Worships fail to assist the secular clergy, it is beyond my comprehension how they may continue to live here, lacking a bishop to govern them and ensure their good reputation, and to keep for them their friends and those places in which they live, receiving neither benefices nor income.

And since the edict of His Most Serene Highness the King (which is in Our Lord's possession) is aimed not so much against religion as against that correspondence with those of his enemies who are intent on the destruction of his state,[226] in obedience to Your Most Illustrious Worships[227] I herewith offer my opinion. The island could be divided up and some two or three bishops created from this clergy, though on condition that these same bishops in no way interfere in matters concerning the Protestant court. Thus His Most Serene Highness will have no cause of complaint, and neither will the Catholic laity. [341r/v]

Every day brings fresh discord between that great lord[228] and his Puritans, and indeed it could not be otherwise, these latter being undisciplined, frenzied people and sworn enemies of all monarchies. Your Most Illustrious Worships could find no better occasion than the

present for his conversion, which could be effected by some learned
and humble man, sent by the Duke of Lorraine or Savoy, for example,
the better to deal with the question.

Several times now I have written to Your Most Illustrious Worships through the resident of the Grand Duke of Tuscany here,[229] and
should Your Most Illustrious Worships have occasion to command me
anything whatsoever, the ambassador of this same duke in Rome[230]
will send all letters safely.

London, 2 July 1629.

Your Most Illustrious and Reverend Worships' most humble
servant,

  frà Simone Stocko

[Following on, in the hand of an official of Propaganda] [346v] London, 2 July 1629. Frà Simon Stoch, Discalced Carmelite. There
being one religious only[231] in the new mission, and others of his
order being unobtainable, two Jesuit fathers have gone thither, from
whom the desired report will be forthcoming. That persecution
increases, however, mainly against the bishop; nor can he imagine
how the clergy may sustain itself without him. And therefore it is necessary to help him. Esteem for the same would follow if the island
could be divided and some two or three other bishops be created, on
condition that they in no way interfere in Protestant affairs, for which
the court is responsible; in this manner neither the Catholic laity nor
the king would have reason for complaint. The persecution having its
origin not only in religion itself as in the correspondence they are said
to hold with the enemies of His Majesty, viz. the Puritans, a fierce and
ungovernable people with whom he is much disgusted, the time
would be ripe for his conversion by means of some learned and humble person from the state of Lorraine or Savoy. That letters be sent
him through the ambassador of the Grand Duke, since he himself uses
the ambassador of His Highness in that city.

[Following on, in Ingoli's handwriting] Die 7 septembris 1629,
congregatio 114, numero 44.[232]

Illustrissimus Dominus Cardinalis Barbarinus retulit litteras
patris Simonis Stoch carmelitani discalceati, missionarii in Anglia, in
quibus significabat: primo, quod ad insulam Avalloniae profecti sunt
duo patres jesuitae, a quibus relatio a Sacra Congregatione petita
habebitur. 2. Quod persecutio in Anglia quotidie magis augetur, et
praesertim contra Episcopum Chalcedonensem. 3. Quod ad eam
sedandam necessarium esset ut duo vel tres alii episcopi in Anglia
constituentur, cum mandato ne se ingerent in causis protestantium,
quod ad forum spectant contintiosum. 4. Quod persecutio anglicana
non tantum habet originem suam a religionis puncto, sed etiam ab

intelligentia qua cum puritanis Regis inimicis a plerisque ex nostris habetur. 5. Denique quod cum dissidia inter puritanos et regem in dies fiant maiora, opportunissima esset occasio procurandi ipsius regis conversionem mediante aliquis viris doctis status Sabaudiae vel Lotharingiae.[233]

Father Stoch to be thanked for his information, which the Sacred Congregation will in good time use for the propagation of our Holy Faith in that kingdom. That he be asked to explain more closely the disputes among the Protestants and about the correspondence with the Puritans which is in part behind the persecution in England.[234]

Discussed by Propaganda on 7 September 1629, in General Congregation no. 114, item no. 44 (*Acta*, vol. 6, ff. 329v-30r). Answered by Propaganda on 15 September 1629 (*Lettere*, vol. 8, f. 147r).

41.   SIMON STOCK TO [PROPAGANDA, IN ROME], LONDON, 9 AUGUST 1629

*SOCG*, vol. 131, ff. 343rv-4rv. B: f. 344r. Autograph letter signed. Italian, Latin. Complete text.

[343r] My Most Illustrious and Reverend Honoured Lords,

Yesterday I was with the ambassador of His Most Serene Majesty the king of France here,[235] and since the king has entrusted him with the negotiations for establishing Monsignor the bishop of Chalcedon here, we spoke at some length about the question and of how it might be accomplished. In the end we were able to find no better way of rendering his jurisdiction acceptable to those of the English nobility who oppose it than to exempt from his jurisdiction all temporal matters which may pertain to Protestant justice (as I have formerly written to Your Most Illustrious Worships). These same nobles may thus recognize him as bishop and superior, and differences among them may be eradicated. It is my wish that Monsignor the bishop will accept this and that they may thus live in peace. And this will be of some satisfaction to His Majesty here, when he sees that [the bishop] is here with no desire to interfere in matters pertaining to the law of the kingdom.

As to the discord between the same Monsignor the bishop and the regulars, these last, as virtuous and obedient children, will content themselves with the system of government which obtains in the Holy Catholic Church the entire world over, when once Your Most Illustrious Worships have issued the sentence. As they are Catholics in all else, they have no wish to be schismatic in this matter of consent seeing most clearly the need here, where, for lack of any such regulation, each [343r/v] does as he wishes, and many much more than they should, and many missionaries here are like unbridled horses, and recognize no superior whatever.

As I have on other occasions written,[236] this year two fathers of the Society of Jesus[237] have gone to the new mission.[238] When their ships return, which will be in September, they will bring to Your Most Illustrious Worships good report therefrom. I now am for the most part in that other new mission[239] of which I have written before to Your Most Illustrious Worships. But since the persecution is great, it bears little fruit, and since it is far off from London, I cannot write as frequently as I would desire. And lastly do I kiss the garments of Your Most Illustrious Worships and most humbly beg your holy benedictions.

9 August 1629, from London.

Your Most Illustrious and Reverend Worships' most humble servant,

Simone Stoch

[Following on, in Ingoli's handwriting] [344v] Holy Office.

London, 9 August 1629. Father Simon Stoch, Discalced Carmelite. The French ambassador having orders from his king to bring about the establishing of the bishop of Chalcedon, he has spoken with him regarding what is to be done, which is that the said bishop must refrain from interference in temporal matters which are the province of that secular justice of the Protestants. That in this manner the nobility may recognize him as their superior, which will be pleasing unto His Majesty, and which course it is to be hoped the bishop will follow. As to the differences between said bishop and the regulars, it is his belief that they will acquiesce in the sentence this court may give, since he maintains that, in matters of consent, they have no wish to create a schism, mostly for the necessity there is in those parts [of a peaceable settlement], each man living as is his wish, and many like unbridled horses. That in the new mission, where he now is working, he can bear little fruit because of the great persecution, and he can write rarely being far off from London.

Die 2 octobris 1629, congregatio 115, *number 22*.[240] Referente Illustrissimo Domino Cardinale Caetano[241] litteras fratris Simonis Stoch carmelitani discalceati, de modo componendi differentias inter Episcopum Chalcedonensem et nobiles Angliae, et de regularium promptitudinem in parendo mandatis Sacrae Congregationis Inquisitionis in causam inter eos et dictum episcopum vertentem, Sacra Congregatio copiam summarii dictarum litterarum iussit remitti ad Congregationem Sancti offitii.[242]

To the father. Acknowledge the receipt, and [request] that he send information constantly about the progress of relations between the bishop of Chalcedon and the English nobles obtained through the mediation of the French ambassador there resident.[243]

Discussed by Propaganda on 2 October 1629, in General Congregation no. 115, item no. 22 (*Acta*, vol. 6, f. 339r). Answered by Propaganda on 12 October 1629 (*Lettere*, vol. 8, ff. 153v–4r).

42. SIMON STOCK TO [PROPAGANDA, IN ROME], LONDON, 1 NOVEMBER 1629

*SOCG*, vol. 132, ff. 244rv–5rv. B: ff.244v–5r. Autograph letter signed. Italian, Latin. Enclosure: letter 43. Summary.

He is satisfied with Rome's decision regarding the dispute between the bishop of Chalcedon and the regulars.[244] Encloses a memorandum giving the reasons for the dispute between English Protestants and Puritans. Persecution continues.

Discussed by Propaganda on 1 February 1630, in General Congregation no. 119, item no. 58 (*Acta*, vol. 7/i, f. 20r). Answered by Propaganda on 20 February 1630 (*Lettere*, vol. 10, ff. 14v–15r).

43. [SIMON STOCK] TO [PROPAGANDA, IN ROME], [LONDON, 1 NOVEMBER 1629]

*SOCG*, vol. 132, ff. 243rv, 246rv. B: f. 246v. Autograph memorandum unsigned. Latin. Enclosed with letter 42. Summary.

In eight points, the reasons for the discord between English Protestants and Puritans. Differences of opinion also exist among the Protestants.

Discussed and answered by Propaganda as in letter 42.

44. SIMON STOCK TO [PROPAGANDA, IN ROME], LONDON, 8 JANUARY 1630

*SOCG*, vol. 132, ff. 249(b)rv, 256rv. B: ff. 249(b)v, 256r. Autograph letter signed. Italian, Latin. Summary.

The Holy Office has considered the question of the dispute between the bishop of Chalcedon and the regulars, establishing that the bishop is not the ordinary of England and thus has no jurisdiction over the laity. Persecution continues, albeit slightly abated. Don Carlos Coloma[245] has arrived in England to negotiate the peace between Spain and England. The king of England, in his turn, has sent an ambassador to Spain.[246]

Discussed by Propaganda on 19 March 1630, in General Congregation no. 121, item no. 39 (*Acta*, vol. 7/i, f. 40r). Answered by Propaganda on 26 March 1630 (*Lettere*, vol. 10, f. 34v).

45. SIMON STOCK TO [PROPAGANDA, IN ROME], LONDON, 1 MARCH 1630

*SOCG*, vol. 132, ff. 250rv, 255rv. B: ff. 250v, 255r. Autograph letter signed. Italian, Latin. Summary.

He has been unable to write as usual because of illness. Like the French ambassador, who has left his appointment,[247] he has been deceived by the rumours concerning the Holy Office's solution to the dispute between the bishop of Chalcedon and the regulars. As persecution abates, scandals among the English clergy increase in inverse proportion.

At the end of the draft of the letter of reply to Stock,[248] Ingoli writes: "And that he remember the report about the state of Avalon, when it is forthcoming."

Discussed by Propaganda on 15 June 1630, in General Congregation no. 124, item no. 48 (*Acta*, vol. 7/i, f. 85r). Answered by Propaganda on 26 June 1630 (*Lettere*, vol. 10, f. 62r)

46. SIMON STOCK TO [PROPAGANDA, IN ROME], LONDON, 28 APRIL 1630

*SOCG*, vol. 132, ff. 251rv. B: ff. 251v, 254r. Autograph letter signed. Italian, Latin. Complete text.

[251r] My Most Illustrious and Reverend Honoured Lords,

Great is my satisfaction that the dispute between Monsignor the bishop of Chalcedon and the regulars has been settled by the Holy Office, since the more they differ, the greater the opposition and differences, and the more (which it greatly pains me to think of) they will write books the one against the other, should Your Most Illustrious Lordships not intervene to pacify them, and this will be greatly to the detriment of the Holy Church's reputation among the infidels. This dispute has now continued for three years, and this delay causes the loss of the court's reputation among the infidels. Great numbers of the Puritan sect have gone from here to live in the northern part of America, 4,000 thousand [sic] or more, and they will infest those infidels with their heresy, who, as I have heard tell from those coming from those parts, are desirous to be Christians, and they are innumerable peoples and near to Europe.[249] Persecution here has increased since the peace was settled between France and England.[250] And lastly do I kiss the garments of Your Most Illustrious Worships, and most humbly beg their holy benedictions.

London, 28 April 1630.

Your Most Illustrious and Reverend Worships' most humble servant,

frà Simone Stoch

[Following on, in the hand of an official of Propaganda] [254v] London, 28 April 1630. Father Simon Stoch. Of the scandal in which the Catholics are involved because of the delay in settling the dispute between the bishop of Chalcedon and the regulars. That a great number of Puritans, as many as 4,000, have gone to the northern parts of America to infest the infidels, who he believes are desirous to be made Christians, and they are innumerable peoples near to Europe. That the persecution has increased following the peace between French and England.

[Following on, in Ingoli's handwriting] Number 20. Die 9 julii 1630, congregatio 126.[251]

Referente Reverendissimo Domino Assessore Sancti Offitii litteras patris Simonis Stoch carmelitani discalceati, de 4 millibus anglis puritanis qui ad inficiendam haeresi calviniana Americam septentrionalem Europae vicinam se transferunt, Sacra Congregatio mandavit scribi Nuntio Belgico[252] ut de praedictis se informet et rescribat, et simul significet an per gallos missionarios possit fieri aliqua provisio contra dictorum anglorum conatus.[253]

Discussed by Propaganda on 9 July 1630, in General Congregation no. 126, item no. 20 (Acta, vol. 7/i, f. 99v).

47. SIMON STOCK TO [PROPAGANDA, IN ROME], LONDON, 30 APRIL 1630

SOCG, vol. 132, ff. 252rv–3rv. Autograph letter signed. Italian. Summary.

He wrote to Propaganda two days previously.[254] Has today received Propaganda's letter of 26 March.[255] Expresses satisfaction at the settlement of the dispute between the bishop of Chalcedon and the regulars. Spoke with the bishop the evening before, who as yet knows nothing of the said settlement. There is a rumour among the regulars that the nuncio in France[256] has all the papers relating to the matter in his hands. Persecution is once more rife.

Possibly discussed by Propaganda on 23 December 1630, in General Congregation no. 133.

48. SIMON STOCK TO [PROPAGANDA, IN ROME], LONDON, 25 JULY 1630
*SOCG*, vol. 132, ff. 257rv, 263rv. B: ff. 257v, 263r. Autograph letter signed. Italian. Summary.

The Holy Office's decree concerning the dispute between the bishop of Chalcedon and the regulars has not yet been made public. The unrest in England is owing to the absence of any formalized jurisdiction. He proposes solving this problem by appointing three or four more bishops, one of whom to be a Benedictine and one a Jesuit.

Discussed by Propaganda on 23 November 1630, in General Congregation no. 132, item no. 10 (*Acta*, vol. 7/i, f. 164v).

49. SIMON STOCK TO [PROPAGANDA, IN ROME], LONDON, 16 SEPTEMBER 1630
*SOCG*, vol. 132, ff. 258rv, 262rv. B: ff. 258v, 262r. Autograph letter signed. Italian, Latin. Summary.

The dispute between regulars and seculars continues, the cause being the absence of formalized jurisdiction. He proposes solving the problem by appointing two more bishops, one a Benedictine, the other a Jesuit, as representatives of the most powerful orders active in England; otherwise the English hierarchy could be answerable to someone living in France or Flanders.

Discussed by Propaganda as in letter 48.

50. SIMON STOCK TO [PROPAGANDA, IN ROME], LONDON, 1 JANUARY 1631

---

*SOCG*, vol. 100, ff. 263rv, 266rv. B: f. 266r. Autograph letter signed. Italian, Latin. Complete text.

[263r] My Most Eminent and Reverend Honoured Lords,

I only received Your Most Eminent Worships' letters of 22 June in late December.[257] And as for matters in Avalon, two fathers of the Society[258] went thither around Easter of the year 1629[259] and returned here before the following feast of the Nativity of Our Lord. They brought with them to England nearly all the Catholics who were there, leaving behind some thirty heretics and two or three Catholic women, with no priest or minister. They say that the winter before their arrival there was extremely cold and the earth sterile. I have spoken with the principal gentleman of that place, and he is sorry to be back and says that it is his intention to return thither once more,[260] and that the fathers of the Society have a mission or a special commission for those places in America.[261]

Since this part of the world is now for the most part at peace, and the English, French and Scots have colonies in those parts of America, if it would please His Holiness to establish in that part of America a colony of Italians, with a bishop and humble religious accustomed to withstanding hardship and privation to plant the Holy Faith in that part of the world, which is as big as Europe and near and opposite Europe and in no part converted, this would be a deed of great honour to the Holy Church, and in time very useful, and it is the most expedient way of converting them.[262]

The decree of the Sacred Congregation concerning Monsignor the bishop of Chalcedon has not been published. Therefore I am unable to write what effect it has had. But when it is published, I shall not fail to give the report you ask for. Both parties write books the one against the other, which is painful and piteous to see. [263r/v] And how grieved are the poor Catholics of this kingdom, and all those with which I have spoken say: If it should please His Holiness to settle the difference, they would be ready to obey his commands, since they truly hold the Holy Apostolic See in great veneration. And lastly I kiss the garments of Your Most Illustrious Worships and most humbly beg your holy benedictions, praying Our Lord that [*illegible*].

London, 1 January 1631.

Your Most Eminent Worships' most humble servant,
frà Simone Stocco

[Following on, in the hand of an official of Propaganda] [266v] London, 1 January 1631. Father Simon Stoch. That at Easter of 1629 two Jesuit friars went to the island of Avalon and returned at Christmas with all the Catholics that were there, having left behind some *30* her-

etics, with no minister, and two or three women. They recount that
the country is sterile and intensely cold. But he has spoken with a
principal gentleman of that land, who expresses his regret at being
returned from thence, [and] wants to return thither, and states that the
Jesuit fathers possess special commissions for those parts of America.
Which, being as big as Europe, with colonies of French, English and
Scots, and no conversion ever having been made there, it would be a
.deed of great moment to send thither a colony of Italians with their
own bishop. That the decree of the Congregation of the Holy Office
concerning the bishop of Chalcedon has not yet been published, but
that both sides write books against each other to the great disgust and
scandal of the Catholics. And they would most willingly obey any
orders that His Holiness may give about this from the great esteem in
which they hold the Apostolic See.

[Following on, in Ingoli's handwriting] *Number 17.*[263]

Eminentissimus Dominus Cardinalis Bentivolus[264] retulit litteras
patris Simonis Stoch carmelitani discalceati, in quibus plura significabat de terra Avvaloniae in America septentrionali, in qua nunc sunt
coloniae gallorum, scotorum et anglorum, et hortabatur Sacram Congregationem ut illuc missionem faceret italorum cum suo episcopo.
Et demum significabat discordias inter Episcopum Chalcedonensem
et regulares quotidie augeri per librorum scripturam ex utraque
parte.[265]

Acknowledge the receipt, and say that he is to keep the Sacred
Congregation informed about Avalon [and] what he will know, the
Sacred Congregation having already ordered thither a mission of English and French Capuchins. And similarly that he inform himself
about the discord between the regular clergy and the bishop of Chalcedon to be thus able to suggest to the Holy Office what means seem
fit to quiet them, which it would indeed be time to do.[266]

Discussed by Propaganda on 25 February 1631, in General Congregation no. 136, item no. 16 (*Acta*, vol. 7/ii, f. 26v). Answered by Propaganda on 8 March 1631 (*Lettere*, vol. 11, f. 22rv).

51.   SIMON STOCK TO [PROPAGANDA, IN ROME], LONDON, 4 FEBRUARY
1631

*SOCG*, vol. 100, ff. 264rv–5rv. B: ff. 264v-5r. Autograph letter signed.
Italian. Summary.

The Holy Office's decree regarding the dispute between the regulars and the bishop of Chalcedon has not yet been made public. If
Propaganda is against the idea of creating new bishops, it should at

least forbid both parties to write books[267] and ask the bishop to send Rome his reasons in writing.

Discussed by Propaganda on 27 March 1631, in General Congregation no. 137, item no. 26 (*Acta*, vol. 7/ii, f. 26v). Answered by Propaganda on 4 April 1631 (*Lettere*, vol. 11, f. 37rv.).

52.   SIMON STOCK TO [PROPAGANDA, IN ROME], CANTERBURY, 5 MARCH 1631

*SOCG*, vol. 100, ff. 269rv, 284rv. B: ff. 269v, 284r. Autograph letter signed. Italian. Summary.

The dispute between the bishop of Chalcedon and the regulars continues. Both parties write books against one another. The last general chapter of his order ruled that a novitiate for English and Scots was to be established in Flanders, but refused the English full electoral rights. In Canterbury the number of converts is growing.

Discussed by Propaganda on 4 July 1631, in General Congregation no. 142, item no. 27 (*Acta*, vol. 7/ii, f. 347r). Answered by Propaganda on 18 July 1631 (*Lettere*, vol. 11, f. 71v)

53.   SIMON STOCK TO [PROPAGANDA, IN ROME], CANTERBURY, 6 APRIL 1631

*SOCG*, vol. 100, ff. 285rv, 288rv. B: ff. 285v, 288r. Autograph letter signed. Italian. Enclosure: letter 54. Summary.

The dispute between the regulars and seculars in England is destined to continue unless the pope makes a decision of some kind. In its present state, his order is in no condition to resolve the quarrel. The general chapter ruled that a novitiate for English and Scots be established, but refused the English electoral rights. He encloses his reasons for believing such rights necessary.

Discussed and answered by Propaganda as in letter 52.

54.   [SIMON STOCK] TO [PROPAGANDA, IN ROME], [CANTERBURY, 6 APRIL 1631]

*SOCG*, vol. 100, ff. 286rv-7rv. Autograph memorandum unsigned. Latin. Enclosed with letter 53. Summary.

His reasons for believing it necessary for the English Discalced Carmelites to have the full electoral rights, in a memorandum entitled "Rationes quare post 10 aut 12 annos in quibus vocibus privati fuerunt, convenit missionariis carmelitarum in Anglia voces suas activas et passivas sicut ceteri religiosi ordines in Gallia et Flandria habere."

Discussed and answered by Propaganda as in letter 52.

55. SIMON STOCK TO [PROPAGANDA, IN ROME], CANTERBURY, 27 APRIL 1631

*SOCG*, vol. 100, ff. 270rv, 283rv. B: ff. 270v, 283r. Autograph letter signed. Italian. Enclosure: letter 56. Summary.

He encloses a draft of the new constitutions for his Order. His superiors wish to send foreign missionaries to England, who, not knowing the language, would do more harm than good. A better plan would be to establish monasteries in Flanders with all the usual rights and privileges.

Discussed and answered by Propaganda as in letter 52.

56. SIMON STOCK TO PROPAGANDA, [IN ROME], [CANTERBURY, 27 APRIL 1631]

*SOCG*, vol. 100, ff. 271rv–82rv. B: ff. 271v, 282r. Autograph memorandum unsigned. Latin, Italian. Enclosed with letter 55. Summary.

In twenty points, a draft of the new constitutions for the English Discalced Carmelites.

Discussed and answered by Propaganda as in letter 52.

57. SIMON STOCK TO [PROPAGANDA, IN ROME], CANTERBURY, 25 JUNE 1631

*SOCG*, vol. 100, ff. 289rv, 298rv. B: ff. 289v, 298r. Autograph letter signed. Italian. Complete text.

[289r] My Most Eminent and Honoured Lords,

I am well pleased to know that the Sacred Congregation has ordered a mission of Capuchin fathers to that part of America.[268] By proceeding with discipline and true observance they will bear much fruit; yet observance in a mission among infidels needs to be different from that in the monasteries. For this reason it is essential that the Sacred Congregation procure for the missionaries full electoral rights, both among themselves and in the election of their superiors, thus establishing a procedure which meets the needs of the mission and resolves the chapters' difficulties. And should the Capuchin fathers observe all this and adapt the way and form of governing to the needs of the mission, they will suffice to convert the whole world.

I have sent to the Sacred Congregation some constitutions for this our English mission[269] and most humbly beg the Sacred Congregation to speak with the fathers of our order, that these or others similar may be adopted, and that they do not work against the common good, both of the Holy Church and of the order.

As for the discord between Monsignor the bishop of Chalcedon and the regulars, it increases always. I can see no other reasons for this discord except ambition and liberty—ambition about who shall be the most great and Lutheran liberty, that no one have jurisdiction to curb these disorders and scandals. If it would please His Holiness to establish our mission, we should set an example of peaceable and orderly living, each in gradu suo. And lastly I kiss your Eminences' garments and most humbly beg your holy benediction.

Canterbury, 25 junii 1631.

Your Most Eminent and Reverend [Worships'] most humble servant,

      frà Simone Stocco

[Following on, in the hand of an official of Propaganda] [298v] London, 25 June 1631. Father Simon Stock. That the Capuchin mission in northern America will bear much fruit, if only the form of observance be changed from that of the monasteries, since the missions require a form of procedure suitable to their particular needs. It is thus necessary that the missionaries have full electoral rights in the election of their superiors. Of the constitutions which he sent for the establishing of his own mission, as he wrote previously, and of the increased discord between the bishop of Chalcedon and the regulars, [he writes] that they have no foundation other than ambition and a spirit of Lutheran liberty, that no one may have the authority to check the scandals. And were his mission to be established there, they would give example of how to live in peace.

[Following on, in the hand of a second official of Propaganda] Die 26 augusti 1631, congregatio 146.[270]

Possibly discussed by Propaganda on 26 August 1631, in General

Congregation no. 145, item no. 33 (*Acta*, vol. 7/ii, ff. 374v-5v).

58. SIMON STOCK TO [PROPAGANDA, IN ROME], LONDON, 1
NOVEMBER 1631
*SOCG*, vol. 100, ff. 290rv, 297rv. B: f. 297r. Autograph letter signed.
Italian. Summary.

His letters to Propaganda and the Congregation's replies have
been made public in England before he himself received the replies.
The bishop of Chalcedon has left England.[271] Stock, who for many
years has been confessor to the Spanish ambassadors and residents in
London,[272] requests the faculties both to consecrate portable altars
and to grant licence to read prohibited and heretical books. He similarly requests indulgences for those who worship in the chapel of
Don Nicolaldi, Spanish resident in London,[273] and his own chapel in
Canterbury. He is obliged to ask Propaganda since he receives no
answer to his letters from his own superiors.

Possibly discussed by Propaganda on 23 December 1631, in General
Congregation no. 150.

59. SIMON STOCK TO [PROPAGANDA, IN ROME], LONDON, 7
DECEMBER 1631
*SOCG*, vol. 150, ff. 284rv, 288rv. B: f. 288r. Autograph letter signed.
Italian. Enclosure: letter 61. Summary.

He encloses the reasons which render necessary full electoral
rights for the English Discalced Carmelites. The difficulties and successes of the English missions of the Dominicans and the Franciscans.
Copy of a letter he sent to the Congregation of the Regulars.[274]

Possibly discussed by Propaganda on 15 March 1632, in General Congregation no. 154.

60. SIMON STOCK TO THE SACRED CONGREGATION OF BISHOPS AND
REGULARS, [IN ROME], [LONDON, 7 DECEMBER 1631]
*Litterae, Stock*, 271.g.3, ff. [1rv-2rv]. Autograph memorandum
unsigned. Latin. Additional copies, addressed to Propaganda: letters
61, 65. Summary.

The reasons which render necessary full electoral rights for the

English Discalced Carmelites, in a memorandum divided into two parts respectively entitled "Rationes quare domus est necessaria pro missione anglicana" and "Rationes quare convenit ut missio anglicana et domus pro missione sint sub definitorio generali et non sub provincia Flandriae."

61.  SIMON STOCK TO [PROPAGANDA, IN ROME], [LONDON, 7 DECEMBER 1631]

*SOCG*, vol. 150, ff. 285rv–7(b)rv. B: ff. 287(a)rv–(b)rv. Autograph memorandum unsigned. Latin. Enclosed with letter 59. Additional copies, to Propaganda: letter 65; to the Sacred Congregation of Bishops and Regulars: letter 60. Summary.

The reasons which render necessary full electoral rights for the English Discalced Carmelites, in a memorandum divided into two parts respectively entitled "Rationes quare convenit ut missio anglicana et domus pro missione sint sub definitorio generali et non sub provincia Flandriae" and "Rationes quare domus est necessaria pro missione anglicana."

Possibly discussed by Propaganda on 29 March 1632, in General Congregation no. 155.

62.  SIMON STOCK TO FRANCESCO INGOLI, SECRETARY OF PROPAGANDA, IN ROME, LONDON, 7 DECEMBER 1631

*SOCG*, vol. 150, ff. 290rv, 297rv. B: ff. 290v, 297rv. Autograph letter signed. Italian. Summary.

The letter begins: "So many good things have I heard of Your Most Illustrious Worship and of your zeal for souls and the sacred missions, that I have taken courage to write to you and ask you to help me in this our mission in Great Britain." Ingoli is to reply through the Spanish ambassador in Rome[275] or through the agent of the Grand Duke of Tuscany.[276] Despite the departure of the bishop of Chalcedon the dispute between seculars and regulars continues, and it will continue to the end unless there is an intervention by the pope to settle it.

Possibly discussed by Propaganda on 15 March 1632, in General Congregation no. 154.

63. SIMON STOCK TO [PROPAGANDA, IN ROME], LONDON, 24 DECEMBER 1631

*SOCG*, vol. 150, ff. 291rv, 296rv. B: ff. 291v, 296r. Autograph letter signed. Italian. Summary.

He wrote some days earlier to Propaganda.[277] Since the bishop of Chalcedon is no longer in England, he requests faculties to consecrate portable altars and chalices, and to grant licence to read prohibited or heretical books.

Discussed by Propaganda as in letter 62.

64. SIMON STOCK TO [PROPAGANDA, IN ROME], LONDON, 28 JANUARY 1632

*SOCG*, vol. 150, ff. 292rv, 295rv. B: ff. 292v, 295r. Autograph letter signed. Italian. Enclosure: letter 65. Summary.

Heresy grows in England, in part aided by the lack of discipline in the Church. The heretics are responsible for a rumour that the pope has been converted to Lutheranism. Since the bishop of Chalcedon is no longer in England, he requests faculties to consecrate portable altars and chalices and to grant licence to read prohibited books.

Possibly discussed by Propaganda on 29 March 1632, in General Congregation no. 155.

65. SIMON STOCK TO PROPAGANDA, [IN ROME], [LONDON, 7 DECEMBER 1631]

*SOCG*, vol. 150, ff. 293rv–4rv. Autograph memorandum unsigned. Enclosed with letter 64. Additional copies, to Propaganda: letter 61; to the Sacred Congregation of Bishops and Regulars: letter 60.[278] Summary.

The reasons which render necessary full electoral rights for the English Discalced Carmelites, in a memorandum divided into two parts respectively entitled "Rationes quare convenit ut missio anglicana et domus pro missione sint sub definitorio generali et non sub provincia Flandriae" and "Rationes quare domus est necessaria pro missione anglicana."

Discussed by Propaganda as in letter 64.

66.   SIMON STOCK TO FRANCESCO INGOLI, SECRETARY OF PROPA- ,
GANDA, [IN ROME], LONDON, 24 MARCH 1632
*SOCG*, vol. 150, ff. 298rv–9rv. Autograph letter signed. Italian. Summary.

He has received the addressee's letter.[279] Requests full electoral rights and the foundation of monasteries, deplores the wicked state of his order's administration. He rejects Propaganda's accusation that what he requests is in any way an innovation. Past difficulties and present successes of the Franciscan and Dominican missions. It is necessary to request the intervention of the Spanish king's resident in England[280] regarding licence to found a monastery in Flanders. It is not true that the constitutions of his order forbid full electoral rights.

Possibly discussed by Propaganda on 31 March 1632, in General Congregation no. 158.

67.   SIMON STOCK TO [PROPAGANDA, IN ROME], LONDON, 24 MARCH
1632[281]
*Litterae, Stock*, 271.g.10, ff. [1rv–2rv]. Autograph letter signed. Italian. Summary.

He asks that the English mission be established in conformity with the dictates of the Council of Trent. For more than twenty-one years[282] he has worked for the establishment of the English mission [of his order], and should his requests not be now approved, he wishes to move to another order.

68.   SIMON STOCK TO PAOLO SIMONE DI GESÙ E MARIA, OCD,
GENERAL, IN ROME, LONDON, 25 JULY 1633
*Litterae, Stock*, 271.g.12, ff. [1rv–2rv]. B: f. [2rv]. Autograph letter signed. Italian. Complete text.

[1r] My Most Illustrious and Reverend Father,
    Pax Christi. It must not be thought that great things are done for Our Lord, especially since a regular and canonical mission cannot obtain here without any participation in the general chapter or observance of the rule of religion as far as possible. It is not a question of lack of confrères here, but of confrères who are observant and of regulars who are friends to poverty and labour and to conformity with the rule.
    The Capuchin fathers work miracles here.[283] They are now build-

ing a church here. And Your Reverences, who were more able than any other order to bear fruit here, sacrifice the order's reputation to mortify me and attempt no remedy, which I am truly sorry about. For this reason I seek the best possible way to help, with no interest other than that of doing good.

When Your Reverences send me the licence to found, granted under these conditions, the resident of the Catholic King here[284] has promised to procure the licence of his king and of Her Most Serene Highness the Infanta, to found in Flanders, at some point on the coast near Great Britain. And once this has been done, I shall procure the promised alms from friends. And at this time Your Reverences might send four to six confrères, who are not English, to set up the monastery. At that point, English confrères may be sent. Once the monastery is established, Italians, Spaniards, or confrères of any nation whatever may be sent, provided that they be men of observance and learned enough for converting heretics. I promise Your Reverences to provide them with all necessities and put them in a way to bear much fruit. But without observance of the rule in those things that may with edification be observed here, they will lose both reputation and spirit and finally their own soul.

The Capuchin fathers have a mission here for Her Most Serene Majesty the Queen, and now they are seeking to establish another here independent of that for the [ir/v] conversion of the kingdom.[285] The fathers of the Society have taken over that mission of Avalon (of which I wrote so much to Your Reverence in times past).[286] This year more will be sent thither, and once they are established thither they will bear much fruit and do great honour to the Holy Church.[287] And it is far easier to bear fruit in a mission of this kind than among heretics.

Persecution is moderating here, being confined to fines, and if a good government existed among the missionaries, one might hope to bear great fruit. But since there is no government, with greater liberty the missionaries will be lost. Now the police are like masters of novices. And lastly do I kiss Your Reverence's garments, and humbly beg the prayers of all the fathers and confrères, and of Your Reverence your holy benediction.

London, 25 Julii 1633.

Your Reverence's most humble servant,

frà Simone Stocco

69. SIMON STOCK TO GIOVANNI MARIA DI SAN GIUSEPPE, OCD, PROC-URATOR GENERAL, IN ROME, [LONDON?], 2 NOVEMBER 1633

*Litterae, Stock*, 271.g.13, f. [1rv]. Autograph letter signed. Latin. Summary.

In compliance with the addressee's request, he is preparing a history of Great Britain which hopes will be ready by Easter.[288] Repeats that the English mission must be established canonically.

70.   SIMON STOCK TO PAOLO SIMONE DI GESÙ E MARIA, OCD, GENERAL, IN ROME, [*illegible*], 3 NOVEMBER 1633
*Litterae, Stock*, 271.g.14, f. [1rv]. B: f. [1v]. Autograph letter signed. Italian. Complete text.

[1r] Jesus Maria Joseph.
   Our Most Reverend Father,
   Pax Christi. If it should please Your Reverence to send me the patent for founding a novitiate for the mission of Great Britain, with a voice in the general chapter, and that the capitular missionaries may have full electoral rights, and hold chapter here and observe the laws of the Holy Church and the primitive rule of the order as far as is possible as much for the edification of their neighbours as for the conversion of other souls and the good of their own, [then] the Catholic king's resident[289] [will] procure licence of his king and of Her Most Serene Highness the Infanta to found a monastery in Flanders, at some spot on the coast near England. And the foundation is not to be for English and Scots only, but for the order's sons of all nations who are concerned with the conversion of Great Britain and the missions here. The missionaries of other orders here operate by provinces, with the same privileges as the provinces in Italy have. The fathers of the Society are once more sending [missionaries] to that mission,[290] of which I have so often written to Your Reverence.[291] And it will be a work of great profit to the Holy Church, because one of those [*illegible*] infidels desires to receive the Holy Faith, and the others will follow his good example. These and other heroic actions are done by the other orders here. And Your Reverences proceed as if it were your desire to plant here epicurism, worthlessness and ignorance. And there is no remedy, but I must to attempt it all the same, since I am filled with pity and shame. I hope that Your Reverence will remedy everything and obliterate my name from all books and papers of the order, and remove me from the congregation. And lastly do I kiss a thousand times the feet of the fathers and of the confrères, begging their prayers, and of Your Reverence your holy benediction.
   [*Illegible*], 3 November 1633.
   Our Father Your Reverence's most humble servant,
      frà Simone Stocco

71. SIMON STOCK TO PAOLO SIMONE DI GESU E MARIA, OCD, GENERAL, IN ROME, LONDON, 3 JANUARY 1634

*Litterae, Stock*, 271.g.16, ff. [1rv–2rv]. B: ff. [1v–2r]. Autograph letter signed. Italian. Summary.

He asks that the English mission be established canonically; otherwise he prefers to transfer to another order.

72. SIMON STOCK TO PAOLO SIMONE DI GESÙ E MARIA, OCD, GENERAL, IN ROME, LONDON, [15 MAY 1634]

*Litterae, Stock*, 271.g.15, ff. [1rv–2rv.] Autograph letter signed. Italian, Latin. Summary.

He asks that the English mission be established canonically. Is unable to travel to Rome, as he would wish, because of his advanced age.

73. SIMON STOCK TO PAOLO SIMONE DI GESÙ E MARIA, OCD, GENERAL, IN ROME, [LONDON, 2 AUGUST] 1634

*Litterae, Stock*, 271.g.18, ff. [1rv–2rv]. B: ff. [1v–2r]. Autograph letter signed. Italian. Summary.

He has waited three weeks for Onophre de Saint-Jacques, who was to visit the mission,[292] and can wait no longer. Asks to be transferred to another order.

74. SIMON STOCK TO PAOLO SIMONE DI GESÙ E MARIA, OCD, GENERAL, IN ROME, LONDON, 2 NOVEMBER 1634

*Litterae, Stock*, 271.g.17, ff. [1rv–2rv]. B: f. [2r]. Autograph letter signed. Italian. Summary.

He deplores the state of the English mission, and in particular accuses the provincial vicar[293] of being "extremely timid, effeminate, irascible, and sly." Asks to be transferred to another order.

75. ELISEUS OF ST. MICHAEL, SIMON STOCK, EDMUND OF ST. MARTIN, ELIAS OF JESUS, FRANCIS OF THE SAINTS[294] TO [FRANCESCO INGOLI, SECRETARY OF PROPAGANDA, IN ROME], LONDON, 14/24 DECEMBER [1634]

*SOCG*, vol. 105, ff. 444rv, 450rv. B: ff. 444v, 450r. Letter not in Stock's handwriting, signed by all. Latin. Summary.

The writers express their thanks for the seminary for English Discalced Carmelites fonded at Louvain. Ask that the decree of the order's penultimate general chapter, regarding the founding of a novitiate, be put into effect. Onophre de Saint-Jacques, who has recently been in England as visitor general,[295] is informed about the matter.

Possibly discussed by Propaganda on 25 June 1625, in General Congregation no. 205.

76. ELISEUS OF ST. MICHAEL, SIMON STOCK, EDMUND OF ST. MARTIN, ELIAS OF JESUS, FRANCIS OF THE SAINTS TO PROPAGANDA, [IN ROME], LONDON, 14/24 JANUARY 1634]
*SOCG*, vol. 105, ff. 445rv, 451rv. B: ff. 445v, 451r. Letter not in Stock's handwriting, signed by all. Latin. Summary.

The writers ask that Onophre de Saint-Jacques, formerly visitor general in England, be consulted on the question of the novitiate.

Possibly discussed by Propaganda on 28 May 1635, in General Congregation no. 204.

77. SIMON STOCK TO PAOLO SIMONE DI GESÙ E MARIA, OCD, GENERAL, IN ROME, LONDON, 7 FEBRUARY 1635
*Litterae, Stock,* 271.g.19, f. [1rv]. Autograph letter signed. Italian. Summary.

The former visitor to England[296] is fully aware of the distressing state of the mission. Should it not be established canonically, he wishes to be transferred to another order. Has sent the addressee the book on the subject of "what our predecessors have done both in the mission and in the conversion of infidels."[297]

78. SIMON STOCK TO PAOLO SIMONE DI GESÙ E MARIA, OCD, GENERAL, IN ROME, LONDON, 13 APRIL [1635]
*Litterae, Stock,* 271.g.20, f. [1rv]. Autograph letter signed. Italian. Summary.

Edmund of St. Martin died on 10 April. He expresses his hopes that the general chapter[298] will approve the reform of the English mission. Has sent the addressee the history of the first Carmelite monks in

Great Britain,[299] which he intends to get printed in Antwerp.


79. SIMON STOCK TO FRANCESCO INGOLI, SECRETARY OF PROPA-
GANDA, [IN ROME], CANTERBURY, 15 OCTOBER 1636
*SOCG*, vol. 135, ff. 164rv, 167rv. B: f. 167r. Autograph letter signed.
Italian. Summary.

Some discord exists between his young confrères and himself.
Onophre de Saint-Jacques, who had promised so much on his visit to
England, has done next to nothing. The English mission is on the
point of collapse. According to Stock, who has suffered sixty years of
persecution, twenty-four of them for the cause of his order,[300] the
blame lies purely with his superiors. Now lives for the most part in
Canterbury, as requested by Propaganda.

After the signature, by way of postscript, appears the sentence:
"Of that mission of Avalon little news reached me, although it yet
progresses. The site is now changed, being towards Virginia."


80. SIMON STOCK TO [FRANCESCO INGOLI, SECRETARY OF PROPA-
GANDA, IN ROME], CANTERBURY, 15 APRIL 1637
*SOCG*, vol. 106, ff. 60rv, 63rv. Autograph letter signed. Italian. Sum-
mary.

A new visitor has arrived in England.[301] The mission is mori-
bund. Conn, the pope's agent,[302] is a most welcome presence. His
greetings to Monsignor Panzani.[303]


81. SIMON STOCK TO [PROPAGANDA, IN ROME], LONDON, 2 JUNE 1637
*SOCG*, vol. 137, ff. 344rv, 349rv. B: ff. 344v, 349r. Autograph letter
signed. Italian. Summary.

He complains of his superiors. The mission is on the verge of
collapse. One confrère has converted to Protestantism. As he wrote the
year before,[304] he has written three books in English against the Protestants, for which he will ask authorization, together with several others on the Church's visible sacrifice, that will be printed.[305] The king
is so good, he should be Catholic.

Discussed by Propaganda on 30 January 1638, in General Congregation no. 240, item no. 37 (*Acta*, vol. 13, f. 21rv). Answered by Propaganda on 13 February 1638 (*Lettere*, vol. 18, f. 15rv).

---

82. SIMON STOCK TO [PROPAGANDA, IN ROME], CANTERBURY, 23 JAN-
UARY 1638

*SOCG*, vol. 137, ff. 341rv, 352rv. B: ff. 341v, 352r. Autograph letter signed. Italian, Latin. Summary.

The English Discalced Carmelites are sending the bearer of the present letter, Anselm of St. Mary,[306] to the order's general chapter, to see that the English mission finally gets established on a correct basis. In default of this, Stock wishes to be transferred to the Carmelites.[307]

Discussed by Propaganda on 20 April 1638, in General Congregation no. 245, item no. 29 (*Acta*, vol. 13, ff. 79v–8or). Answered by Propaganda on 24 April 1638 (*Lettere*, vol. 18, f. 50v).

83. SIMON STOCK TO [PROPAGANDA, IN ROME], [LONDON OR CAN-
TERBURY, 1638]

*SOCG*, vol. 347, ff. 637rv–4orv. Autograph memorandum signed. Latin. Another copy: letter 84. Summary.

Suggestions concerning the administration of the English mission in a memorandum in three parts, respectively entitled "Rationes quare missionariis nostris in Anglia convenit vocibus suis activis et passivis gaudere," "Rationes quare novitiatum requirunt," and "De rebus pro missione absolute necessariis."

Possibly discussed by Propaganda on 24 May 1638, in General Congregation no. 246, item no. 13 (*Acta*, vol. 13, f. 92[b]r).

84. SIMON STOCK TO [PROPAGANDA, IN ROME], [LONDON OR CAN-
TERBURY, 1638]

*SOCG*, vol. 347, ff. 644rv–9rv. Autograph memorandum signed. Latin. Another copy: letter 83.[308] Summary.

Suggestions concerning the administration of the English mission in a memorandum in three parts, respectively entitled "Rationes quare missionariis nostris in Anglia convenit vocibus suis activis et passivis gaudere," "Rationes quare novitiatum requirunt," and "De rebus pro missione absolute necessariis."

Discussed by Propaganda as in letter 83.

85. SIMON STOCK TO [PROPAGANDA, IN ROME], LONDON, 23 JUNE 1638
*SOCG*, vol. 137, ff. 342rv, 351rv. B: ff. 342v, 351r. Autograph letter signed. Italian. Summary.

Should his superiors not heed the requests of the English Discalced Carmelites, he wishes to be transferred to the Carmelites. He asks that Anselm of St. Mary, at present in Rome, be heard to this effect.

Possibly discussed by Propaganda on 9 August 1638, in General Congregation no. 249

86. SIMON STOCK TO FRANCESCO INGOLI, SECRETARY OF PROPAGANDA, [IN ROME], LONDON, 23 JUNE 1638
*SOCG*, vol. 137, ff. 343rv, 350rv. B: ff. 343v, 350r. Autograph letter signed. Italian. Summary.

Since the English Discalced Carmelites have no other protector in Rome, their protests against the order's superiors are addressed to the addressee.

Discussed by Propaganda as in letter 85.

87. SIMON STOCK TO [FRANCESCO INGOLI, SECRETARY OF PROPAGANDA, IN ROME], CANTERBURY, 8 APRIL 1639
*SOCG*, vol. 138, ff. 194rv, 198rv. B: ff. 194v, 198r. Autograph letter signed. Italian. Summary.

He expresses his concern at the addressee's anger towards him.[309] The kingdom is labouring under the rebellion of the Scottish Puritans.[310] Asks to be transferred to the Carmelites.

88. SIMON STOCK TO [PROPAGANDA, IN ROME], CANTERBURY, 22 FEBRUARY 1641
*SOCG*, vol. 84, f. 111rv. Autograph letter signed. Italian, Latin. Enclosure: letter 89. Summary.

He encloses the Scots' profession of faith. Their apostasy will inevitably pass through England, Ireland, Holland, Germany and France, finally reaching Rome. He is beset by increasing persecution, but above all by that of his superiors.

---

Discussed by Propaganda on 10 June 1641, in General Congregation no. 277, item no. 31 (*Acta*, vol. 14, f. 357v). Answered by Propaganda on 20 June 1641 (*Lettere*, vol. 20, ff. 164v–5r).

89.   [SIMON STOCK] TO [PROPAGANDA, IN ROME], [CANTERBURY, 22 FEBRUARY 1641]
*SOCG*, vol. 84, ff. 120rv, 125rv. B: f. 125r. Copy not in Stock's handwriting. Latin. Enclosed with letter 88. Summary.

Copy of the Scots' profession of faith, entitled "Confessio fidei in Scotia nuper edita, et publica auctoritate recepta et stabilita, et per Angliam quoque sparsa."[311]

Discussed and answered by Propaganda as in letter 88.

90.   [SIMON STOCK] TO [PAOLO SIMONE DI GESÙ E MARIA, OCD, GENERAL, IN ROME], [CANTERBURY, AFTER 21 APRIL 1641 OR 1643]
*Litterae, Stock*, 271.g.1, ff. [1rv–3rv]. B: ff. [2v, 3v]. Autograph letter unsigned. Italian, Latin. Summary.

An autobiographical letter, written by Stock "in obedience to Your Reverence." Tells of the childhood of the missionary, his first contacts with the Discalced Carmelites, his novitiate, and his time with the English mission. The dispute with his superiors "has lasted many years, and greatly have I travailed, and yet it is not ended." Tells of his having written seven books that have been published, "and some upon request of divers people as yet unpublished."[312]

91.   ANSELM OF ST. MARY, SIMON STOCK, ELIAS OF JESUS, JOSEPH OF ST. MARY, GERVASIUS OF THE BLESSED SACRAMENT, JOHN BAPTIST OF MOUNT CARMEL[313] TO [FRANCESCO INGOLI, SECRETARY OF PROPAGANDA, IN ROME], LONDON, 19 JUNE 1649
*SOCG*, vol. 297, ff. 101rv, 116rv. B: f. 116r. Letter not in Stock's handwriting, signed by all. Latin, Italian. Enclosure: letter 92. Summary.

Following Onophre de Saint-Jacques' visit of the year before, the English Discalced Carmelites met in London in June 1649. They now request that Propaganda intercede in the question of the novitiate to be founded at the French-Belgian border or, if possible, in England. The reply must be addressed to Anselm of St. Mary at the Spanish embassy.

---

92.    ANSELM OF ST. MARY, SIMON STOCK, ELIAS OF JESUS, JOSEPH OF
ST. MARY, GERVASIUS OF THE BLESSED SACRAMENT, JOHN BAPTIST OF
MOUNT CARMEL TO PROPAGANDA, [IN ROME], LONDON, 19 JUNE 1649
*SOCG*, vol. 297, ff. 102rv. 115rv. B: f. 115r. Letter not in Stock's hand-
writing, signed by all. Latin, Italian. Enclosed with letter 91. Sum-
mary.

The writers request the intervention of Propaganda in favour of
the novitiate to be founded for English Discalced Carmelites.


93.    SIMON STOCK TO PROPAGANDA, IN ROME, LONDON, 28 JUNE 1649
*SOCG*, vol. 297, ff. 103rv, 114rv. B: ff. 103v, 114r. Autograph letter
signed. Italian. Summary.

He asks that Propaganda intercede with his superiors, as
requested in his last letter sent through the Spanish ambassador.[314]

# Notes to Part One

## CHAPTER TWO

1 Zimmerman, *Carmel in England*, 23–9. Zimmerman's is the only published work which deals with the Discalced Carmelites in England. On the female communities, see Hardman, *English Carmelites*.

2 [Biagio della Purificazionc], "Missioni Inghilterra" [1705], AOCD, Ms. 277; also [Biagio della Purificazione], "Missiones Europa Anglia. Historia Missionis 1614/83", [1705], AOCD, Ms. 271.d. Zimmerman simply copies the material in Biagio della Purificazione, occasionally inserting information about the documents in the order's archives which are used in the present work.

3 Letter 90. See Zimmerman, *Carmel in England*, 23–31.

4 On the Venerable English College, see Williams, *Venerable English College Rome*; and particularly Kelly, ed., *Liber Ruber* (the short biographical note concerning Stock is in no. 37, 146–7). See also A. Kenny, ed., *Responsa Scholarum* (where, strangely, Stock is not mentioned).

5 According to Zimmerman, Stock was born in 1574 (*Carmel in England*, 23). When, however, Stock entered the Venerable English College in Rome in October 1606, he is said to be "annos natus circiter 30" (Kelly, ed., *Liber Ruber*, 146), that is, born around 1576. On 15 November 1636, in a letter to the secretary of Propaganda, Francesco Ingoli, Stock states: "[S]ono 60 anni ch'ho patito persecutione per la Santa Fede" (letter 79). If these sixty years are to be taken as indicating the year of his birth, they also refer to 1576, which corresponds exactly with the date in the Venerable English College entry. In 1624 Stock speaks of himself as being almost "sexaginario" (letter 9), obviously an exaggeration, since he could have been no more than forty-eight or fifty.

6 In his autobiographical letter, referring to the years of his youth, Stock writes: "Essendo sortito d'Inghilterra con grande difficultà, stava con pensiero dubioso, si potesse adiutare l'afflictione d'Inghilterra più con essere

soldato o scolare, et per molto tempo mi pareva che sarebbe più con essere soldato" (letter 90).

7 Stock was admitted to the Venerable English College in October 1606 and ordained priest on 2 May 1610. He left shortly afterwards to begin his novitiate with the Discalced Carmelites, with whom he stayed for nine months without completing his studies (Kelly, ed., *Liber Ruber*, no. 37, 146–7; letter 90; [Biagio della Purificazione], "Missioni Inghilterra," 20–6; Zimmerman, *Carmel in England*, 27).

8 [Biagio della Purificazione], "Missioni Inghilterra," 20–6; Zimmerman, *Carmel in England*, 29.

9 AOCD, *Acta CG*, vol. 1, f. 28v (23 April 1614).

10 Eliseus of St. Michael (William Pendryck), 1583–1650, was provincial vicar of the English Discalced Carmelites from 1618 to 1625 and from 1626 to 1635. He is the author of *Application of the Lawes of England*, which appeared anonymously in 1623. He is mentioned in [Biagio della Purificazione], "Missioni Inghilterra," 37–9; Zimmerman, *Carmel in England*, 40–56; Allison, "Bibliographical Notes," 93. See also Stock's scathing comments on him (ch. 4 n28).

11 Edmund of St. Martin (Edmund Standford), ?–1635. He is mentioned in [Biagio della Purificazione], "Missioni Inghilterra," 40–1, 103; Zimmerman, *Carmel in England*, 56–60. In a letter to the general, his confrère Bede of the Blessed Sacrament mentions that he fell from his horse (Bede to Paolo Simone di Gesù e Maria, London, 13 March 1626, AOCD, *Litterae, Bede*, 271.h.13, f. 13r). Stock too mentions his death (letter 78).

12 [Panzani], "Relazione Dello Stato della Religione Cattolica in Inghilterra," 1637, APF, *SOCG*, vol. 347, ff. 495r, 499v.

13 Signing "Religious Man of the Congregation of S. Elias," in 1618 Stock published *Practise how to finde Ease, First Part* and in 1619 *Practise how to finde Ease, Second Part*. As "Iohn Hunt," Stock published *Humble Appeale* in 1620, and *Briefe Discoverie* in 1621. Under the name "S.S. of the Congregation of S. Elias," then there appeared in 1623 *Practise of the Presence of God, Third Part*. Subsequently, in 1637 and 1638, the two volumes *Of the Visible Sacrifice* appeared under the pseudonym "Anonymous Eremita." In his autobiographical letter, Stock mentions having published seven volumes and written "some upon request of divers people as yet unpublished" (letter 90). Zimmerman's list is incomplete (*Carmel in England*, 37–8), as are those of [Cosma a S. Stephano], *Bibliographia Carmelitana*, and of [Bartolomeo di S. Angelo and Enrico del SS. Sacramento], *Collectio Scriptorum*. For an up-to-date list, see Allison and Rogers, "Catalogue of English Books 1558–1640," 182–3. See also Allison, "Bibliographical Notes," 90–3. For a complete list of Stock's works, see the bibliography.

14 Letter 12; Elias of Jesus to Isidoro di San Giuseppe [*c.* 1648], AOCD, "Missiones Europa Anglia. Brevis relatio missionariorum 1614/48," Ms. 271.c.1, f. [1r].

15 On Stock's relations with the Spanish embassy, see Zimmerman, *Carmel in England*, 32–3.

16 Gee, *Foot out of the Snare*, sig. P2. In his denunciation of English Catho-

lics, Gee also gives the name of one "F. Simons a Carmelite," obviously Stock, "Author of divers late foolish Pamphlets" (ibid., sig. P3). Of Stock's works, Gee mentions those of 1618, 1619 and 1623 (ibid., 94; see ch. 2 n13). Stock is mentioned at another point, this time as "F. Doughty" (ibid., sig. P3). Gee probably failed to realize that "Simons" and "Doughty" were the same person.

17 Gillow, *Bibliographical Dictionary*, 2: 109; letter 72.

18 Zimmerman, *Carmel in England*, 32.

19 Zimmerman, pretending to quote from Stock's autobiographical letter (letter 90), has him say he was "attendant upon Mr. Anthony Roper, of Eltham" (*Carmel in England*, 25). Subsequently, Stock was a frequent visitor at the Roper house in Chelsea, and he then moved to Canterbury with the family. Eliseus of St. Michael lived with another branch of the Roper family, that of John Roper, Baron Teynham, accommodation Stock had procured for him (ibid., 42).

20 No one has ever made use of the letters Stock wrote to the order, with the exception of his autobiographical letter (letter 90). The letters to Propaganda have so far been put to best use by historian Raymond J. Lahey ("Role of Religion"). They had earlier been used by T.A. Hughes, *History of the Society of Jesus*; Schmidlin, "Project eines Nordamerik"; Lenhart, "Important Chapter in American Church History"; Lenhart, "Capuchin Prefecture of New England"; O'Neill, "North American Beginnings," in Metzler, ed., *Memoria Rerum*, I/2, 713-726. Some of Stock's letters are listed in the calendars of Carl Russell Fish (*Guide*) and Finbar Kenneally (*United States Documents*). For his part in English affairs, Stock was certainly known to Philip Hughes (*Rome and Counter-Reformation*) and to Maurus Lunn, "Benedictine Opposition to Bishop Smith." None of the authors mentioned, however, is familiar with more than a small part of Stock's correspondence, while Lahey is the only one to realize its potential importance.

21 Letters, 7, 14, 17. In one of his letters Stock dates the origin of his battles back to 1611 (letter 66).

22 Letters 2-3, 7.

23 Letter 10. On La Fuente, see letter 9n15.

24 Propaganda's policy is later explained to Stock: "[Q]uesta Sacra Congregatione ha per costume di non violentar li superiori delle religioni, trovando che col andar contro la loro volontà si difficultano sempre grandemente li negoti" ([PF] to SS, Rome, 17 July 1627, APF, *Lettere*, vol. 6, f. 94v).

25 Although the matter was without sequel, the case of Charles Camus Duperon, aged thirty-three, a nobleman of Lyons, is revealing about Propaganda's need and desire to create a network of informers and men of trust in the mission countries who would be outside the influence of the various religious orders. Duperon had asked to be sent, at his own expense, as a missionary to Canada. Propaganda's secretary, Ingoli, commented as follows: "Stimo sia bene mandarvi questo soggetto, [perché] presto sarà necessario far in Canada un vescovo, per li progressi ch'ivi si fanno. E di più è bene che la Sacra Congregatione habbia una persona

colà, dalla quale possa esser avvisata degl'andamenti di quei religiosi, poiché si vede ch'in cotesti luoghi lontani, li religiosi, per facilitar le conversioni servendosi della theologia, condescendono nella predicatione del Vangelo a cose che da questa Santa Sede non sono state approvate, come s'è veduto nel Giapone e si vedrà da quello che riferirà il signor cardinal Pamphilio sulla China" (Charles Camus Duperon to PF, [Lyons, 1641], APF, *SOCG*, vol. 402, ff. 200rv, 202rv; Ingoli's comments are in f. 202v). Duperon's request was discussed in the General Congregation of 26 February 1641 (APF, *Acta*, vol. 14, f. 281r, no. 24). Propaganda's reply to Duperon is [PF] to Duperon, Rome, 4 May 1641, APF, *Lettere*, vol. 9, ff. 136v–7rv.

26 The original bull is in APF, *Miscellanee Diverse*, vol. 22, ff. 1rv–4rv. Pope Gregory XV called the new Congregation into existence on 6 January 1622, and the cardinals met for the first time on 14 January. Although the bull is dated 22 June, it was probably printed in September and was certainly ready by 6 October. See Metzler, *Inventory* 13; Metzler, "Foundation of the Congregation 'de Propaganda Fide' by Gregory XV," in Metzler, ed., *Memoria Rerum*, I/1 86–93.

27 On Ingoli, see Metzler, "Francesco Ingoli," in Metzler, ed., *Memoria Rerum*, I/1, 197–243.

28 For an idea of Propaganda's world strategy, see the first subdivision of the world by means of which the cardinals of the Congregation divided their respective responsibilities (APF, *Acta*, vol. 3, ff. 3rv–5rv [8 March 1622]). In that subdivision North America is missing completely. Other world subdivisions in APF, *Acta*, vol. 24, ff. 37rv–8rv, no. 9 (12 July 1655); *Acta*, vol. 26, 125–9, no. 7 (14 June 1657).

29 On the problems of English Catholicism in Stock's time, see P. Hughes, *Rome and Counter-Reformation*. See letter 38n206.

30 Davies, *North Atlantic World*, 11–13.

31 On the history of Newfoundland, see Cell, *English Enterprise in Newfoundland*, a thorough and stimulating compendium of all the author's previous works; the many works by David Beers Quinn, particularly *England and the Discovery of America* and *North America from Earliest Discovery to First Settlement*, especially 347–68, 417–28. Outdated, but useful for the odd detail, is Howley, *Ecclesiastical History of Newfoundland*. Rowe, *History of Newfoundland and Labrador* is a useful survey.

32 For the history of these early ventures, see Cell, *English Enterprise in Newfoundland*, 61–91.

33 For the origin of the name Ferryland, see Seary, *Place Names of the Avalon Peninsula*, 27–8.

34 See [Mason], "Newfound Land," a map published in Orpheus Iunior [Vaughan], *Cambrensium Caroleia*, which came out again the following year in Orpheus Iunior [Vaughan], *Golden Fleece*. See also Cell, *English Enterprise in Newfoundland*, 92; Coakley, "Calvert and Newfoundland," 5; Lahey, "Role of Religion," 494.

35 Coakley, "Calvert and Newfoundland," 2–3; Lahey, "Role of Religion," 493; Quinn, *England and the Discovery of America*, 393–4; Krugler, "Eng-

lish and Catholic," 1; Kingsbury, *Records of the Virginia Company*, 3:81.

36 Quinn, *England and the Discovery of America*, 394.

37 [Wynne], *Letetr* [*sic*] *written by Captaine Edward Winne*, 1621; [Wynne], *Letter from Captain Edward Wynne*, 1622, also published in the appendix to the 1622 edition of Whitbourne, *Discourse and Discovery*, and later in [Purchas], *Purchas His Pilgrimes*, 4: 1889–90. As late as 1628 Wynne still viewed his experience in a favourable light (see "The British India," BL, Royal Mss. 17 A LVII).

38 Grant to Sir George Calvert of the whole country of Newfoundland, PRO, CO 1/2/14 (31 December 1622/10 January 1623).

39 Grant to Sir George Calvert of the province of Avalon, PRO, CO 1/2/23 (7/17 April 1623); Charter of Avalon, BL, Sloane Mss. 170 (7/17 April 1623). On Calvert's grants, see Coakley, "Calvert and Newfoundland," 6–9; Lahey, "Role of Religion," 496; Cell, *English Enterprise in Newfoundland*, 92–3; Krugler, "English and Catholic," 2.

40 Quinn, *England and the Discovery of America*, 384–6. See a somewhat different interpretation of Persons's attitude towards expansion in Bossy, "Reluctant Colonists," in Quinn, ed., *Early Maryland*, 152–9.

41 Hunt [Stock], *Humble Appeal*, 56, 59, 67; Hunt [Stock], *Briefe Discoverie*, 33.

42 Letter 12.

43 If one accepts that the conversion actually took place and that the person in question was really a member of the Privy Council (and there is no reason to doubt either of Stock's statements), then it must be someone who before August/September 1624 was neither secretly nor publicly Catholic. This automatically excludes important figures such as Thomas Hamilton, earl of Melrose, Edward Somerset, earl of Worcester, and Richard Weston, who had all become Catholic prior to that date. The person in question could easily have come into contact with Stock through the Spanish embassy in London because of the Spanish marriage negotiations. He must then have either disappeared completely or even died, since Stock makes no further mention, even implicitly, of such a councillor. James, marquis Hamilton, would seem to fit all these characteristics. He took an active part along with Calvert in the Spanish marriage negotiations. Furthermore, he died suddenly, on 2/12 March 1624/25, "a Catholique," according to the Reverend John Southcote ("Notebook of John Southcote," Catholic Record Society, no. 1 [(1905]: 100). Another, more remote possibility, would be Edward Wotton, Baron Wotton, removed by Charles I from the Privy Council precisely on the accusation of Catholicism ([Birch, ed.], *Court and Times of Charles the First*, 1: 7–8; *DNB* 21: 966). Wotton died early in 1626, but from the moment of his leaving the Privy Council, he had retired to Boughton Malerbe. For the members of the Privy Council, see *APC 1623–25*, 1–2; *1625–26*, 1–2.

44 In the whole of his correspondence, Stock never mentions Calvert by name. No doubt whatsoever, however, exists concerning his identity.

45 No complete biography of Calvert exists other than the entry in *DCB* 1: 162–3, written by Allan M. Fraser. James W. Foster never completed his

intended biography, but historian John D. Krugler is currently making at a full-scale study of Calvert. For the time being, see his very useful and well-documented articles, "Sir George Calvert's Resignation as Secretary of State"; " 'The Face of a Protestant, and the Heart of a Papist.' " "Lord Baltimore, Roman Catholics, and Toleration"; "The Calvert Family, Catholicism, and Court Politics"; " 'With promise of Liberty in Religion' "; "English and Catholic." See also Coakley, "Calvert and Newfoundland"; Lahey, "Role of Religion"; Lahey, "Avalon. Lord Baltimore's Colony in Newfoundland," in Story, ed., *Early European Settlement and Exploitation in Atlantic Canada*, 115-37.

46 Dudley Carleton to Sir Dudley Carleton, 4/14 April 1624, *CSP, Dom. 1623-25*, 208.

47 John Chamberlain to Sir Dudley Carleton, London, 8/18 January 1624/25, in [Birch, ed.], *Court and Times of James the First*, 2: 490.

48 *APC 1623-25*, 453-54 (9/19 February 1624/25).

49 Chamberlain to Sir Dudley Carleton, London, 12/22 February 1624/25, in [Birch, ed.], *Court and Times of James the First*, 2: 490; McClure, ed., *Letters of Chamberlain*, 2: 600.

50 *Calendar of Patent and Close Rolls, Ireland, Reign of Charles the First*, 36-7. On the origin of the name, see H. Kenny, "Baltimore: New Light on a Old Name," 116-18. On Calvert's favourable terms upon leaving office, see Krugler, "English and Catholic," 4.

51 *APC 1623-25*, 453-4 (9/19 February 1624/25).

52 Chamberlain to Sir Dudley Carleton, London, 9/19 April 1625, in [Birch, ed.], *Court and Times of Charles the First* 1: 7-8; McClure, ed., *Letters of Chamberlain*, 2: 608.

53 George Cottington to John Finet, 7/17 April 1628, BL, Sloane Mss. 3827, f. 124v.

54 Letters 10, 12. Using different sources, Krugler reached the same conclusions, dating Calvert's conversion between July 1624 and January 1625 ("Face of a Protestant," 529). Later, Krugler was able to date it more precisely as being between 20 August and 5 November 1624 ("English and Catholic," 4).

55 Chamberlain to Sir Dudley Carleton, London, 26 February/8 March 1624/25, in [Birch, ed.], *Court and Times of James the First*, 1: 501; McClure, ed., *Letters of Chamberlain*, 2: 603. Krugler, who did not know Stock's correspondence at the time he wrote, believed in Matthew's influence over Calvert ("Calvert's Resignation," 252). See also Mathew and Calthrop, *Life of Sir Tobie Matthew*, 290. See also T[homas] R[oper] to [Thomas More, in Rome], [London?], 21 February 162[5], WDA, *B*, vol. 47, no. 181, ("Sir G. Coluerte I am tolde is rectus in C[atholic] R[eligion] and it is sayed he intende to goe on a uiagge [voyage] to the neu founde land where he hathe a share in that plantation").

57 Chamberlain to Joseph Mead, London, 13/23 April 1625, in [Birch, ed.], *Court and Times of Charles the First*, 1: 10.

58 Krugler, "Face of a Protestant"; Krugler, "Calvert's Resignation," 252-4; Krugler, "English and Catholic," 1-5. On Calvert's boyhood, see Foster, "Calvert: His Yorkshire Boyhood."

CHAPTER THREE

1 Letter 14. Other confrères in England with Stock were Edmund of St. Martin and Eliseus of St. Michael.

2 Letters 14–15.

3 George Calvert to John Coke, 15/25 March 1624/25, *CSP. Col. Addenda 1574–1674*, 68, no. 138; HMC, Cowper Mss., 1: 187.

4 George Villiers, duke of Buckingham, to Coke, Theobalds, 17/27 March 1624/25, HMC, Cowper Mss., 1: 187.

5 Stock refers to Lord Baltimore for the first time in letter 12 (15 November 1624). Since his preceding letter is of 30 August (letter 10), their meeting, like Lord Baltimore's conversion, probably took place some time between those two dates.

6 He mentions Lord Baltimore's plans for the first time in letter 14. The first extant letter to the order to mention Avalon appears in the following year (letter 32), but it seems to imply some previous correspondence on the subject which has not survived.

7 None of the available sources make any reference to Catholic elements in Lord Baltimore's Newfoundland colony before this time. If anything, the reverse seems to be true. One of the early requests of the first governor, Edward Wynne, was for a "learned and . . . religious Minister" (*Letetr* [*sic*] *written by Captaine Edward Winne*, 20).

8 Letter 14.

9 See [Holinshed], *Chronicles of England*, 1: 9; [Dodsworth and Dugdale], *Monasticon Anglicanum*, 1: 2–3. For a more recent interpretation, see Phelps, *History and Antiquities of Somersetshire*, 1: 38–40.

10 [Lloyd], *State Worthies*, 750–2. This interpretation of the origin of the name Avalon with regard to Newfoundland appears here for the first time in print.

11 Account of Lord Baltimore's Colonizing Ventures in North America, c. 1670, BL, Sloane Mss. 3662, f. 24r.

12 [Wynne], *Letter from Captain Edward Wynne*. On the name Avalon and the matter of Lord Baltimore's concessions, see also Charter of Avalon, BL, Sloane Mss. 170 (7/17 April 1623); Coakley, "Calvert and Newfoundland," (1976). 6–9.

13 Lahey, "Role of Religion," 72: 496–7.

14 Letters 14–15.

15 For sixteenth-century works on Newfoundland, see Quinn, *North America from Earliest Discovery to First Settlement*, 347–68, 417–28, 594–5; Cell, *English Enterprise in Newfoundland*, 34–52. Also Taylor, *Stuart Geography*; Taylor, *Late Tudor and Early Stuart Geography*; Parker, *Books to Build an Empire*, 1965.

16 [Mason], *Briefe Discourse of the New-found-land*.

17 Whitbourne, *Discourse and Discovery*; Whitbourne, *Discourse Containing a Loving Invitation*.

18 [Wynne], *Letetr* [*sic*] *written by Captaine Edward Winne*; [Wynne], *Letter from Captain Edward Wynne*.

19 [T.C.], *Short Discourse of the New-Found-Land*.

20 Alexander, *Encouragement to Colonies*.

21 Eburne, *Plain Pathway to Plantations*. For an accurate introduction to all the works appearing between 1620 and 1624, see Louis Booker Wright's introduction to Eburne's *Plain Pathway to Plantations* (1962), ix–xxxvi. References to this work are from this edition.

22 Whitbourne, *Discourse and Discovery*, Epistle Dedicatory; [T.C.], *Short Discourse of the New-Found-Land*, [4]; Eburne, *Plain Pathway to Plantations*, 136.

23 Mason, *Briefe Discourse of the New-found-land*, [4]; Whitbourne, *Discourse and Discovery*, 1; Whitbourne, *Discourse Containing a Loving Invitation*, To the Reader; [T.C.], *Short Discourse of the New-Found-Land*, [10]. The meridian that Stock has in mind is the "prime meridian," as it is now called. Before Greenwich was established, the prime meridian varied from country to country and from map to map. Stock is referring to the prime meridian which passes through the Azores, with respect to which England is east, and Newfoundland (Avalon) west and which is, as Stock says, "three degrees nearer to the meridian than England." Gerard de Jode's 1593 atlas uses the same prime meridian for the maps of America and Europe, while the world map in the same atlas gives a prime meridian located in the Pacific Ocean (*Speculum Orbis Terrae*). Stock had seen Gerard de Jode's atlas before the summer of 1625, but not before 31 May 1625 (letter 18). Two considerations support this conclusion. First, he did not use the information from the map before summer. Second, his knowledge of the meridian would presuppose the identification of Avalon with Newfoundland, which is still at this point to be excluded. The information must therefore have been passed on to Stock by someone (perhaps Lord Baltimore himself) who had probably got it from Gerard de Jode's atlas and who then showed Stock the atlas itself. For the history of the prime meridian, see Howse, *Greenwich Time*, 127–8.

24 Soon afterwards, Stock was in close contact with Sir Arthur Aston, future governor of Avalon. Judging from his letters to Propaganda, Stock could have only met Aston some time between March and early May 1626 (letters 15–16). Aston cannot therefore have been his initial source.

25 As late as the end of May, Stock is still making a clear distinction between Avalon and the places in which "the heretical English ministers have sown their heresy," that is, New England, New Scotland, Virginia, Bermuda and Newfoundland, this last being quite clearly considered a separate place from Avalon (letters 17–18). Stock's misunderstanding is yet further proof of his total ignorance of existing literature on Newfoundland.

26 Letters 16–17.

27 *APC 1625–26*, 33 (26 April/6 May 1625).

28 On 24 May 1625, Stock states that Lord Baltimore is about to leave for Ireland (letter 17). On 31 May he writes that "of those that thought to go [to Avalon] . . . some have gone to Ireland," obviously a reference to Lord Baltimore (letter 18). Lord Baltimore must therefore have left between 24 and 31 May 1625.

29 Charles I to Henry Cary, Viscount Falkland, Westminster, 29 May/8 June

1625, *Calendar of Patent and Close Rolls, Ireland, Reign of Charles the First*, 36.

30 Letter 16.

31 In Ireland Lord Baltimore did not stay on his own property in County Longford, but at Cloghammon, in County Wexford, where he had purchased Sir Richard Masterson's estate. See David Roth, bishop of Ossory, to Peter Lombard, archbishop of Armagh, 17 September 1625, HMC, Franciscan Mss., 81; also Lahey, "Role of Religion," 499n31.

32 According to William Vaughan, Wynne had spent four winters in Newfoundland (Orpheus Iunior [Vaughan], *Cambrensium Caroleia*, [67], that is, from the summer of 1621 to the end of the winter of 1624-25. For an esetimation of his administration, see Lahey, "Role of Religion," 499-500; *DCB* 1: 672.

33 *APC 1625-26*, 20 (5/15 April 1625). It is probably more than a coincidence that permission was granted on the recommendation of Albertus Morton, who had taken Lord Baltimore's place as secretary of state.

34 On receiving the first news from Avalon after the summer, Stock writes to Rome: "The island ... is so pleasing to this knight, our dear friend, ... that he is established there, and I have procured him the governorship of the same island" (letter 24). The obvious implication is that Aston accepted the post only after spending some time in Ferryland. More problematic is Stock's part in Lord Baltimore's choice of Aston. On 2 May 1625 Stock still seems not to know Aston (letter 15). Aston received permission to leave for Newfoundland on 5/15 April (*APC 1625-26*, 20). On 10 May Stock refers to Aston as "a Catholic knight and dear friend" (letter 16). If Stock did influence Lord Baltimore, it must have been at some point between March and early May 1625.

35 On 24 May 1625 Stock states that Aston is about to leave for Avalon (letter 17). On 31 May he writes that "of those that thought to go [to Avalon] some have departed" (letter 18), obviously meaning Aston.

36 Shaw, *Knights of England*, 2: 134.

37 *CSP, Dom. 1603-10*, 146, no. 20 (23 August/2 September 1604).

38 Thomas Locke to Sir Dudley Carleton, 23 April/3 May 1621, *CSP, Dom. 1619-23*, 249, no. 107.

39 *APC 1621-23*, 180-1 (29 March/6 April 1622).

40 Ibid., 244 (6/16 June 1622).

41 Ibid., 246 (7/17 June 1622).

42 Ibid., 252 (16/26 June 1622).

43 A short biography of Aston, based on the above sources, is in Lahey, "Role of Religion," 500n38.

44 See ch. 2 n34.

45 Letter 16.

46 Letter 17.

47 On the direct link between English expansion and the Protestant religion, see Wright, *Religion and Empire* (first ed.: 1943), in particular, 134-9. See the concern over the conversion of the Indians in Newfoundland and the New World in Whitbourne, *Discourse and Discovery*, sig. B2, 14-15; Whit-

bourne, *Discourse Containing a Loving Invitation*, sig. A2v; [T.C.], *Short Discourse of the New-Found-Land*, [3]; Eburne, *Plain Pathway to Plantations*, 25.

48 On the English Catholics' attitude towards expansion in America, see Quinn, *England and the Discovery of America*, 364–97.

49 [Hakluyt], *Principal Navigations*. On Hakluyt, see Wright, *Religion and Empire*, 33–56.

50 Whitbourne, *Discourse and Discovery*, frontispiece.

51 Wright, *Religion and Empire*, 137–40.

52 Ibid., 141–9; Wright's introduction to Eburne, *Plain Pathway to Plantations*, xxvi–xxxiv.

53 [Purchas], *Purchas His Pilgrimes*. On Purchas, see Wright, *Religion and Empire*, 115–33.

54 Hunt [Stock], *Humble Appeal*, 56.

55 Arias, "Señor. El Doctor Iuan Luis Arias dize" [1609], in *Papeles Tocantes la Iglesia Española*, BL (Dept. of Printed Books), 4745.f.11 (8), sig. A. An English translation of Arias is given in Major, ed., *Early Voyages to Terra Australis*, 2–3 (the original is in Spanish). Major, however, does not indicate precisely where the document is to be found, merely mentioning a "collective volume in the British Museum" (1).

56 Whitbourne warns: "But if this designe of a Plantation [in Newfoundland] should not be entertained, and throughly prosecuted, it may be iustly doubted, that some other Prince will step in, and undertake the same" (*Discourse and Discovery*, 16–17). Eburne similarly mentions the need for a thorough and far-reaching Protestant influence over the idolaters (*Plain Pathway to Plantations*, 25).

57 Letter 15.

58 Letter 14.

59 Letter 16.

60 Letters 17–18.

61 Letter 17. See also letters 12, 16.

62 The Isle of Man was united to the Church of England at the end of the sixteenth century, although the proceedings had met with some opposition (Kinvig, *History of the Isle of Man*, 125–6). The Isle of Wight had become Catholic under Mary I, but reverted to Protestantism under Elizabeth I (R.L.P. Jowitt and D.M. Jowitt, *Isle of Wight*, 9–10). The Channel Islands (Jersey, Guernsey, Alderney, Sark and some of the minor islands) had continued under the jurisdiction of the diocese of Coutances, in France, even when the English throne had attempted to transfer them to Salisbury and Winchester at the end of the fifteenth century. In 1613 James I decided to bring the islands into the Church of England, and by 1623 normalization in Jersey was almost attained, although in Guernsey it did not take place until 1662 (Eagleston, *Channel Islands under Tudor Government*, 49–55, 131, 139–40, 142–5). The end of Catholicism in these island was thus relatively fresh in the English Catholics' collective consciousness. This should help explain for the modern reader the otherwise curious analogy between these islands and their far-off counterparts in the New World.

63 Letter 17. If this project ever existed, nothing is known of it today, nor have I been able to trace Stock's source.

64 Letter 18. This is probably Charles I's proclamation "for settling the plantation of Virginia" (*CSP, Dom. 1625-26*, 22, no. 52 [13/23 May 1625]). Stock states the proclamation was issued later than his letter of 24 May (letter 17), but, in fact, it had already been made public on 13/23 May. Possibly Stock simply was not aware of the proclamation date but knew of it by 31 May.

65 Letter 18.

66 See Codignola, "America del Nord nei documenti di Propaganda," in Codignola, ed., *Canadiana*, 34-5.

67 Stock's letters took respectively 34 days (letter 17), 42 days (letter 14), 48 days (letter 16), 51 days (letter 18), and 61 days (letter 15). Propaganda's replies to Stock were sent off from four to eight days after the date of the General Congregation in which they were discussed.

68 Appendix to letter 14.

69 [PF] to SS, Rome, 26 March 1625, APF, *Lettere*, vol. 4, f. 52v.

70 Ibid., f. 53r.

71 APF, *Acta*, vol. 3, f. 208v, no. 18 (22 May 1625).

72 [PF] to SS, Rome, 7 May 1625, APF, *Lettere*, vol. 4, f. 76r.

73 Ibid. Millini had been in contact with the general since the end of the previous year over the question of the novitiate. Millini himself had informed Stock of these negotiations (see letter 5).

74 [PF] to SS. Rome, 5 July 1625, APF, *Lettere*, vol. 4, f. 106v. It should be recalled that Propaganda had known of this since at least 27 June, when the draft of the reply to Stock was prepared (in appendix to letter 16).

75 APF, *Acta*, vol. 3, ff. 3rv-5rv, no. 2 (8 March 1622). Of the lands in America, mention is made only of Brazil and the West Indies, linked to Portugal and Spain respectively.

76 Metzler, "Orientation, programme et premières décisions," in Metzler, ed., *Memoria Rerum*, I/1: 156-8.

77 [Bolìvar], "Relaçion de la Virginia por fr. Gregorio de Bolivar menor observante Predicator de la Yndia Ocidental,' APF, *Miscellanee Varie*, vol. 6, f. 194rv (the original is in Spanish). On Bolìvar's report, see Metzler, "Der älteste Bericht über Nordamerika in Propaganda-Archiv," *Neue Zeitschrift für Missionswissenschaft* 25 (1969): 29-37, which also gives a transcription of the report itself. From a comparison of the respective dates, I would say that Stock's information on North America is slightly earlier than Bolìvar's or at least contempoary. However, Stock deals with Newfoundland; Bolìvar, with Virginia.

78 "[Q]uella nuova isola Avolonia [*sic*], da lei [Stock] così chiamata" ([PF] to SS, Rome, 26 March 1625, APF, *Lettere*, vol. 4, f. 52v).

79 Newfoundland is in fact omitted in the summary appearing in the appendix to Stock's letter of 31 May (letter 18).

80 Davies, *North Atlantic World*, 38.

CHAPTER FOUR

1 Letters 18.
2 Letter 19.
3 C. de Jode, "Americae Pars Borealis," in [G. de Jode], *Speculum Orbis Terrae*, 1593. The first edition of the atlas, entitled *Speculum Orbis Terrarum*, [1578], bears, in fact, very little relation to the 1593 edition. The maps of America, including Cornelis de Jode's, are absent. Stock's words ("the geographers write" [letter 19]) seem to indicate that he had access to the whole atlas, not just the map of America, and that he was aware that there were two de Jodes. On this point, see ch. 3 n23. On de Jode, see van Ortroy, *Oeuvre cartographique de De Jode*, particularly 96–8.
4 Letter 19; C. de Jode, "Americae Pars Borealis."
5 For example, see this caption: "In his montibus habitant diversae nationes, homines fieri et sine lege: quique continuis bellis inter se conflictantur, Avanares scilicet Albardi, Calicuaz, Tagiz, Apalche, Chilaga Mocosa, pluresque aliae" (C. de Jode, "Americae Pars Borealis").
6 Stock's transcription is very faithful to the original Cornelis de Jode. See Stock: "[Q]ui inter Floridam et terram Bacalaos habitant, omnes uno nomine Canadenses appelantur, sed diversae nationes populorum, Mechelaga, Hongueda, Corterealis, prae caeteris benigni et humani" (letter 19). And de Jode: "Qui inter Floridam et terram Baccalaos habitant, hi uno nomine Canadenses appellantur: sed diversae nationes populorum, ut sunt Hochelaga, Hongueda, Corterealis, prae caeteris beningni [*sic*] et humani" ("Americae Pars Borealis").
7 The bibliography on the image of the Indians in sixteenth- and seventeenth-century Europe, and England in particular, is vast. Among the most recent (1975–85) works, see Jennings, *Invasion of America*; Jaenen, *Friend and Foe*; Porter, *Inconstant Savage*; Fishman, *How Noble the Savage*; Kupperman, *Settling with the Indians*; Sheehan, *Savagism and Civility*; Axtell, *European and Indian*; Salisbury, *Manitou and Providence*; Jaenen, *French Relationship with Native Peoples*; Dickason, *Myth of Savage*; Trigger, *Natives and Newcomers*; and Axtell, *Invasion Within.*
8 C. de Jode, "Americae Pars Borealis."
9 Letter 19. An estimation shared by all contemporary commentators on Newfoundland. See [Mason], *Briefe Discourse of the New-found-land*, [8]; Whitbourne, *Discourse and Discovery*, Epistle Dedicatory, To his Maiesties good Subiects, 1, 47; Whitbourne, *Discourse Containing a Loving Invitation*, To the Reader; [T.C.], *Short Discourse of the New-Found-Land*, [10]. Stock gives no intimation of knowing any of these.
10 Letter 19 ("inter Canadenses").
11 Ibid.
12 See ch. 5.
13 Letter 19. On 31 May 1625 Stock had first mentioned the easy passage from America to Japan, China, the Philippines and the East Indies (letter 18). It is thus possible that at that date he was already in touch with the Catholic pilot. On the other hand, speculations about the existence of a North-

west passage were already in the air, and it had become a chief factor underlying voyages to America. So Stock may merely have heard of it.

14 G. de Jode, "Totius orbis cogniti Universalis Descriptio," 1589, in *Speculum Orbis Terrae*. A caption states that "Regiones hae multum adhuc sunt incognitae, neque eo ob intensissimum frigus, adnavigare licet" (ibid.).

15 C. de Jode, "Americae Pars Borealis."

16 [PF] to SS, Rome, 5 July 1625, APF, *Lettere*, vol. 4, f. 106v. In February of the following year Propaganda is still insisting that the two missionaries were destined by the order for the Avalon mission.

17 According to Benedict Zimmerman, Bede of the Blessed Sacrament and Elias of Jesus arrived in London in the summer of 1625 (*Carmel in England*, 67, 101). They had certainly not arrived before 31 March, when Stock writes to Propaganda for the last time before the summer pause (letter 18). Their arrival can thus be fixed betwen 31 May and 29 August, which is the date of the first extant letter of Bede from England (Bede to Paolo Simone di Gesù e Maria, London, 29 August 1625, AOCD, *Litterae, Bede*, 271.h, f. 1rv).

18 Bede of the Blessed Sacrament (John Hiccocks), c. 1588–1647, had been superior of the monastery of English, Irish and Dutch Discalced Carmelites in Louvain since 1621 (the year the monastery was founded). He was provincial vicar in England from 1625 to 1626 and from 1635 to 1642. On Bede, see [Biagio della Purificazione], "Missioni Inghilterra" [1705], AOCD, Ms. 277, 63–97; Zimmerman, *Carmel in England*, 61–94. The originals of nineteen of his letters are preserved in the archives of the Discalced Carmelites ("Missiones Europa Anglia. P. Beda a SS. Sacr.: Litterae & relationes 1622/27," AOCD, MS. 271.h).

19 Elias of Jesus (Edward Bradshaw), ?–1652, had probably come, like Bede, from Brussels. On Elias, see [Biagio della Purificazione], "Missioni Inghilterra," 63; Zimmerman, *Carmel in England*, 95–107. The signed originals of five of his letters are preserved in the archives of the Discalced Carmelites ("Missiones Europa Anglia. P. Elias a Jesu: Litterae & relationes 1627/41," AOCD, Ms. 271.i), together with a report giving the history of the order in England, which is in his hand, although unsigned (Missiones Europa Anglia. Brevis relatio missionariorum 1614/48," AOCD, Ms. 271.c.1).

20 Stock, Eliseus of St. Michael and Edmund of St. Martin.

21 Letters 19, 23, 27.

22 Letters 24, 27. Although the plague had been claiming victims since March of that year, with more than eight hundred dying daily, none of Stock's confrères seem to have been affected. See [Southcote], "Notebook of John Soutcote," in Catholic Record Society, no. 1 (1905): 101; Bede of the Blessed Sacrament to Paolo Simone di Gesù e Maria, London, 28 August 1625, AOCD, *Litterae, Bede*, 271.h, f. 1r.

23 Letter 90.

24 Letter 5.

25 Thus Stock wrote to Bede: "Veramente farà bene Vostra Riverenza di non mettersi in cose di questa missione, perché non le intende, et in loco

d'adiuto augmentarà il travalio. Et [Vostra Riverenza deve] metersi un poco di studiare un compendio di logico et case di conscienza, per essere habile di venire qua" (letter 8).

26 Letters 24–5.

27 Letter 32.

28 Bede of the Blessed Sacrament to Paolo Simone di Gesù e Maria, [London, 6 February 1626], AOCD, *Litterae, Bede*, 271.h, f. 9v; Bede of the Blessed Sacrament to Paolo Simone di Gesù e Maria, London, 13 March 1626, ibid., f. 13r. Stock similarly takes no care to mince his words when speaking of another provincial vicar, Eliseus, whom he describes as "extremely timid, effeminate, irascible, and sly" (letter 74).

29 Bede of the Blessed Sacrament to Paolo Simone di Gesù e Maria, London, 10 October 1625, AOCD, *Litterae, Bede*, 271.h, f. 2rv; Bede of the Blessed Sacrament to Paolo Simone di Gesù e Maria, [London, 6 February 1626], ibid., f. 9v; Bede of the Blessed Sacrament to Paolo Simone di Gesù e Maria, London, 6 February 1626, ibid., f. 1r; Bede of the Blessed Sacrament to Paolo Simone di Gesù e Maria, London, 13 March 1626, ibid., f. 13r; Bede of the Blessed Sacrament to Paolo Simone di Gesù e Maria, London, 2 July 1626, ibid., f. 17r.

30 Bede of the Blessed Sacrament to Paolo Simone di Gesù e Maria, London, 29 August 1625, ibid., f. 2v.

31 That is, about February 1625 (see letter 14).

32 Bede of the Blessed Sacrament to Paolo Simone di Gesù e Maria, London, 29 August 1625, AOCD, *Litterae, Bede*, 271.h, f. 1r.

33 Bede of the Blessed Sacrament to Paolo Simone di Gesù e Maria, London, 10 October 1625, ibid., f. 2r; Bede of the Blessed Sacrament to Paolo Simone di Gesù e Maria, London, 24 October 1625, ibid., f. 3rv.

34 Bede of the Blessed Sacrament to Paolo Simone di Gesù e Maria, London, 10 October 1625, ibid., f. 2rv. Strangely enough, Bede writes: "[I]o mi ho informato dalli marinari et d'un piloto che venne questo anno da quelle parte, però non voglio replicare quello che io ho saputo di quelle paese" (f. 2v).

35 Bede of the Blessed Sacrament to Paolo Simone di Gesù e Maria, London, 24 October 1625, ibid., ff. 3rv–4rv.

36 Letters 25–26.

37 This is a continual *leitmotif* in Stock's letters, both to Propaganda and to the order. In 1633 Stock accuses his superiors of proceeding "as if it were your desire to plant here epicurism, worthlessness and ignorance" (letter 70). He later asks to be transferred to another order, then to the jurisdiction of the bishop of Chalcedon, and later still to the Carmelite order.

38 Letter 27. See also [Southcote], "Note-book of John Southcote," 101.

39 Letter 28.

40 Ibid.

41 Letter 24.

42 Letter 23.

43 Appendix to letter 23.

44 Appendix to letter 27. The order obviously still continued to allow Propaganda to believe that Bede and Elias were destined for Avalon.

45 The doctored report is [Bede of the Blessed Sacrament] to [Paolo Simone di Gesù e Maria], [London, 24 October 1625], APF, *SOCG*, vol. 189, ff. 347rv–8rv. Although the title may have been added by Propaganda officials, the presence of the two names "Virginia" and "Nuova Inghilterra," which are contained in the original report but not in the doctored version, makes it more probable that it was the order itself that gave the title. One of Propaganda's clerks adds a further title at the end of the abstract: "Relatione dell'isola della Nuova Inghilterra, dove si tratta di far missioni." Ingoli, after the words "Nuova Inghilterra," was careful to add "sive Avvalonia." If Stock's ideas of American geography were somewhat vague, they were much better than Propaganda's.

46 Bede of the Blessed Sacrament to Paolo Simone di Gesù e Maria, London, 6 and 23 January 1626, APF, *SOCG*, vol. 101, ff. 46rv–7rv. The original of the letter of the 23rd is not extant, while the original of the letter of the 6th is in AOCD, *Litterae, Bede*, 271.h, ff. 5rv–6rv. In his letter, Bede states (I quote from Propaganda's copy): "In questa prigione siamo sei prigionieri, tra quali vi è uno che mi disse che *questa [e] state* venne un sacerdote da quell'isola della quale ha trattato il padre frà Simone, et che essendogli offerto da quel cavalier qualche buono stipendio per andar là, vi rispose che non vi *andarebbe* ancor che li desse la metà della sue possessioni" (italics added). Thus, according to Bede's informer, this priest returned from Avalon during the summer of 1625—a statement that goes counter to every other piece of evidence. No missionary accompanied Aston to Newfoundland or returned to England prior to the end of the year. Stock would have been the first to know of it. "Quel cavalier" who had to offer "qualche buono stipendio" was obviously Lord Baltimore, but Lord Baltimore was in Ireland and thus not there to make the offer. Two further considerations. Why, in his letter of 24 October 1625, does Bede mention having met "un pilotto che venne da lì," but fail to mention the priest who was said to be returned that very summer? And why, speaking of the priest, does Bede talk of going ("andarebbe") rather than coming back, which would have been far more obvious if he really had been there? Clearly, this priest is a figment of Bede's imagination.

47 Propaganda officials do not seem particularly interested in discussing Bede's report or letters. See APF, *Acta*, vol. 4, f. 30r, no. 6 (17 March 1626); ibid., f. 39rv, no. 18 (31 March 1626).

48 It must be remembered that, because of the royal patronage, Propaganda had no jurisdiction over Spanish and Portuguese America and that the Congregation's efforts could thus only be directed at French and English America. See Ting Pong Lee, "Actitud de la Sagrada Congregación frente al Regio Patronato," in Metzler, ed., *Memoria Rerum*, I/1: 353–438. Nothing had so far been done about French America. The Avalon colony would thus be the first in an absolute sense.

49 Letter 19. Stock had already advanced this hypothesis on 31 May, without, however, backing it up with any direct evidence (letter 18).

50 [PF] to SS, Rome, 15 November 1625, APF, *Lettere*, vol. 4, ff. 190v–1r.

51 [Ortelius], *Theatrum Orbis Terrarum*. The Italian edition referred to here appeared in 1608 ([Ortelius], *Teatro del mondo*). It included a map of the

world ("Typus Orbis Terrarum," 1587) and a map of America ("Americae sive Novi Orbis," 1587), both signed by Ortelius. Ortelius's atlas is still in the Biblioteca Apostolica Vaticana in Rome in various editions, including the abovementioned 1608 Italian edition. It is the only atlas of all those mentioned in the present work to be found there.

52 Note that the name "San Lorenzo" refers only to the gulf, while the river is nowhere called by any name (Ortelius, "Typus Orbis Terrarum").

53 Ortelius, "Americae sive Novi Orbis."

54 Ortelius, "Typus Orbis Terrarum."

55 Ortelius, "Americae sive Novi Orbis."

56 [PF] to Giulio Sacchetti, bishop of Gravina, nuncio in Spain, Rome, 15 November 1625, APF, *Lettere*, vol. 4, f. 186r; [PF] to Giovanni Francesco Guidi di Bagno, archbishop of Patras, nuncio in Flanders, Rome, 15 November 1625, ibid., f. 186rv.

57 Ibid. (in both letters).

58 Guidi di Bagno to Cardinal Ludovico Ludovisi, prefect of Propaganda, Brussels, 3 January 1626, APF, *SOCG*, vol. 101, ff. 117rv, 127rv; Sacchetti to Ludovisi, Madrid, 1 February 1626, ibid., ff. 70rv, 79rv.

59 Metzler, "Francesco Ingoli," in Metzler, ed., *Memoria Rerum*, I/1: 197–243.

60 Letter 19.

61 Ibid.

62 It is doubtful whether the letter, probably delivered to Stock by one "of those Catholics" whose return was expected (ibid.), was intended for Lord Baltimore, who was still in Ireland.

63 On Stock's part in Aston's appointment, see ch. 3 n34.

64 Letter 24. The small numbers of Indians in Newfoundland is underlined by other sources ([Mason], *Briefe Discourse of the New-found-land*, [9]; Whitbourne, *Discourse and Discovery*, 2, 47–8; Eburne, *Plain Pathway to Plantations*, 137), as is their mild disposition (Whitbourne, *Discourse and Discovery*, To his Maiesties good Subiects, 2, 4; Eburne, *Plain Pathway to Plantations*, 55). Undoubtedly, the most authoritative report of the first inhabitants of Newfoundland, the Beothuks, is that of John Guy, who had direct contact with them in 1612. Guy's impression too is favourable. Guy's manuscript has only recently been published, and Stock certainly did not know it (Journal of John Guy, Lambeth Palace, Ms. 250, ff. 406rv–12rv; printed in Ritchie, ed., *New World*, 52–64). On Guy's account, see Cell, *English Enterprise in Newfoundland*, 68–9, which also gives new sources on this point; Porter, *Inconstant Savage*, 260–2).

65 Letter 27. In 1619 the Virginia Company had given ten thousand acres of land for a university to be founded at Henrico. In 1620 a school was planned at Southampton Hundred for the conversion of the Indians. In 1621 the so-called East India School was founded in Charles City as a college dependent on Henrico. All of these projects fell through, as did an Academia Virginiana et Oxoniensis, which was launched in 1624 but never went beyond the project stage. On the various attempts, see Wright, *First Gentlemen of Virginia*, 95–101; Davis, *Intellectual Life in Colonial South*, 276–9; Porter, *Inconstant Savage*, 434–45. Until Stock's source is

discovered, it is impossible to know which of these projects Stock was referring to. In *Declaration of the State of the Colonie and Affaires in Virginia*, published in 1620, a whole chapter is devoted to the project of a *"college* to be erected in *Virginia* for the conversion of *Infidels"* (36–7).

66 Letter 27.

67 The general's letter is not extant, but Stock mentions it in letter 32.

68 APF, *Acta*, vol. 4, f. 30r (30 March 1626).

69 [PF] to SS. Rome, 21 March 1626, APF, *Lettere*, vol. 5, f. 51rv.

70 This is to be deduced from a sentence appearing in the draft of the reply to Stock (see ch. 4 n69), but which is absent from the actual reply, whether because of a clerk's mistake or second thoughts on Propaganda's part, is not known: "[W]ith this knowledge it will not then be difficult to find suitable subjects for the mission in other orders" (appendix to letter 27).

71 Of the 1625–26 winter, nothing is known beyond what can be inferred from Stock's letters, that is, that Aston considered his experience in an essentially favourable light, at least up until the moment the letter Stock mentions was written, around September/October 1625. To this impression could be added the account of William Vaughan, whose involvement in Newfoundland to some extent compensates for the fact that he was not an eyewitness. In 1626 Vaughan writes of how the "generous" Aston is working zealously for his colony, at the ame time defending it from "wild Boares" (Orpheus Iunior [Vaughan], *Golden Fleece*, Third Part, 21).

CHAPTER FIVE

1 Letter 24.

2 Letters 32, 29.

3 Letter 30.

4 [PF] to SS. Rome, 21 March 1626, APF, *Lettere*, vol. 5, f. 51rv.

5 The general's letter reached Stock shortly before 22 April 1626 (see letters 31–2).

6 Letters 31–2.

7 Letters 33–4. With these, Stock encloses a transcription of the twenty-three articles of law in force against English Catholics (letter 35).

8 Letter 31. See also letter 32.

9 P. Hughes, *Rome and Counter-Reformation*, in particular, 329–46; Bossy, *English Catholic Community*, 54–7; Allison, "Smith, Richelieu and French Marriage," 193–7; D. Lunn, *English Benedictines*, 151–4.

10 [PF] to SS, Rome, 15 November 1625, APF, *Lettere*, vol. 4, ff. 190v–1r.

11 Letter 29.

12 Letter 28.

13 Unfortunately, all the maps Stock sent to Propaganda have disappeared from the archives. For the seventeenth and eighteenth centuries generally they contain very few maps, and none are of North America. Since all the maps cannot have been purloined or mislaid, the most probable explanation is that an entire section of the Propaganda archives was transferred to some other as yet unidentified archive.

14 For the history of the Northwest Passage, see Dodge, *Northwest by Sea*,

which gives a chronological list of voyages (vi–xi). See also Quinn, *North America from Earliest Discovery to First Settlements*, 369–84; Taylor, *Late Tudor and Early Stuart Geography*; Parker, *Books to Build an Empire*.

15 Letter 29.

16 Clearly an Englishman, although Stock does not mention his nationality.

17 It is equally possible that the son who had accompanied him in his explorations was the same one who eventually became a priest.

18 Letter 29. See also letters 19, 39.

19 [PF] to SS, Rome, 15 November 1625, APF, *Lettere*, vol. 4, f. 191r.

20 Letter 29.

21 Ibid.

22 Letter 39.

23 Propaganda had written to the nuncio: "Un piloto inglese catolico ha significato a frà Simon Stoch carmelitano scalzo, missionario in Inghilterra, d'haver passato per li fiumi dell'America settentrionale da un capo all'altro, e che aprendosi quel camino dall'Inghilterra alla China s'andarebbe in quattro mesi. . . . [D]esidera questa Sacra Congregatione de Propaganda Fide che Vostra Signoria s'informi et avvisi se costà si ritrova alcun rincontro di questa navigatione" ([PF] to Giulio Sacchetti, bishop of Gravina, nuncio in Spain, Rome, 15 November 1625, APF, *Lettere*, vol. 4, f. 186r). The nuncio had then scrupulously "fatto particolar diligenza per trovar persone in questa corte" to supply him with information and had received replies from several of these people (Sacchetti to Cardinal Ludovico Ludovisi, prefect of Propaganda, Madrid, 1 February 1626, APF, *SOCG*, vol. 101, f. 70r).

24 Letter 29. Bruneau seems to have done next to nothing about Avalon. It is however possible that the supposed discovery of the Catholic pilot reached Spain through Bruneau or that he had a hand in identifying the pilot. Bruneau, c. 1576–1634, was the resident of the king of Spain in London from October 1624 to January 1626, and he is defined a man of some experience by the Venetian ambassadors (Zuane Pesaro and Alvise Valaresso to Doge and Senate, London, 4/14 October 1624, *CSP, Ven. 1623-25*, 451; Pesaro to Doge and Senate, Kingston, 2/12 January 1625/26, *CSP, Ven. 1625-26*, 271). On Bruneau, see the short entry in *Biographie Nationale de Belgique*, 3: 110–14. Stock had been his confessor (letter 12). On the remote possibility of Bruneau being "signor Brune," see letter 3n4.

25 Letter 29.

26 Whitbourne, *Discourse and Discovery*, 16; [T.C.], *Short Discourse of the New-Found-Land*, sig. C3, [18]; Alexander, *Encouragement to Colonies*, 23–4.

27 [Hakluyt], *Principal Navigations*, 3: 11–29; [Purchas], *Purchas His Pilgrimes*, 3: 809–14, 827–31, 836–53.

28 Gilbert, *Discourse for a Passage to Cataia*.

29 Letter 29.

30 Hakluyt's transcription gives Gilbert's entire work, with the exception of the first part, containing George Gascoigne's introduction, his "Prophetical Sonet," and a letter of Humphrey Gilbert's to his brother John, dated

June 1566 (*Principal Navigations*, 3: 11–24). Stock discovered Hakluyt independently of Purchas, as we shall see.

31 Naturally, Stock makes no direct reference to Hakluyt or Gilbert. Gilbert's influence, however, is clearly recognizable throughout, even in the very concept of America as an island. This fact has been grasped by the majority, but it was still unclear in the hazy mind of Stock, who applies it only to North America, even though North and South America had been drawn as unified from the maps of Martin Waldseemüller onwards (letter 29; [Hakluyt], *Principal Navigations*, 3: 11, 13–14). Another point of contact between Gilbert and Stock is the latter's reference to "the ebbing and flowing of the sea and the currents" (letter 29), which corresponds to Gilbert's marginal notes on the three tidal movements ([Hakluyt], *Principal Navigations*, 3: 14). A study of the tides and movements of the sea was considered a vital factor in the search for the Northwest Passage. Francis Bacon had written of it in his treatise "De Fluxu et Refluxu Maris," which Stock could not have known since it was not published until 1653, although it was written in 1612 (Bacon, *Scripta in Naturali and Universalis Philosophia*, 178–207). Stock is certainly quoting Gilbert in his precise reference to the Northeast Passage ("until the time of Henry VII, king of England, the English were unaware of a passage to Russia, which is now a most common thing" [letter 29]), even though Gilbert gives the king of England as Edward VI ([Hakluyt], *Principal Navigations*, 3: 13). This last fact is also mentioned by T.C., who seems to have been unknown to Stock although he wrote in 1623 ([T.C.], *Short Discourse of the New-Found-Land*, [16]-sig. C3).

32 Letter 29.

33 Letter 19. This is the most probable hypothesis concerning the Dutch maps. Although it is not to be ruled out that the maps were newer ones, such as that of Peter Keer ("Americae Nova Descriptio," 1614), it is impossible to establish it with certainty from Stock's scanty information.

34 Speed, *Prospect of the Most Famous Parts of the World*.

35 [Speed], "America with those known parts," ibid. The map of the scientist Henry Briggs published in Purchas is clearly the influence behind the part concerning North America ("North part of America," in [Purchas], *Purchas His Pilgrimes*, 2: 852–3).

36 [Speed], "New and Accurat Map of the world," in *Prospect of the Most Famous Parts of the World*.

37 Stock's letter speaks of "newly printed English and Dutch maps," but he does not specify which of the two he sent to Propaganda. The problem is solved by the clerk of Propaganda, who states precisely that it was a "new map compiled by the English" (letter 29).

38 The longitude of Plymouth is not $320^0$ West (letter 31), but $312^0$ West ([Speed], "New and Accurat Map of the world") or $310^0$ West ([Speed], "America with those known parts"). The Straits of Le Maire, which Stock claims were discovered "three or four years ago" (letter 29), were according to Speed discovered in 1616, that is ten years previously ([Speed], "America with those known parts").

39 Letters 29, 31, 39.

40 On Plymouth, see p. 38.

41 Letter 29. In a caption, Speed states that "[t]his West-mediterranean sea was first found by Mr. Hudson" ("New and Accurat Map of the world").

42 A meridian which in Speed's two maps appears slightly more to the west of "Hubberts" or "Hubbarts Hope" and "Porte Nelson."

43 Letter 29.

44 [Speed], "America with those known parts." "Buttons bay" will become Hudson Bay, while "Hudsons Bay" will be renamed James Bay. See Skelton, *Explorers' Maps*, 134.

45 Namely, the present-day Pacific Ocean. By "The Pacificke Sea" Speed intends only that part of the ocean south of the Tropic of Capricorn ("New and Accurat Map of the world").

46 For a clear identification of climatic zones in Stock, see both [Gilbert], "A General Map, Made Onelye for the Particuler Declaration of This Discovery," and [Speed], "New and Accurat Map of the world."

47 The present-day Straits of Le Maire separate Tierra del Fuego from Staten Landen. Barnevelt Island is to the south of the present-day Lennox and Nueva islands in the Tierra del Fuego. On Jacob Le Maire, see van der AA, *Biographisc Woordenboek der Nederlanden*, 5: 26.

48 Letter 39.

49 Precise reference is made, for example, in the map of John Mason published by William Vaughan that same year, which mentions both Lord Baltimore and "Avalonia"; and the map William Alexander published in 1624 (untitled) and reprinted by Purchas in 1625, which mentions Avalon but not Lord Baltimore. See [Mason], "Newfound Land," in Orpheus Iunior [Vaughan], *Golden Fleece*; Alexander, *Encouragement to Colonies*; [Purchas], *Purchas His Pilgrimes*, 4: 1872-3.

50 "You may likewise see that island of which I have written formerly and the excellence of its position" (letter 31).

51 Letter 19. See also it mentioned briefly in letter 29.

52 Letter 31.

53 Ibid.

54 [Smith], *Generall Historie of Virginia*.

55 Smith depicts the Indians as "generally tall and straight, of a comely proportion, and of a colour browne when they are of any age, but they are borne white.... They are very strong, of an able body and full of agilitie, able to endure to lie in the woods under a tree by the fire, in the worst of winter, or in weedes and grasses, in Ambuscado in the Sommer" (*Generall Historie of Virginia*, 30). On Smith's description, see Porter, *Inconstant Savage*, 319; Fishman, *How Noble the Savage*, 69, 81-3.

56 [Purchas], *Purchas His Pilgrimes*, 4: 1697.

57 John Guy: "[T]hey are of reasonable stature, of an ordinary middle sise ... their faces something flat and broad, red with Oker, as all their apparell is, and the rest of their body: they are broad brested, and bould, and stand very upright" ([Purchas], *Purchas His Pilgrimes*, 4: 1881). Richard Whitbourne: "The Natives of the Countrey have great store of red Oaker, which

they use to colour their Bodies" (ibid., 1887; original in Whitbourne, *Discourse and Discovery*, A conclusion).

58 Stock is writing in 1626; Smith, in 1624. It is then possible that Stock regarded Smith's information as referring to 1623, that is, to three years before.

59 Letter 31.

60 "In the towne upon a high Mount they have a Fort well built . . . where is planted their ordnance: Also a faire watch-tower, partly framed for the Sentinell." The governor of Plymouth was William Bradford, but, what more interested Stock, "their Preachers are Master William Bruster and Master Iohn Layford" ([Smith], *Generall Historie of Virginia*, 247).

61 Hondius [de Hondt], "Americae Descrip.," in [Purchas] *Purchas His Pilgrimes*, 3: [858]. Purchas published many of de Hondt's maps.

62 Ibid., 4: 1872-3.

63 [Briggs], "North part of America."

64 [Briggs], "Treatise of the North-west passage," in [Purchas], *Purchas His Pilgrimes*, 3: 852-3. Brigg's treatise had originally been published in [Waterhouse], *Declaration of the state of Virginia*, 45-50, but without the map.

65 [Purchas], *Purchas His Pilgrimes*, 4: 1877-90.

66 [PF] to SS, Rome, 9 May 1626, APF, *Lettere*, vol. 5, ff. 92v-3r; appendix to letter 29. The whole draft of the letter to Stock is in Ingoli's handwriting, while the summary was written by one of Propaganda's clerks.

67 See [PF] to SS, Rome, 26 March 1625, APF, *Lettere*, vol. 4, f. 53r.

68 In consequence of Stock's letters (letters 17-18), Propaganda had decided to contact the superiors of the Dominicans, the Franciscans, the Augustinians and the Jesuits about the possibility of establishing missions in North America (APF, *Acta*, vol. 3, f. 245rv, no. 25 [21 July 1625]; [PF] to [Muzio Vitelleschi, SJ, General], Rome, [26 July 1625], APF, *SOCG*, vol. 259, f. 203rv; [PF] to [Serafino Secchi, OP, General], [Rome, 26 July 1625], APF, *Miscellanee Diverse*, vol. 22, f. 348r). The only reply known came from the general of the Jesuits, Vitelleschi, who wrote that three Jesuits and two lay brothers had gone to Canada that very year, repeating the attempt of eleven years previously, which had not, however, been successful (Vitelleschi's answer is written on Propaganda's letter). Subsequently, the Jesuits were to act independently in North America. Relations with the Capuchins were contemporary with the failure of the Avalon venture. On 22 November 1630 Propaganda decided to solicit the procurator general of the French and English Capuchins, Francesco da Genova, to intervene through François-Joseph Du Tremblay (better known as Joseph de Paris, the famous Eminence Grise), in a bid to stop the Puritan advance in America (APF, *Acta*, vol. 7/i, f. 87rv, no. 10 [22 November 1630]). The following year, Propaganda considered the possibility of sending a Recollet bishop to Canada (ibid., vol. 7/ii, f. 87rv, no. 18 [4 July 1631]). For these early attempts, see Campeau, *Établissement à Québec*, 60-4.

69 Appendix to letter 31.

70 Letter 39.

71 Appendix to letter 29.

### CHAPTER SIX

1 Letter 37.
2 Letter 36. Stock wrote no letters to Rome from 30 June 1626 (letters 33–5) to 12 February 1627 (letter 36).
3 Letter 36. Stock's first letter concerning Avalon was that of 8 February 1625 (letter 14).
4 Letters 36–7.
5 [Southcote], "Note-Book of John Southcote," in Catholic Record Society, no. 1 (1905): 100.
6 P. Hughes, *Rome and Counter-Reformation*, 336, 351.
7 Ibid., 355–6; *DNB* 18: 511; Gillow, *Bibliographical Dictionary*, 5: 512.
8 *DNB* 18: 511. See also letter 3n4.
9 *DNB*, 17: 216.
10 Letter 37.
11 Letter 36. It is perhaps no coincidence that of the extant correspondence between Stock and his order, five letters belong to the period up to 1624, only one to the years 1625–31 (of 1626), and the remaining ten to 1632 onwards. Relations had been practically severed.
12 Letter 37. On the dispute between Bishop Smith and the regulars, see P. Hughes, *Rome and Counter-Reformation*, 347–77; D. Lunn, *English Benedictines*, 151–4. The sequel to the dispute is sufficiently well-known. The English government issued a proclamation for Smith's arrest on 11/21 December 1628 and on 24 March offered a reward of £100 to whomever managed to capture him. Outlawed in England, abandoned by the pope (who ordered an end to the controversy in his brief *Britannia* of 9 May 1631), Smith left for France that same year, never to return to England. Gregorio Panzani's English mission of 1634 put an official end to his episcopate. An excellent account of the whole affair is to be found in Philip Hughes, who uses Propaganda's sources and some of Stock's letters to the Congregation.
13 Letter 36.
14 This is to be deduced from the dates of Stock's letters (letters 33–4, 36).
15 Letter 15.
16 Letter 36.
17 Lord Baltimore explains in his letter to Edward Nicholas, secretary to George Villiers, duke of Buckingham, that Aston was unable to return to the colony while the state of war necessitated the requisitioning of his ships (Lord Baltimore to Edward Nicholas, Savoy, 7/17 April 1627, PRO, CO 1/4/19).
18 A decision made between 7/17 April and 21/31 May 1627, judging from two letters of Lord Baltimore's (Lord Baltimore to Nicholas, 7/17 April 1627; Lord Baltimore to Thomas Wentworth, Savage, 21/31 May 1627, in Knowler, ed., *Strafforde's Letters and Dispatches*, 1: 39; also in Cooper, ed., *Wentworth Papers*, 258. On 21/31 May Lord Baltimore had announced his imminent departure for Newfoundland.

19 *CSP, Dom. 1625–49 Addenda*, 232, no. 12. Aston's wife was granted a pension of £50 for life (*CSP, Dom. 1627–28*, 525, no. 30), her right to which was disputed by the Polish Ambassador Jan Racotzki in August 1631, probably because of her husband's past activity ([Southcote], "Note-Book of John Southcote," 107.

20 Alvise Contarini to Doge and Senate, 12 March 1627, *CSP Ven. 1626–28*, 147; Gardiner, *History of England*, 6: 162–3.

21 Lord Baltimore to Nicholas, 7/17 April 1627.

22 See ch. 6 n18.

23 Lord Baltimore to Wentworth, 21/31 May 1627.

24 Ibid. On Lord Baltimore's dissatisfaction with the way his colony was being run, see also Propositions made to Charles I by Robert Hayman concerning Newfoundland, [1628], BL, Egerton Mss. 2541, f. 166r; Account of Lord Baltimore's Colonizing Ventures in North America, c. 1670, BL, Sloane Mss. 3662, ff. 24v–5r.

25 [Southcote], "Note-Book of John Southcote," 103. As chaplain to Lady Aston, Southcote was kept well-informed about the Avalon colony. The date of arrival is also confirmed by the Reverend Erasmus Stourton (PRO, CO 1/4/59).

26 The fact is certainly strange. It should be remembered, however, that one of Stock's two letters was written prior to Lord Baltimore's arrival in England and the other before his return from Avalon. Also that two months elapsed between the two (letters 36–7).

27 It is unlikely that Stock would not have mentioned Lord Baltimore's return in his letter (letter 37), if it had already taken place.

28 The fact of his return is similarly unknown to William Payne, who writes to Katherine Conway, Edward Conway's wife, recommending that she invest in land in Newfoundland (2/12 November 1627, *CSP, Dom. 1627–28*, 421, no. 13).

29 *APC 1627–28*, 216.

30 [Southcote], "Note-Book of John Southcote," 103.

31 Letter 37. From what Stock says, it appears that while all the survivors of the original fifteen or twenty to leave with Aston had returned to England (letter 36), some twenty or more ("approximately twenty") had taken their places and had left with Lord Baltimore and the two seculars (letter 37). Once again, this information is present in no other source.

32 Anderson, ed., *Book of Examinations and Depositions*, 2: 38.

33 PRO, CO 1/4/59.

34 On Longville, see PRO, CO 1/4/59. Anstruther, *Seminary Priests*, 2: 202–3; Gillow, *Bibliographical Dictionary*, 4: 328. Kelly, ed., *Liber Ruber*, no. 37, 185–6; A. Kenny, ed., *Responsa Scholarum*, no. 54, 310–11; [Southcote], "Note-Book of John Southcote," 103; Foley, ed., *Records of the English Province of the Society of Jesus*, 6: 284, 509, 512. P. Hughes, *Rome and Counter-Reformation*, 412–13; Caraman, *Morse Priest of the Plague*, 22–4, 142; Coakley, "Calvert and Newfoundland," 11; Lahey, "Role of Religion," 504.

35 On Pole, see [English College] to [Fabio de Lagonissa, archbishop of Conza, nuncio in Flanders], [Douai, August 1630], APF, *SOCG*, vol. 259,

f. 2rv; [Panzani], "Relazione Dello Stato della Religione Cattolica in Inghilterra," 1637, ibid., vol. 347, f. 500r (where Pole is mentioned as Rivers, his other alias); PRO, CO 1/4/59. Henson, ed., *Register of the English College at Valladolid*, 107–8; Stanfield, ed., "Archpriest Controversy," in *Miscellanea XII*, 170; Conway to Richard Wainwright, John Griffin and John Curay, 7/17 January 1625/26, *CSP, Dom. 1625-26*, 215, no. 19; Alvise Contarini to Doge and Senate, London, 18 December 1626, *CSP, Ven. 1626-28*, 63; Anderson, ed., *Book of Examinations and Depositions*, 2: 38–41; [Southcote], "Note-Book of John Southcote," 103; Foley, ed., *Records of the English Province of the Society of Jesus*, 7: 609. Allison, "Gerard and Gunpowder Plot," 52–5; Coakley, "Calvert and Newfoundland," 11; Lahey, "Role of Religion," 504–5.

36 Letter 37.

37 This is also historian Raymond J. Lahey's opinion ("Role of Religion," 504).

38 In 1631, Lord Baltimore was to write a treatise taking the Jesuits' part against bishop Smith (L.B. [Lord Baltimore], *Answere of a Catholike Lay Gentleman*). It must be remembered, however, that Lord Baltimore had for years been friend with the Jesuit Tobie Matthew.

39 Stock's two letters of 1627 took 150 days (letter 36) and 101 days (letter 37) respectively. The replies to Stock were dispatched five and nine days respectively after the date of the General Congregation in which they were discussed.

40 Appendix to letter 38.

41 P. Hughes, *Rome and Counter-Reformation*, 365.

42 [PF] to SS, Rome, 17 July 1627, APF, *Lettere*, vol. 6, f. 94v.

43 [PF] to SS, Rome, 28 January 1628, ibid., vol. 7, f. 9rv.

44 [PF] to SS, Rome, 17 July 1627, ibid., vol. 6, f. 94v.

45 [PF] to SS, Rome, 28 January 1628, ibid., vol. 7, f. 9r.

46 Enclosed with letter 29 was one of John Speed's maps, probably "America with those known parts," 1626, or "New and Accurat Map of the world," 1626, both of which are in Speed, *Prospect of the Most Famous Parts of the World*.

47 [PF] to SS, Rome, 28 January 1628, APF, *Lettere*, vol. 7, f. 9r.

### CHAPTER SEVEN

1 Charles I to Henry Cary, Viscount Falkland, Lord Deputy in Ireland, Whitehall, 19/29 January 1627/28, *CSP, Ireland 1625-32*, 305, no. 905.

2 Lord Baltimore to John Harrison, Bristol, 5/15 February 1627/28, BL, Stowe Mss. 743, ff. 76rv–7rv. Also Coakley, "Calvert and Newfoundland," 11.

3 Lord Baltimore to Thomas Wentworth, Cloghammon, 17/27 April 1628, in Cooper, ed., *Wentworth Papers*, 291–2.

4 Baltimore's last letter to Wentworth is dated 17/27 April. The first letter in which Stock speaks of Lord Baltimore's departure is dated 27 June (letter 38).

5 PRO, CO 1/4/59; Account of Lord Baltimore's Colonizing Ventures in

North America, c. 1670, BL, Sloane Mss. 3662, f. 25r; Scisco, "Calvert's Proceedings against Kirke," 134 (the document here examined by Scisco is remarkably similar to the Account of Lord Baltimore's Colonizing Ventures in North America). Lord Baltimore married Anne Mynne (?–1622) in 1604. They had eleven children, six boys (Cecil, 1606–75; Leonard, 1610/11–47; John, ?–1619; Francis, ?–1629/32; Henry, 1617–34/35; George, 1613–34) and five girls (Anne, 1607–after 1672; Dorothy, 1608–23; Elizabeth, 1609–before 1629; Grace, 1611–72; Helen, 1615–after 1655). Between 1622 and 1625 Lord Baltimore married Joane (of whom nothing else is known), who bore him a son (Philip, 1624/25–82/83). On the death of his father, Cecil became the second Baron Baltimore. Around 1628 he married Anne Arundell, daughter of Thomas Arundell, Baron Arundell of Wardour. Sir Robert Talbot married Grace Calvert in 1627 or 1630. William Peaseley married Anne Calvert around 1628/29. On the Calvert family, see Wroth, "Tobacco or Codfish," 523–4; Nicklin, "The Calvert Family"; Hastings, "Calvert and Darnell Gleanings."

6  Both the Reverend Erasmus Stourton and Stock claim that Lord Baltimore was accompanied by a secular priest in 1628. According to Stourton, this was someone by the name of Hacket (PRO, CO 1/4/59; letter 38). According to Raymond J. Lahey ("Role of Religion," 505n70), this Hacket was none other than the priest Anthony Whitehair; see also Anstruther, *Seminary Priests*, 2: 354–5).

7  Letters 38–39. Nine months had elapsed since his last letter; eleven more were to pass before his next (letter 40).

8  Letter 37; [PF] to SS, Rome, 28 January 1628, APF, *Lettere*, vol. 7, f. 9rv.

9  Letter 38.

10  Letter 39.

11  PRO, CO 1/4/59.

12  On the origins of Lord Baltimore's Catholic settlers, see Lahey, "Role of Religion," 505–6. See also letter 27 ("Many of our Catholic friends would go to live there if there were sufficient members of the clergy to accompany them"). In general, see Handcock, "West County Migrations to Newfoundland."

13  Letter 38.

14  See ch. 7 n6.

15  There is a complete absence of references to other Catholic priests in all other sources, particularly in the accounts given in Southampton the following year, which are otherwise well-informed and include Pole, *alias* Smith's activity (Anderson, ed., *Book of Examinations and Depositions*, 2: 39–41). After giving information about the two secular priests in 1627, Stock then seems to have lost track of them. He last refers to them in letter 38.

16  [PF] to SS, Rome, 28 January 1628, APF, *Lettere*, vol. 7, f. 9r ("un altro mappa come quello che mandò, essendosi per certo accidente perduto"). Stock had enclosed it with letter 29. See also ch. 6 n46.

17  Letter 38.

18  Ibid.

19  Appendix to ibid.

20 Henry Briggs's map, for example, gives the impression that there is a large group of islands opposite the estuary of the St. Lawrence, of which New-foundland is the largest ("North part of America," in [Purchas], *Purchas His Pilgrimes*, 3: 852–3).

21 For example, both Briggs (ibid.) and Speed ("America with those known parts," in *Prospect of the Most Famous Parts of the World*; [Speed], "New and Accurat Map of the world," in ibid.).

22 [Ortelius], *Teatro del mondo*.

23 Appendix to letter 38.

24 [Smith], *Generall Historie of Virginia*. The map of Bermuda is to be excluded, as not being of interest to Stock. That of Virginia is dated 1606, that of New England, 1614.

25 Alexander, *Encouragement to Colonies*.

26 If we accept this hypothesis, we have to assume that Stock came across Alexander's map in *Encouragement to Colonies* and deduced the date of the map from the volume's publication date, since Purchas republishes it undated (*Purchas His Pilgrimes*, 4: 1872–3).

27 Waterhouse, "Treatise of the North-west passage," in *Declaration of the state of Virginia*, 45–50; also in [Purchas] *Purchas His Pilgrimes*, 3: 852–3. Should this hypothesis prove correct, we would then know for sure that Stock had finally made the acquaintance of *Purchas His Pilgrimes*, and with it not only Briggs's "Treatise of the North-west passage," but also the long and important accounts of Newfoundland written by Richard Whitbourne, John Guy, and Edward Wynne (ibid., 3: 852–3; 4: 1877–90). It would then be possible to credit Stock with an adequate and updated picture of America.

28 Letter 39.

29 Stock speaks of one map only which he had sent to Propaganda several days previously ("Many days past"), that is, not a month before (ibid.).

30 See ch. 6 n46; ch. 7 n16.

31 Note, particularly, the co-ordinates of Newfoundland ("That island of which I have written") and the information on the "Mediterranean Sea" (letter 39).

32 [PF] to SS, Rome, 20 January 1629, APF, *Lettere*, vol. 8, f. 15v.

33 [PF] to SS, Rome, 2 December 1628, ibid., vol 7, f. 163v.

34 [PF] to SS, Rome, 20 January 1629, ibid., vol. 8, f. 15v.

35 With reference to the two maps Stock had sent (letter 38), Propaganda wrote that they had been "così grate, che Sua Santità n'ha voluta una" ([PF] to SS, Rome, 2 December 1628, ibid., vol. 7, f. 163r). This explains why, at least in this case, the map is not to be found in the archives of Propaganda.

36 Letter 38.

37 Abate Alessandro Cesare Scaglia was ambassador of Savoy in London from May 1625 to August 1628.

38 Letter 39.

39 [PF] to SS, Rome, 20 January 1629, APF, *Lettere*, vol. 8, ff. 15v–16r.

40 [PF] to SS, Rome, 2 December 1628, ibid., vol. 7, f. 163v.

### CHAPTER EIGHT

1 Lord Baltimore to George Villiers, duke of Buckingham, Ferryland, 25 August/4 September 1628, PRO, CO 1/4/57.

2 Raymond de La Ralde, fl. 1621–32, lieutenant to Guillaume and Émery de Caën, had the charge of protecting the de Caën monopoly from the frequent violations perpetrated by Basque, Flemish, Spanish and French ships in the Gulf of the St. Lawrence. On La Ralde, see *DCB* 1: 419.

3 Lord Baltimore to the duke of Buckingham, 25 August/4 September 1628.

4 For a detailed account of military operations in the summer of 1628, see Coakley, "Calvert and Newfoundland," 12. His sources are Lord Baltimore to Charles I, Ferryland, 25 August/4 September 1628, PRO, CO 1/4/56; Lord Baltimore to the duke of Buckingham, 25 August/4 September 1628.

5 See ch. 8 n4. Lord Baltimore could not know that the duke of Buckingham had been assassinated on 28 August/2 September 1628, two days before he sent off his request for assistance from Ferryland.

6 Lord Baltimore to Charles I, 25 August/4 September 1628.

7 Lord Baltimore to the duke of Buckingham, 25 August/4 September 1628.

8 Francis Cottington to Richard Weston, Lord Treasurer, 13/23 December 1628, PRO, CO 1/4/60.

9 William Peaseley to Lords Commissioners of the Admiralty, [December?] 1628, PRO, CO 1/4/61.

10 Anderson, ed., *Book of Examinations and Depositions*, 2: 38n4.

11 *CSP, Dom. 1629-31*, 152. Obviously, Leonard Calvert had also accompanied Peaseley to England at the end of 1628.

12 PRO, CO 1/4/63; *id.* 1/4/64. See also Coakley, "Calvert and Newfoundland," 13.

13 Vaughan, *Newlanders Cure*, 1: 69.

14 Lord Baltimore to [Francis Cottington], Ferryland, 18/28 August 1629, in Wroth, "Tobacco or Codfish," 527. The original of the letter, of which Wroth also gives a photograph, is preserved in The New York Public Libary, Arents Tobacco Collection.

15 Lord Baltimore to Charles I, Ferryland, 19/29 August 1629, PRO, CO 1/5/27.

16 Probably scurvy. See Vaughan, *Newlanders Cure*, 1: 67.

17 Lord Baltimore's house is most probably that which Doctor James Yonge identifies in his sketch some years later as the house of Lady Kirke (Poynter, ed., *Journal of James Yonge*, 80). On Lord Baltimore's house, see also Harper, "In Quest of Lord Baltimore's House"; Lahey, "Role of Religion," 506–7n77; Barakat, "Some Comments on Lord Baltimore's House at Ferryland, Newfoundland."

18 Lord Baltimore to Charles I, 19/29 August 1629. The winter of 1628-29 was particularly harsh. The two Jesuits who went to Avalon in 1629 also commented that "the winter before their arrival there was extremely cold and the earth sterile" (letter 50).

19 *APC, Col. 1613-80*, 133, no. 222 (25 February/6 March 1628/29); also *APC 1628-29* (25 February/6 March 1628/29).

20 Anderson, ed., *Book of Examinations and Depositions*, 2: 38-41.

21 PRO, CO 1/4/59.

22 [English College] to [Fabio de Lagonissa, archbishop of Conza, nuncio in Flanders], [Douai, August 1630], APF, *SOCG*, vol. 259, f. 2v ("haeretici sua peragebant").

23 On Stourton, see *DCB* 1: 614. Stourton arrived in the summer of 1627 and stayed until 28 August/7 September 1628, when he was forcedly put on board the *Victory*. He landed at Plymouth on 26 September/6 October of the same year, and here, on 9/19 October, gave evidence against Lord Baltimore (PRO, CO 1/4/59). The only favourable account of Stourton comes from Robert Hayman, at that time governor of the colony of Bristol's Hope. Hayman, speaking of Stourton as "Preacher of the Word of God, and Parson on Ferry Land," describes him as *"Apostle* of this Land" (R.H. [Hayman], *Quodlibets*, 37, no. 102).

24 A certain William Poole, of Renews, gave evidence in 1652 in the dispute between the Kirke and Calvert families. While describing Lord Baltimore as a "papist" and stating specifically that he had preferred the Protestant David Kirke, Poole does not mention the enforced baptizing of his son (Scisco, "Testimony Taken in Newfoundland," 246). If this is the same William Poole Stourton mentions, the Anglican minister's accusation is clearly unfounded.

25 Lord Baltimore to [Cottington], 18/28 August 1629, in Wroth, "Tobacco or Codfish," 527.

26 Lord Baltimore to Charles I, 19/29 August 1629.

27 Lord Baltimore to [Cottington], 18/28 August 1629, in Wroth, "Tobacco or Codfish," 527.

28 Lord Baltimore to Charles I, 19/29 August 1629.

29 Lord Baltimore to [Cottington], 18/28 August 1629, in Wroth, "Tobacco or Codfish," 527; Joseph Mead to Sir Martin Stuteville, Christ's College, 23 January/2 February 1629/30, in [Birch, ed.], *Court and Times of Charles the First*, 2: 53. The anonymous author of Account of Lord Baltimore's Colonizing Ventures in North America, c. 1670, BL, Sloane Mss. 3662, f. 25r, is wrong in affirming that Lord Baltimore's wife Joane and all the sons who "were left with her" perished in a shipwreck. On the problem of the fate of Lord Baltimore's wife and family, the definitive account is probably to be found in Wroth, "Tobacco or Codfish," 529-31n5. See also ch.7n5.

30 Of the one hundred settlers who spent the terrible winter of 1628-29 with Lord Baltimore, nine or ten died, while forty or so, Lord Baltimore writes, accompanied him to Virginia. When he later returned to England, Lord Baltimore left in Ferryland about thirty Protestants and two or three Catholic women (letter 50). All the others, including his numerous family, apparently returned to England before Lord Baltimore left for Virginia. As for the missionaries, the only one of whom anything is subsequently heard is Pole (Anderson, ed., *Book of Examinations and Depositions*, 2: 38-41).

31 Lord Baltimore to Charles I, 19/29 August 1629; Lord Baltimore to [Cottington], 18/28 August 1629, in Wroth, "Tobacco or Codfish," 527. As Lawrence C. Wroth points out, and Kenneth Gordon Davies confirms,

there was no comparison between the relative simplicity of tobacco cultivation and the dangers of fishing (Wroth, "Tobacco or Codfish," 531n10; Davies, *North Atlantic World*, 147–9).

32 Lord Baltimore to Charles I, 19/29 August 1629; Lord Baltimore to [Cottington], 18/28 August 1629, in Wroth, "Tobacco or Codfish," 527. Forty Catholics had accompanied Lord Baltimore to Avalon in 1628 (PRO, CO 1/4/59). Once again it is Stock who informs us that Lord Baltimore returned to England with "nearly all the Catholics who were there [in Avalon], leaving behind some thirty heretics and two or three Catholic women, with no priest or minister" (letter 50). We may presume that almost all the remaining members of the original group of forty Catholics went with Lord Baltimore in Virginia.

33 Letter 50.

34 Letter 50; also letter 40. In 1629, Easter fell on 15 April.

35 Stock, as usual, fails to give their names. That they were Baker and Rigby is the supposition of the Jesuit historian Thomas Aloysius Hughes (*History of the Society of Jesus*, 1: 198–9).

36 Anderson, ed., *Book of Examinations and Depositions*, 2: 38. The departure date of the *Saint-Claude* two weeks after Easter would seem to tally with Stock's statement. It is somewhat strange, however, that the evidence published by Roger Charles Anderson, so fierce against Pole and Thomas Walker, makes no mention of the two Jesuits' presence in Ferryland.

37 Letter 50.

38 Letter 40.

39 On Matthew's influence over Lord Baltimore and that of the Jesuits generally, see also [Panzani], "Relazione Dello Stato della Religione Cattolica in Inghilterra," 1637, APF, *SOCG*, vol. 347, f. 511r.

40 T.A. Hughes, *History of the Society of Jesus*, 1: 244–52.

41 See ch. 6.

42 In his letter to Francis Cottington, Lord Baltimore explains that his original intention had been to return with the others to England, but that on that very day he had changed his mind and decided to sail for Virginia. He was thus "overtaken wth tyme and busynesse that I can write no more at this tyme" (Lord Baltimore to [Cottington], 18/28 August 1629, in Wroth, "Tobacco or Codfish," 529). The implication is that he will leave Ferryland in a very short time.

43 Ibid., 527; Lord Baltimore to Charles I, 19/29 August 1629.

44 They were eventually to return to England at the end of 1629 (letter 50).

45 Since Baker and Rigby returned to England around Christmas 1629, they clearly could not have accompanied Lord Baltimore's sons, who had left some time around August (Lord Baltimore to [Cottington], 18/28 August 1629, in Wroth, "Tobacco or Codfish," 529).

46 Lord Baltimore to Charles I, 19/29 August 1629.

47 Letter 50.

48 Scisco, "Testimony Taken in Newfoundland," 242, 245. Another testimony has it that Lord Baltimore entrusted his property to "William Poole, George Leese, Sydney Taylor, Sydney Hill, Planters" (ibid., 247).

49 John Pott, Samuel Mathews, Roger Smith, William Claiborne to the Privy

Council, 30 November/10 December 1629, PRO, CO 1/5/40, ff. 101rv-2rv.

50 Letter 50. The date of Lord Baltimore's return is based on the supposition that Baker and Rigby, the two Jesuits, had accompanied him from Ferryland to Jamestown and from Jamestown to England. This is what Stock seems to imply. On Lord Baltimore's unfortunate journey to Virginia, see Coakley, "Calvert and Newfoundland," 16-17; Lahey, "Role of Religion," 509. According to Coakley, Lord Baltimore reached Virginia around the beginning of October.

51 Charles I to Lord Baltimore, Whitehall, 22 November/2 December 1629, PRO, CO 1/5/39.

52 Lord Baltimore to [Dudley Carleton, Viscount Dorchester, secretary of state], [February 1630], PRO, CO 1/4/62. The dating of this document in *CSP, Col. 1574-1660*, 95, no. 62, about 1628 is evidently wrong. On this, see Lahey, "Role of Religion," 509n88; Coakley, "Calvert and Newfoundland," 17n63.

53 As we have seen, Joane Calvert had accompanied her husband from Ferryland to Jamestown. She had evidently not returned with him in England, however, and Lord Baltimore was now busy arranging her journey back (Lord Baltimore to [Viscount Dorchester], [February 1630]; John Pory to Joseph Mead, London, 12/22 February 1629/30, in [Birch, ed.], *Court and Times of Charles the First*, 2: 54). Joane probably drowned that same year, 1630, when the ship that was carrying her back to England was shipwrecked. On the whole question, see Wroth, "Tobacco or Codfish," 529-31n5.

54 Of his three letters to Propaganda in 1629, only two (letters 41-42) make any mention of Avalon, and this is only to announce the departure of the two Jesuits. None of the six letters of 1630 mentions Avalon, even though on one occasion Stock speaks of matters pertinent to America (letter 46).

55 [PF] to SS, Rome, 26 June 1630, APF, *Lettere*, vol. 10, f. 62r. The letter requesting information of Avalon was drafted by Propaganda's secretary, Francesco Ingoli (appendix to letter 45).

56 Letter 50. In this letter Stock refers to Ingoli's letter of 26 June 1630 (see ch. 8 n55), although he wrongly dates it 22 June.

57 Ibid.

58 Andrews, *Colonial Period of American History*, 1: 374-99; Porter, *Inconstant Savage*, 509-11.

59 F. Higginson, *New-Englands Plantation*.

60 T.W.S. Higginson, *Life of Francis Higginson*, 89.

61 Letter 46.

62 Letter 50.

63 René de L'Escale, 1588-1648, Capuchin, in religion Pacifique de Provins, had been for many years missionary in Persia before he quarrelled with his superiors, particularly with the powerful François-Joseph Du Tremblay (better known as Joseph de Paris), and was forced to ask to be sent to Canada. Propaganda appointed him prefect of Canada, but at the moment of departure he refused to go, preferring the more promising territory of the French West Indies. He could hardly be said to have found great fortune

there either, dying lost in the Guyanan jungle. This writer is preparing an edition of Pacifique's letters.

64 Speaking of the founding of a seminary at Les Saintes, near Guadeloupe, "immediatamente dependente del Papa," Pacifique writes: "perché [Holy See officials] si affatigano tanto per domandare al re, a suoi ministri, et mendicare d'alcune compagnie una terra o isola, massima[mente] per fine di adoprar la salute delle anime, già che non solo il Papa lo puol, ma anche Vostra Signoria Illustrissima [the Nuncio in France]? Perché vogliamo suffrire che il Summo Pontefice et la Santa Chiesa lascia perire la sua authorità? Vostra Signoria Illustrissima mi crede. Faccia a modo mio, et conforme al mio parere" (Pacifique de Provins to Niccolò Guidi di Bagno, archbishop of Athens, nuncio in France, Nantes, 2 November 1647, APF, *SOCG*, vol. 145, ff. 71rv–2rv).

65 Pacifique did not even receive an answer (see APF, *ACTA*, vol. 17, f. 580rv, no. 18 [17 December 1647]), while the reply to Stock makes no mention of Stock's proposal ([PF] to SS, Rome, 8 March 1631, APF, *Lettere*, vol. 11, f. 22rv).

66 See Ch. 5.

67 [PF] to Fabio de Lagonissa, archbishop of Conza, nuncio in Flanders, Rome, 20 July 1630, APF, *Lettere*, vol. 10, ff. 78v–9r.

68 Lagonissa to [PF], Brussels, 21 September 1630, APF, *SOCG*, vol. 259, f. 1rv. With Lagonissa's letter was enclosed a report on New England prepared by the English College in Douai, which mentions Lord Baltimore's presence in Newfoundland ([English College] to [Lagonissa], [Douai, August 1630], ibid., f. 2rv).

69 APF, *Acta*, vol. 7/i, f. 164v, no. 10 (22 November 1630).

70 On the history of the Capuchins in Acadia, see Candide de Nant, *Pages glorieuses*; Lenhart, "Capuchin Prefecture of New England."

71 [PF] to SS, Rome, 8 March 1631, APF, *Lettere*, vol. 11, f. 22v.

72 Letter 57.

CHAPTER NINE

1 Letter 68. See also letter 70.

2 Letter 79.

3 Stock does not write to Propaganda in the years 1633, 1635, 1640, 1642–48. It is probably worth noting that it is in those years (1633, 1635) that Stock intensifies his correspondence with his Order.

4 Letters 68, 70.

# Notes to Part Two

1 Stock settled in England permanently in April 1615 (see ch. 1).
2 The general chapter took place in Loano, Italy, in May 1623 (see AOCD, (*Acta CG*, vol. 1, f. 67r).
3 Giovani Francesco Guidi di Bagno, 1578-1641, archbishop of Patras, was nuncio in Flanders from 1621 to 1627 and nuncio in France from 1627 to 1630. He was appointed cardinal on 19 November 1629. See Biaudet, *Non-ciatures Apostoliques Permanentes*, 269; Cauchie and Maere, éds., *Recueil des instructions*, xxxiii–xxxv, 100–135; de Meester, éd., *Correspondence*, particularly, 2: 720-1; Raffaeli Cammarota, "L'archivio Guidi di Bagno," *Clio*, 12 (1967): 235-43.
4 I have been unable to establish the identity of this mysterious person Stock afterwards refers to as "signor Brune" (letter 12). Stock mentions him four more times (letters 4, 9, 12–13) and was almost certainly speaking of him when he affirms that "[m]oney with which to purchase the site and to found it [the novitiate] is ready" (letter 18). "Signor Brune" would seem to point to Jacques Bruneau, the Spanish resident in London (see ch. 5n24), as would the fact that Bruneau was in Flanders at the same time as "signor Brune" from what Stock says in letter 9. I am, however, inclined to believe that they are not the same person. Stock later speaks explicitly of a "signore seretario [*sic*] agente di Spagna" (letter 12) as someone distinct from "signor Brune." Furthermore, Stock gave "signor Brune" letters of introduction to take with him on his journey to Rome at the beginning of 1625 (letter 13), a time when Bruneau was involved in his diplomatic duties in London. Bruneau's only documented journey is that to Brussels in October 1624 (Marcantonio Padavin to Doge and Senate, Vienna, 19 October 1624, *CSP, Ven. 1623-25*, 465). Another possibility is that "signor Brune" is Anthony Browne, Viscount Montague, whom certainly Stock knew — but to date the only evidence is the similarity of the two names.
5 On Sunday, 5 November 1623, there had been a serious accident at Hundson House, Blackfriars, the residence of the French ambassador in London, Tanneguy Leveneur, Count of Tillières. Part of the roof fell in, kill-

ing the Jesuit Robert Drury, his confrère William Whittingham, and a hundred or more of the congregation gathered to celebrate mass. The accident was given ample coverage in the correspondence of many personalities of the time, and a number of published accounts of it exist. Lord Baltimore, at that time secretary of state and member of the Privy Council, was one of those to comment on the incident (Lord Baltimore to Edward Conway, St. Martin's Lane, 26 October/5 November 1623, *CSP, Dom. 1623-25*, 104, No. 103). For a summary of the incident, see Foley, ed., *Records of the English Province of the Society of Jesus*, 2: 76-98. For a Protestant viewpoint, see John Chamberlain to Joseph Mead, London, 29 October/8 November 1623, in [Birch, ed.], *Court and Times of James the First*, 2: 426-31. By the Gregorian Calendar (New Style), which the English Catholics used, the incident took place on 5 November. By the Julian Calendar (Old Style), used at that period in England, it was 26 October. Here, as always in his correspondence, Stock uses New Style.

6 "Signor Brune."
7 See ch. 4.
8 Edmund of St. Martin and Eliseus of St. Michael.
9 The letter Stock mentions is not extant.
10 Stock left Belgium for England in April 1615 ([Biagio della Purificazione], "Missioni Inghilterra," [1705], AOCD, Ms. 277, 26; Zimmerman, *Carmel in England*, 29). His request for a novitiate must therefore date back to this time.
11 Probably letter 3.
12 Paolo Simone di Gesù e Maria (Rivarola), 1571-1643, was general of the Order of the Discalced Carmelites in the years 1623-26, 1632-35, and 1641-43 (see AOCD, *Acta CG*, vol. 1, ff. 69r, 141r, 185v). This was one of his customary visits to the French and Belgian monasteries. Stock had on several occasions invited him to visit England personally (letters 4-5, 11).
13 See ch. 2n5.
14 Edmund of St. Martin and Eliseus of St. Michael.
15 The Dominican Diego de La Fuente, known in England as "Father Maestro," formerly chaplain to the Spanish ambassador in London, Diego Sarmiento de Acuñas, later Count Gondomar (see n25), was a key figure in European diplomatic circles in the years 1617-24. From 1618, when he took Count Gondomar's place as Spanish resident in London, La Fuente exerted considerable influence at court (Piero Contarini to Doge and Senate, London, 5/15 October 1618, *CSP, Ven. 1617-19*, 330). On Count Gondomar's return to England towards the end of 1620, La Fuente left London for Spain via Brussels (Girolamo Lando to Doge and Senate, London, 30 October/10 November 1621, *CSP, Ven. 1619-21*, 458). In February 1621 he left Madrid and went to Rome (Alvise Corner to Doge and Senate, Madrid, 19 February 1621, ibid., 569), where he remained till the beginning of 1624, negotiating with the Pontifical Court over the dispensations for the Spanish marriage. He was suggested as a likely candidate for the post as bishop in England or even as the new Spanish ambassador (Alvise Valaresso to Doge and Senate, London, 2/12 September 1622, *CSP,*

*Ven. 1621–23*, 403; Corner to Doge and Senate, Madrid, 1 February 1624, *CSP, Ven. 1623–25*, 207; Valaresso to Doge and Senate, London, 23 February/4 March 1624, ibid., 219). The marriage negotiations broke down, and La Fuente was in London briefly in early April 1624 prior to returning to Spain early in July of the same year (Valaresso to Doge and Senate, London, 5/15 April 1624, ibid., 262; Valaresso to Doge and Senate, London, 5/15 July 1624, ibid., 373). The letter Stock mentions here was written by La Fuente in Brussels on his way back to Spain. Stock, who was on excellent terms with the Spanish Embassy in London, replaced La Fuente as ordinary chaplain of the embassy on the latter's departure in October 1620 (letter 12). The meeting of which Stock speaks in the following letter (letter 10) must therefore have taken place during La Fuente's second brief stay in London between April and July 1624.

16 Probably letter 7.

17 "Signor Brune."

18 See n12.

19 Ottavio Bandini, 1557/58–1629, a cardinal, was a founding member of Propaganda and was among those concerned to bring about the Spanish marriage. We know for certain that Stock sent at least one letter to Bandini (letter 13) whom he had probably known through La Fuente, but it is probable that all those Stock sent to a particular person in Propaganda in the years 1624–26 were addressed to him. Another possibility is that Stock's correspondent was Cardinal Giovanni Garcia Millini, who was similarly involved in the Spanish marriage negotiations. Certainly, Stock's first letter to be addressed directly to Propaganda's secretary, Francesco Ingoli, was considerably later (letter 62). On the addressees of Stock's letters, see the Introductory Note.

20 See n15.

21 Eliseus of St. Michael was provincial vicar from 1618 to 1625, and orders for his confrères probably went through him. The general's letter mentioned here is not extant.

22 [PF] to SS, Rome, 12 [October 1624], APF, *Lettere*, vol. 3, f. 176r.

23 This was the very brief visit to England made by the prior of the Paris monastery of the Discalced Carmelites, Bernard de Saint-Joseph, as ordered by the general, Paolo Simone di Gesù e Maria. Bernard was very well-known to Eliseus of St. Michael, one of the three Discalced Carmelites in England at that time since he had been his teacher in Paris between 1611 and 1613 ([Biagio della Purificazione], "Missioni Inghilterra," AOCD, Ms. 277, 52–3; Zimmerman, *Carmel in England*, 41–3). The meeting between Bernard and his three English confrères (Stock, Eliseus and Edmund of St. Martin) took place in Eltham, a village close to London (Hasted, *Country of Kent*, 1: 48–64), where Eliseus was living with a branch of the Roper family to whom Stock had introduced him ([Biagio della Purificazione], "Missioni Inghilterra," 53; Zimmerman, *Carmel in England*, 25, 42).

24 See ch.2.

25 Count Gondomar was Spanish ambassador in London from 1613 to 1618

and from 1620 to 1622. In the interim from 1618 to 1620, his place was taken by La Fuente. On Count Gondomar, see *Correspondencia oficial de Gondomar*, ed. Ballestreros y Beretta.

26 Carlos Coloma, 1566-1637, was Spanish ambassador in London from 1622 to 1624 and from 1630 to 1631. When he left London in 1624, his place was taken by Bruneau. On Coloma, see the short entry in *Diccionari Biogràfic*, 1: 594; Turner, *Some Aspects of Coloma*.

27 Bruneau. On Bruneau, see ch. 5n24.

28 "Signor Brune."

29 Lord Baltimore.

30 The average voyage time from England to Newfoundland was about four weeks, but it could take as little as seventeen days (Cell, *English Enterprise in Newfoundland*, 5). According to David Kirke, later the Calvert family's rival in Newfoundland, Ferryland (i.e. Avalon) was the "neerest plantation and not above 15 dayes sayle, a safe passage Free from Rocks shoals or Sands" (Scisco, "Kirke's Memorial on Newfoundland," 49). Richard Eburne gives a similar account of a rapid and easy journey (*Plain Pathway to Plantations*, ed. Wright, x). According to T.C., the journey from the west coast of Ireland to Newfoundland took twelve to fourteen days (*Short Discourse of the New-Found-Land*, [10]). Later on, when Stock had become pessimistic about the whole Avalon venture, he emphasized the great distance separating the colony from England, giving it at some two thousand miles (letters 27, 31).

31 It was hardly possible for Lord Baltimore "to return to his land," that is, to Avalon, since he had never been there. Rather than a mistake, I am inclined to read this as a white lie on Stock's part, intended to underline Lord Baltimore's familiarity with the country.

32 The Discalced Carmelites in England at that time, besides Stock, were Eliseus of St. Michael and Edmund of St. Martin. Stock had already informed his general (letter 5) and Bede of the Blessed Sacrament (letter 8) of their illnesses. Edmund's sickness is unknown, but Eliseus was "ill with stone" (Bede of the Blessed Sacrament to Paolo Simone di Gesù e Maria., London, 20 March 1626, AOCD, *Litterae*, Bede, 271.h, f. 15r).

33 Stock generalizes an ignorance of Newfoundland which is in fact only his own. At least up until the great wave of colonial activity in the 1620s, which was only just beginning when Stock wrote, the island of Newfoundland was one of the places the Europeans knew best of all North America. His problem, here as elsewhere, is that he fails to realize that Avalon is in Newfoundland.

34 See ch. 3.

35 See ch. 3n23.

36 These are well-known facts on Newfoundland. (See, for example, [Wynne], *Letter from Captaine Edward Wynne*, sig. C; Whitbourne, *Discourse and Discovery*, 10, 52-9; Whitbourne, *Discourse Containing a Loving Invitation*, To the Reader, 6, 9, 37; [T.C.], *Short Discourse of the New-Found-Land*, [6-8], [10]; Eburne, *Plain Pathway to Plantations*, x; [Purchas], *Purchas His Pilgrimes*, 4: 1877-8; Orpheus Iunior [Vaughan], *Cambrensium Caroleia*, Augustissimae Regiae Maiestati.)

37 See ch. 3. Both William Alexander and T.C., whom Stock evidently does not know, list Lord Baltimore's colony among those already established in Newfoundland. (See [T.C.], *Short Discourse of the New-Found-Land*, [5]; Alexander, *Encouragement to Colonies*, 25.)

38 See n10.

39 See n23.

40 Marginal note: "Vide decretum in actis congregatio 22 martii 1625."

41 Stock's letter was discussed in General Congregation no. 33, 22 March 1625.

42 Giovanni Garcia Millini, 1572–1629, cardinal, member of Propaganda.

43 Guidi di Bagno. The letter is [PF] to Guidi di Bagno, Rome, 26 March 1625, APF, *Lettere*, vol. 4, f. 55rv.

44 The last paragraph is the draft of the reply to Stock.

45 See ch. 3.

46 Stock still lived in London, but he began to go frequently to Canterbury, where he lived as a guest of the Roper family from 1633 to the time of his death (Zimmerman, *Carmel in England*, 33, 36). The Ropers had property both in Eltham (see n23, and in Canterbury (Hasted, *County of Kent*, 1: 323–4, 369, 407). From Stock's letters one gathers that he went to Canterbury whenever he could and that he later spent "the most part" of his time there (letter 41; see also letters 16, 79). There are letters he sent to Propaganda from Canterbury in 1631, 1636–39, and 1641. According to a recent study, the spread of Catholicism in Kent and particularly Canterbury was not quite so rapid as Stock's descriptions would suggest, the Roper family being the centre of one of the few Catholic circles in the region (Chalklin, *Seventeenth-Century Kent*, 229).

47 Stock's letter was discussed in General Congregation no. 35, 2 May 1625.

48 Guidi di Bagno.

49 The last paragraph is the draft of the reply to Stock.

50 Probably [PF] to SS, Rome, 26 March 1625, ibid., ff. 52v–3r.

51 Sir Arthur Aston. See ch. 3. The "two faithful servants" Stock mentions here and elsewhere (letter 17) are unidentified.

52 Lord Baltimore.

53 The distance from London to Canterbury was forty-three miles according to the contemporary Raphael Holinshed (*Chronicles of England*, 1:125), but it is in fact sixty-two miles. For other estimates, see also [Fisher], *Kentish Traveller's Companion*, 144; Hasted, *County of Kent* 4:389bis.

54 George Abbot, 1562–1633, archbishop of Canterbury from 1611 to 1633.

55 Jamestown, the first English colony in mainland North America, was founded in 1607. Bermuda had come to the attention of the English when George Somers was shipwrecked there in 1609. In 1620 the *Mayflower* docked in what was to become Plymouth. The territory named New Scotland was given to Alexander in 1621 by James I and included present-day Nova Scotia, New Brunswick and the area between New Brunswick and the St. Lawrence River.

56 See ch. 3n62.

57 It should be noted that Stock never mentions the general of the Discalced Carmelites in his letter. Ingoli, however, who summarized the letter, knew

perfectly well of his contacts with the general, and Propaganda's letters had mentioned them to Stock. (See [PF] to SS, Rome, 26 March 1625, APF, *Lettere*, vol. 4, f. 52v.)

58 Stock does not mention a "popolo" in his letter, although in a preceding one he speaks explicitly of "inhabitants . . . gentiles and English heretics" (letter 14).

59 The problem of the novitiate, here only briefly touched on, had been raised in all his previous letters.

60 This letter and the last of 24 May (letter 17) were both discussed in General Congregation no. 38, 27 June 1625.

61 See also letter 17.

62 Bede of the Blessed Sacrament and Elias of Jesus arrived in England between 31 May and 29 August 1625. See ch. 3n17.

63 Guidi di Bagno.

64 The last paragraph is the draft of the reply to Stock.

65 According to Richard Whitbourne, the first ships left for Newfoundland in February, although the dangers of the sea in winter would have made it more prudent to wait until at least 25 March/4 April (Whitbourne, *Discourse and Discovery*, 21–3). The number of ships Stock gives is totally implausible, even as the sum total of ships coming "from different parts" and not just the English. According to Kirke, 800 ships left annually for Newfoundland (300 of which were English). T.C. and Whitbourne put the figure at 650 (of which 250 were English, with 5,000/6,000 men). According to Whitbourne, it was possible to reach the figure of 500 English ships with a total of 10,000 men. (See Scisco, "Kirke's Memorial on Newfoundland," 50; [T.C.] *Short Discourse of the New-Found-Land*, sig. B2, [11]; Whitbourne, *Discourse and Discovery*, 11–12; Whitbourne, *Discourse Containing a Loving Invitation*, 19,45.)

66 Lord Baltimore.

67 Aston.

68 See ch. 3.

69 See ch. 3n63.

70 See ch.3n62.

71 See n10.

72 Stock is quoting from memory a well-known passage in canonical law. (See Friedberg, ed., *Corpus Iuris Canonici*, 2: 310–11.)

73 This letter was discussed in General Congregation no. 39, 21 July 1625.

74 Letter 17.

75 See ch. 3n64. Stock's judgment of King Charles I is here somewhat severe, but he afterwards warmed to him, to the point of stating that "un re così bono deve essere catolico" (letter 81). A similar hope was expressed a few years later by a Capuchin annalist, Zaccaria da Saluzzo, in his *Orthodoxa Consultatio*.

76 See ch. 3.

77 In his previous letter (letter 17), Stock had made no mention of the "passage." For obvious security reasons, it is unlikely that Stock kept a copy of his letters, and he was unable to recheck what he had written on other

occasions. This, then, is a mistake on Stock's part, and this letter must be taken as his first mention of the Northwest passage.

78 Aston had left for Avalon; Lord Baltimore, for Ireland. Exactly who "the others . . . dispersed here and there" were is not known. Very probably it refers to no one in particular. This has to be taken as a tacit underlining of the difficulties caused by the lack of missionaries from Propaganda.

79 James I, 1566–1625, king of England and Ireland from 1603 to 1625, died on 27 March/6 April 1625.

80 There is a vast literature dealing with anti-Catholic persecution in England. For a detailed description of the fines and punishments, see Aveling, "Documents Relating to the Northern Commissions," in Talbot, ed., *Miscellanea Recusant Records*, 291–307. On education, see Beales, *Church under Penalty*, particularly 91–101. See also [Pendryck], *Application of the Lawes of England*. William Pendryck was Stock's confrère, Eliseus of St. Michael.

81 Stock's letter was discussed in General Congregation no. 39, 21 July 1625.

82 Guidi di Bagno.

83 The last paragraph is the draft of the reply to Stock.

84 Lord Baltimore.

85 Bede of the Blessed Sacrament and Elias of Jesus. See ch. 4.

86 Stock refers to Aston's departure between 24 and 31 May 1625.

87 Since this is English America and since there was little record of any problems with the Indians in French America, by "other Americans" Stock probably means the Indians under Spanish rule. This would tally with the fact that on the map of Cornelis de Jode that Stock had in front of him while writing this letter, the only favourable captions regard the "Canadenses." All the other Indians mentioned in the captions are in Spanish territory, and are referred to in negative terms (see C. de Jode, "Americae Pars Borealis," in [G. de Jode], *Speculum Orbis Terrae*). In general, Stock's comments on the American Indians are favourable, though he seems to know very little about them.

88 See ch. 4.

89 See ch. 5.

90 See ch. 4n9.

91 While at first glance this seems the usual list of American place-names given by Stock, in fact it differs significantly from the preceding ones, as the following table shows:
— Virginia, Bermuda, New England, New Scotland (letter 16);
— New England, New Scotland, Virginia, Bermuda (letter 17);
— Virginia, Bermuda, New England, New Scotland, Newfoundland (letter 18);
— Virginia, New England, New Scotland, the Canadians (letter 19).
    In the last instance, "the Canadians" replaces Bermuda and Newfoundland. This addition is almost certainly owing to the information on Cornelis de Jode's map. The disappearance of Bermuda is probably the result of the same source — Bermuda is nowhere represented on Gerard de Jode's map of the world and appears tiny and at a considerable distance from

North America on the map of America (see C. de Jode, "Americae Pars Borealis"; C. de Jode, "Totius orbis cogniti Universalis Descriptio," in *Speculum Orbis Terrae*). The disappearance of Newfoundland presents a different problem. Although it could be put down to an Avalon-New-foundland identification, the general sense of the letter seems to go against this. It can therefore only be assumed that Stock simply forgot to include it.

92  See letter 21 (the proclamation), letter 20 (the translation into Italian), letter 22 (the translation into Spanish). The Spanish version was obviously prepared in the Spanish Embassy in London, given Stock's close relations with them. The Italian version was prepared in Rome.

93  See n96.

94  Marginal note: "Nuntio Hispania et Fiandra."

95  Stock's letter was discussed in General Congregation no. 46, 11 November 1625.

96  This letter was discussed at the same time as letter 23.

97  See ch. 4.

98  Guidi di Bagno.

99  The last paragraph is the draft of the reply to Stock.

100  See [PF] to Giulio Sacchetti, bishop of Gravina, nuncio in Spain, Rome, 15 November 1625, *Lettere*, vol. 4, f. 186r; [PF] to Guidi di Bagno, Rome, 15 November 1625, ibid., f. 186rv.

101  "Signor Brune."

102  Left blank in the original. The reference, obviously to be filled after checking the information in the archives, is probably [PF] to Guidi di Bagno, Rome, 26 March 1625, APF, *Lettere*, vol. 4, f. 55rv.

103  Stock writes from Chelsea on 14 September and 30 October. On 2 December he was back in London (see, besides the present, letters 24, 26). In Chelsea Stock probably lived with the Roper family. They had inherited a house from Thomas More through his daughter Margaret, who, around 1525, had married William Roper, More's first biographer. More had purchased it in 1520 "for its vicinity to London, for the salubrity of the air, for the pleasantness of the situation, and for the incomparably sweet, delightful, and noble River Thames, gently gliding by it" (Faulkner, *Historical and Topographical Description of Chelsea*, 1: 114). On the Roper family, see *DNB* 17: 215-16.

104  [PF] to SS, Rome, 5 July 1625, APF, *Lettere*, vol. 4, ff. 106v-7r; [PF] to SS, Rome, 26 July 1625, ibid., f. 115r. Stock dates the second of the two letters wrongly. Both must have reached him as he was about to depart for Chelsea, since they are not mentioned in the letter of the preceding day (letter 19).

105  Bede of the Blessed Sacrament and Elias of Jesus.

106  Stock, together with Eliseus of St. Michael, had been granted his previous faculties in 1621. They were then sent back to the order at some point and are still preserved in the order's archives (AOCD, Ms. 250.i.1). On 11 November 1625 Propaganda's secretary, Francesco Ingoli, prepared a memo for the Holy Office, responsible for granting faculties to missionaries, asking that Stock be granted what he requested (as indicated in the

appendix to the present letter). On 15 November Propaganda writes to Stock assuring him that the faculties will be sent as soon as they are received from the Holy Office ([PF] to SS, Rome, 15 November 1625, APF, *Lettere*, vol. 4, f. 191r). On 7 March Stock still did not have them (letter 29). When they finally arrived on 22 March, he deemed them insufficient (letter 30).

107 Stock's letter mentions neither the general nor Avalon. Ingoli, however, was fully informed of Propaganda's attempts to convince the order to send missionaries to the colony.

108 Obviously Avalon. The Avalon-Newfoundland confusion persists.

109 See ch. 3n34.

110 See ch. 4.

111 See n122.

112 Elias of Jesus, the infirm missionary, and Bede of the Blessed Sacrament, the provincial vicar.

113 Stock's letter was discussed in General Congregation no. 52 (and not no. 51, as Ingoli writes), 6 February 1626.

114 See n42.

115 Obviously a mistake on Propaganda's part. Almost certainly influenced by the extract from Bede of the Blessed Sacrament's report (see ch. 4) and by their contacts with the order, they add Lord Baltimore to Aston.

116 The last paragraph is the draft of APF, *Acta*, vol. 4, ff. 14v–15r, no. 5 (6 February 1626).

117 Avalon.

118 Marginal note in Ingoli's handwriting: "Persecutione in Inghilterra e mission nell'Avalonia."

119 A reference to the general situation. He only mentions the imprisoned confrères, Bede and Elias, in letter 29.

120 See n92.

121 See ch. 4.

122 See [PF] to SS, Rome, 26 March 1625, APF, *Lettere*, vol. 4, ff. 52v–3r. Stock's date is wrong.

123 Elias of Jesus.

124 Richard Smith, bishop of Chalcedon.

125 A relatively precise figure; the shortest distance between Ireland and Newfoundland by modern calculation is 1,823 miles. See also n30.

126 Stock's letter was discussed in General Congregation no. 53, 17 March 1626.

127 Letter 26. Probably referring to a classification of Propaganda archives which no longer exists.

128 This last sentence was added by Ingoli some time after he had prepared the summary of Stock's letter. Propaganda was obviously in close contact with the general, Paolo Simone di Gesù e Maria. The news of the imprisonment of Bede and Elias is passed on to Propaganda by the general, independently of Stock, who only mentions it later (letter 29). Propaganda received the information from the general between 6 February and 17 March (APF, *Acta*, vol. 4, ff. 14v–15r, no. 5; ibid., f. 30r, no. 6). Bede was imprisoned on 26 December 1625 ([Biagio della Purificazione], "Mis-

sioni Inghilterra," AOCD, Ms. 277, pp. 72–3). His first letter from prison is of 6 January 1626 (Bede of the Blessed Sacrament to Paolo Simone di Gesù e Maria, London, 6 January 1626, AOCD, *Litterae Bede*, *Ms.* 271.h, ff. 5rv–6rv). In the intervening days Elias must have been seized, since by 9 January he was in prison with Bede (Bede of the Blessed Sacrament to Paolo Simone di Gesù e Maria, London, 9 January 1626, ibid., f. 8r). It is not known exactly when they were freed. On 2 July Bede and Elias were still in prison, but, according to Zimmerman, they were set free at some point in July (Bede of the Blessed Sacrament to Paolo Simone di Gesù e Maria, London, 2 July 1626, ibid., f. 17rv; [Biagio della Purificazione], "Missioni Inghilterra," 95; Zimmerman, *Carmel in England*, 97, 101). Bede left England for Calais and then went to Brussels. Elias went with Bede as far as Calais and then continued to Paris.

129 See n42.

130 Letters 26–7.

131 This refers to a "poi" ("then") which originally came after "ringratia" ("thanks") and was afterwards crossed out.

132 The last paragraph is the draft of the reply to Stock.

133 It is difficult to imagine what letters Stock is referring to since the extant letters present no apparent break in sense between one letter and the next.

134 In November 1625 the English attached Cadiz. Stock had up to that moment conveyed his correspondence through the Spanish Embassy in London. He afterwards proposed to Propaganda their using the Tuscan embassies in London and Rome as an alternative (letters 36, 40, 42).

135 Philippe de Bethune, Count de Selles, 1561–1649, French ambassador in Rome from 1624 to 1626.

136 Bernardino Spada, 1593–1661, bishop of Tamiathis, nuncio in France from 1623 to 1627.

137 Jean de Varinières, Marquis of Blainville, ambassador extraordinary in London from the end of October 1625 to mid-May 1626.

138 The only letter of the "14" is letter 23. This reference on Ingoli's part is difficult to understand since Propaganda had in the meantime received another letter from Stock (letter 24), discussed on 6 February 1626 (APF, *Acta*, vol. 4, ff. 14v–15r, no. 5). Yet another of his letters (letter 27) had not arrived at this point, and it is not discussed until some time later (APF, *Acta*, vol. 4, f. 30r, no. 6 [21 March 1626]).

139 General Congregation no. 52 did take place on 3 March 1626, but there is no mention in the *Acta* of any discussion of Stock's letter (see ibid., ff. 21v–8rv).

140 [PF] to SS, Rome, 15 November 1625, APF, *Lettere*, vol. 4, ff. 190v–1r.

141 Bruneau. See ch. 5n24; n4.

142 See ch. 4. The request for information is in [PF] to SS, Rome, 15 November 1625, APF, *Lettere*, vol. 4, ff. 190v–1r.

143 See ch. 5.

144 See ibid., Stock's last few words are syntactically obscure in the original Italian version.

145 Avalon.

146 The "old maps" which Propaganda refers to in [PF] to SS, Rome, 15

November 1625, APF, *Lettere*, vol. 4, f. 190v. (See ch. 4.)

147 See ch. 5.

148 Bede of the Blessed Sacrament and Elias of Jesus. See n128.

149 See n106.

150 Stock's letter was discussed in General Congregation no. 56, 4 May 1626.

151 It was in fact a year. Stock's first letter mentioning Avalon is letter 14.

152 Ingoli is thinking of letter 19, in which Stock had briefly mentioned the Catholic pilot.

153 [PF] to SS, Rome, 21 March 1626, APF, *Lettere*, vol. 5, f. 51rv.

154 See ch. 5.

155 The last paragraph is the draft of the reply to Stock.

156 [PF] to SS, Rome, 6 December 1625, APF, *Lettere*, vol. 4, f. 201v.

157 Marginal note in the hand of an official of Propaganda: "Licenza ordinaria."

158 Stock's letter was discussed in General Congregation no. 68, 18 December 1626.

159 The map was enclosed with letter 29.

160 See ch. 5.

161 See ibid.

162 Ibid.

163 See ch. 5n38.

164 See ch. 3; ch. 5n50. The "island" is Avalon/Newfoundland. Stock had obviously identified them as one and the same place. Note that the name "Avalon" nowhere appears in any of Speed's maps.

165 See ch. 5n4-5.

166 Confrères in England besides Stock were Bede of the Blessed Sacrament and Elias of Jesus (both in prison), Eliseus of St. Michael and Edmund of St. Martin (both ill).

167 Stock's letter was discussed in General Congregation no. 68, 18 December 1626.

168 The general's letter is no longer extant.

169 Bede of the Blessed Sacrament and Elias of Jesus. See n128.

170 Bede of the Blessed Sacrament. See also ch. 4.

171 Propaganda's cardinals.

172 Avalon.

173 Stock here does not state explicitly that he himself has been chosen to go to Avalon, although he tells Propaganda that same day (letter 31).

174 [PF] to SS, Rome, 26 March 1625, APF, *Lettere*, vol. 4, ff. 52v-3r.

175 [PF] to SS, Rome, 6 December 1625, ibid., f. 201v.

176 Letter 31.

177 Whatever letter Stock is referring to is no longer extant.

178 See n106.

179 Stock's letter was discussed in General Congregation no. 68, 18 December 1626 (see APF, *Acta*, vol. 4, f. 157r, no. 5).

180 The first letter in which Stock mentions Avalon is in fact letter 14.

181 See ch. 6.

182 Stock made his profession of faith on 6 October 1613 (Zimmerman, *Carmel in England*, 29). He therefore dates his persecution at the hands of

his superiors back to the very moment of his profession. He is afterwards to say that from the moment of his profession he had made it clear to his superiors that he considered service in the English mission an essential element of his vocation (letter 37).

183 Amerigo Salvetti Antominelli, resident in London from 1618 to 1657.

184 Francesco Niccolini, resident in Rome from 1621 to 1644.

185 Stock's letter was discussed in General Congregation no. 77, 17 July 1627.

186 Because of the way the sheet is folded, the reader at this point has to move on to another column. Hence "Turn over" ("Volta").

187 "[C]reates much difficulty in negotiations" replaces the original "non è di profitto alla propagatione della Fede" ("is not useful to the propagation of the Faith"), obviously omitted because considered too strong.

188 The last paragraph is the draft of the reply to Stock.

189 Stock's last letter was eight months earlier (letter 36).

190 The two seculars are Thomas Longville and Anthony Pole, *alias* Smith or Rivers (see ch. 6). For the number of Catholics in Newfoundland, see ch. 6n31.

191 See n182.

192 Stock's letter was discussed in General Congregation no. 85, 19 January 1628.

193 The map Propaganda refers to is the one Stock had enclosed with letter 29, i.e., one of Speed's. See ch. 5.

194 "[A]lthough" refers to a sentence which Ingoli later changed, forgetting to cross out the "although."

195 The last paragraph is the draft of the reply to Stock.

196 See ch. 7.

197 Avalon.

198 Longville and Pole.

199 "[H]e of whom I did write" is Lord Baltimore. For an interpretation of "others went the same year," see ch. 7.

200 See ch. 7.

201 Stock's letter was discussed in General Congregation no. 100 item no. 22 (not "20," as indicated by Ingoli), 24 November 1628.

202 Francesco Barberini, 1597–1679, cardinal, member of Propaganda, protector of England from 1626 to 1679.

203 The last paragraph is the draft of APF, *Acta*, vol. 6, f. 168rv, no. 22 (24 November 1628).

204 See ch. 4.

205 Urban VIII (Maffeo Barberini), 1568–1644, was pope from 1623 to 1644.

206 On the death of Cardinal William Allen (1532–94), the pope appointed not a bishop but an archpriest in the person of George Blackwell (1545?–1613). Blackwell remained in office from 1598 to 1608, when he was replaced by George Birkhead (?–1614), in turn replaced by William Harrison (1553–1621). When Harrison died, William Bishop was sent to England with the title of bishop of Chalcedon *in partibus infidelium*. (See Stanfield, ed., "Archpriest Controversy," in *Miscellanea XII*, 132–86. See also ch. 2.)

207 F. Barberini.

208 Pius IV (Angelo Medici), 1499–1565, was pope from 1559 to 1565. The Council of Trent ended during his pontificate.

209 On the Minim Brown, see [Panzani], "Relazione Dello Stato della Religione Cattolica in Inghilterra," APF, *SOCG*, vol. 347, f. 500r.

210 Stock's letter and Ingoli's memorandum were discussed in General Congregation no. 100, 24 November 1628.

211 A copy of Speed's map which Stock had already enclosed with letter 29. See ch. 5.

212 Avalon/Newfoundland.

213 See ch. 5.

214 Letter 29.

215 See ch. 5.

216 Avalon. Note that, a few lines back, Stock spoke of an "island," and now he speaks of this "new mission." Although he was by now perfectly aware that Avalon and Newfoundland were the same place, he continued to treat them as if they were two different places.

217 On the relations between Charles I and the Puritans, see French, *Charles I and Puritan Upheaval*.

218 See ch. 7n37.

219 Note the optimistic tone of Propaganda's words ("it can be navigated further into lands unknown") as opposed to Stock's ("Whether it is possible to navigate yet further, this is not yet known").

220 Stock's letter was discussed in General Congregation no. 103, 12 January 1629.

221 F. Barberini.

222 The last paragraph is the draft of APF, *Acta*, vol. 6, f. 198v, no. 31 (12 January 1629).

223 The last paragraph is the draft of the reply to Stock.

224 Alexander Baker and Lawrence Rigby (see ch. 8). Only Stock, on this and two successive occasions (letters 41, 50), gives news of the two Jesuits' journey to Newfoundland. Information is also conveyed implicitly in letters 68, 72.

225 Stock was not the only Discalced Carmelite in England at this moment. Even though they took no active part in the life of the mission, Eliseus of St. Michael and Edmund of St. Martin were also there. Eliseus, who after Bede of the Blessed Sacrament's departure was again provincial vicar (1626–35), was still living with the Roper family in Eltham, where remained until 1636, "doing much in a limited sphere of action." Of Edmund, "harassed by the Puritans," nothing is known from April 1626 till 26 July 1633 ([Biagio della Purificazione], "Missioni Inghilterra," AOCD, Ms. 277, 39–41; Zimmerman, *Carmel in England*, 44, 58).

226 Stock seems here to be referring to a lost letter of his which should come between letter 39 and the present one. For the royal proclamation, see *CSP, Dom. 1628–29*, 244, 519.

227 A reference to Propaganda's request (see [PF] to SS, Rome, 20 January 1629, APF, *Lettere*, vol. 8, f. 16r).

228 Charles I.

229 Salvetti Antominelli.

230 Niccolini.
231 Propaganda confuses Stock's information on Avalon with that on England.
232 Stock's letter was discussed in General Congregation no. 114, 7 September 1629.
233 The last paragraph is the draft of ibid..
234 The last paragraph is the draft of the reply to Stock.
235 Charles d'Aubespine, Marquis of Châteauneuf, 1580–1653, was French ambassador in England from July 1629 to April 1630. The meeting then took place, according to Stock, on 8 August.
236 Letter 40.
237 Baker and Rigby.
238 Avalon.
239 Canterbury.
240 Stock's letter was discussed in General Congregation no. 115, 2 October 1629.
241 Luigi Caetani, 1595–1642, cardinal, member of Propaganda.
242 The last paragraph is the draft of APF, *Acta*, vol. 6, f. 339r, no. 22 (2 October 1629).
243 The last paragraph is the draft of the reply to Stock.
244 In 1630 and 1631 the dispute was at its height. For the whole question and its development, see P. Hughes, *Rome and Counter-Reformation*, 347–430.
245 See n26.
246 Francis Cottington, 1578?–1652, was ambassador in Spain from November 1629 to January 1631.
247 The Marquis de Châteauneuf.
248 [PF] to SS, Rome, 26 June 1630, APF, *Lettere*, vol. 10, f. 62r.
249 The settlers headed by the Reverend Francis Higginson (1629) and John Winthrop (1630). See ch. 8.
250 The peace treaty signed by Charles I at Windsor and Louis XIII at Fontainebleau on 16 September 1629.
251 Stock's letter was discussed in General Congregation no. 126, 9 July 1630.
252 Se [PF] to [Fabio de Lagonissa], archbishop of Conza, nuncio in Flanders, Rome, 20 July 1630, APF, *Lettere*, vol. 10, ff. 78v–9r.
253 The last paragraph is the draft of APF, *Acta*, vol. 7/i, f. 99v, no. 20 (9 July 1630).
254 Letter 46.
255 [PF] to SS, Rome, 26 March 1630, APF, *Lettere*, vol. 10, f. 34v.
256 Guidi di Bagno.
257 [PF] to SS, Rome, 26 June 1630, APF, *Lettere*, vol. 10, f. 62r. Stock wrongly dates the letter "22."
258 Baker and Rigby.
259 In 1629 Easter fell on 5/15 April.
260 Lord Baltimore.
261 On the whole question, see ch. 8. It is not known what "special commission" the Jesuits had. Stock is probably referring to negotiations between Lord Baltimore and the Society, which had already resulted in the depar-

ture of Baker and Rigby for Newfoundland. Not by chance were Jesuits the first missionaries in Maryland. See the detailed account of Lord Baltimore's relationship with the Society of Jesus in Bossy, "Reluctant Colonists," in Quinn, ed., *Early Maryland*, 161–4.

262 See ch. 8.

263 Stock's letter was discussed in General Congregation no. 136, item no. 16 (not "17," as Ingoli writes), 25 February 1631.

264 Guido Bentivoglio, 1577–1644, cardinal, member of Propaganda.

265 The last paragraph is the draft of APF, *Acta*, vol. 7/ii, f. 26v, no. 16 (25 February 1631).

266 The last paragraph is the draft of the reply to Stock (see [PF] to SS, Rome, 8 March 1631, APF, *Lettere*, vol. 11, f. 22rv).

267 For the list of these books, see [Panzani], "Relazione Dello Stato della Religione Cattolica in Inghilterra," ff. 492rv–3r.

268 Stock is alluding to the information conveyed in [PF] to SS, Rome, 8 March 1631, APF, *Lettere*, vol. 11, f. 22v. For the history of the Capuchins in Acadia, see Candide de Nant, *Pages glorieuses*; Lenhart, "Capuchin Prefecture of New England."

269 See letter 56.

270 In *Acta* there is no mention of Stock's letter having been discussed. On 26 August 1631 General Congregation no. 145 was held, but the only item regarding England is no. 33 (APF, *Acta*, vol. 7/ii, ff. 366rv–76r). On 9 September 1631 General Congregation no. 146 took place, and no reference whatsoever was made to England (ibid., ff. 376v–83r).

271 Smith left England on 24 August/3 September 1631 ([Southcote], "Note-Book of John Southcote," Catholic Record Society, no. 1 [1905]: 107).

272 On this occasion, Stock writes that "Ha piaciuto alli embussatori et residenti del re di Spagnia per molti anni di elegermi qua per loro confessore ordinario." Stock enjoyed close relations with the Spanish Embassy in London from the time of his arrival in England. In October 1620 he took La Fuente's place as ordinary chaplain. Then he was confessor to Count Gondomar (1620–22), Coloma (1622–24), and Bruneau (1624–26) (see ch. 5n24; letter 12; nn25–6). These terms of familiarity obviously continued after Bruneau's departure and certainly still obtained in 1631, when the present letter was written. Stock's correspondence went through the Spanish Embassy at least until 15 December 1625, when he advised Propaganda against the use of "that channel" because of the war. On 7 December 1631 Stock informed them that letters to him might once again go through the Spanish diplomatic channels. As late as 28 June 1649, the date of his last letter, Stock refers to a previous letter of his forwarded through the Spanish ambassador in London (see letters 28, 62, 72, 93).

273 Juan de Nicolaldi was Spanish resident in London from the end of July 1631 to September 1637.

274 The original of this letter is not known, but it was almost certainly enclosed with letter 60.

275 Manuel de Azevedo, Count of Monterey.

276 Niccolini.

277 Letter 59.

278 On this copy there is an additional reference to General Congregation no. 155, 29 March 1632, in which Stock's memorandum was discussed. However, the *Acta* of that date contain no reference whatsoever to it (see APF, *Acta*, vol. 8, ff. 47rv–5or).

279 The last letter from Propaganda of which a copy is still extant is [PF] to SS, Rome, 18 July 1631, APF, *Lettere*, vol. 11, f. 71v. It is possible, however, that other letters were sent to Stock without copies being kept.

280 Nicolaldi.

281 This letter, undoubtedly addressed to Propaganda, afterwards ended up in the order's archives and was never sent back. At f. [2rv] there is the typical summary of Propaganda's clerks. This is the only letter originally addressed to Propaganda which is today to be found in the archives of the order.

282 From 1611, therefore. This was probably Stock's first stay in England (see ch. 2).

283 See n285.

284 Nicolaldi.

285 These were the Capuchins in the private service of Queen Henrietta Maria, wife of Charles I. The papal envoy Panzani mentions nine in his report on England ("Relazione Dello Stato della Religione Cattolica in Inghilterra," f. 499v).

286 Unfortunately, there remains no trace of these previous letters of Stock's to the general, either in the archives of the order or in Propaganda.

287 Stock is obviously referring to a previous departure of Jesuits for Avalon, not to that of Baker and Rigby, who did not stay long in the colony. For the next departure of Jesuits (though for Maryland, not Avalon), see n290.

288 This history, which never got further than the manuscript stage, was entitled "Sancti Palladii Scotorum Apostoli" (AOCD, Ms. 317.e). It was finally completed not by Easter (27 March 1634), but on 13 January 1635, as Stock writes in the dedicatory epistle. Shortly afterwards Stock sent it off to the order (see letters 77–8).

289 Nicolaldi.

290 As on previous occasions (see chs. 8 and 9, letters 50, 68), Stock confuses the original Avalon mission with the plan to found Maryland and a Maryland mission — a project shared by the Jesuits and the Calvert family. The Jesuits Baker and Rigby had gone to Avalon. On 22 November 1633, a few days after the date of the present letter, two more Jesuits, Andrew White and John Gravener (*alias* Altham), together with their lay brother Thomas Gervase, left the Isle of Wight for Maryland to become the founders of the Maryland Jesuit mission. For a detailed account, see T.A. Hughes, *History of the Society of Jesus*, 1: 244–347.

291 See n286.

292 See n295.

293 Eliseus of St. Michael was provincial vicar for a second term from 1626 to 1635.

294 Francis of the Saints (Christopher Leigh), 1600?–41, made his profession

of faith in Brussels on 7 November 1621 and returned to England in 1631/ 32 (see Zimmerman, *Carmel in England*, 108–13).

295 Onophre de Saint-Jacques's visit took place between the end of 1634 and the end of January 1635. Zimmerman gives extracts from his report (ibid., 49–51). See also letters 73, 77.

296 See n295.

297 See n288.

298 The general chapter of the Order met in Rome from 27 April 1635 (see AOCD, *Acta CG*, vol. 1, f. 154r).

299 See n288.

300 See ch. 2n5; n182.

301 According to Zimmerman, Bede of the Blessed Sacrament made his visit on returning in England in 1636 (*Carmel in England*, 105).

302 George Conn, ?–1640, arrived in England as papal agent on 17/27 July 1636 and stayed on until the summer of 1639. He took the place of Panzani. Subsequently, Carlo Rossetti, archbishop of Tarsus, took over from Conn.

303 Gregorio Panzani, c. 1576–1662, was in England as papal envoy extraordinary from 1634 to 1636, when Conn took his place. He was the author of the "Relazione Dello Stato della Religione Cattolica in Inghilterra," extant in various manuscript copies. Among them are the one cited, in the archives of Propaganda and the one in BL, *Add. Mss.* 15389, ff. 99rv–126rv.

304 In the letter of the year before (letter 79) there is no mention of Stock's books. We must therefore presume that at least one letter from 1636 was lost.

305 See ch. 2 n13; Bibliography.

306 Anselm of St. Mary (John Hansom), ?–1679, made his profession of faith on 5 September 1625. He was provincial vicar in England from 1647 to 1655 (see Zimmerman, *Carmel in England*, 118–36).

307 Before electing the new general, the order's general chapter, meeting in Rome from 23 April to 7 May 1638, voted against the request advanced by the English confrères (see AOCD, *Acta CG*, vol. 1, f. 169r).

308 This copy, unlike the other, contains a reference to General Congregation no. 246, 24 May 1638, in which Stock's memorandum was discussed. The *Acta* of the same date make no mention of this discussion. The only possibility is that the memorandum was discussed with item no. 13, relating to England (see APF, *Acta*, vol. 13, f. 92[b]r, no. 13 [24 May 1638]).

309 Stock writes: "Ho inteso che Vostra Signoria Eccellentissima sta disgustato meco, et mi doleo molto, et humilissimamente supplico Vostra Signoria Eccellentissima di farmi il favore di significare la causa." This would seem to indicate that he had only been told of his being in disfavour with Ingoli secondhand, rather than that Ingoli himself had written to him.

310 The dispute between Charles I and the Scottish Puritans came to a head after Alexander Henderson and Archibald Johnson drew up the National Covenant in Edinburgh at the end of February 1638. The first skirmishes

in what came to be known as the Bishops' Wars (May–June 1639) were recorded soon after the date of Stock's letter (see French, *Charles I and Puritan Upheaval*, 223–4).

311 The National Covenant. See n310.

312 See the list of Stock's works in the Bibliography. Stock's comments on his works are one of the few elements which permit an approximate dating of this letter. Stock's last work, "Advertisement of old Anonimous Eremita," BL, *Add. Mss.* 22645, is dated 1640. Since this letter seems to be addressed to the general, Paolo Simone di Gesù e Maria, whose third and last mandate began on 21 April 1641 (AOCD, *Acta CG*, vol. 1, f. 185v), it seems reasonable to conclude that the letter was written shortly after that date and certainly prior to 1643, when the general died.

313 Joseph of St. Mary (Nicholas Rider), 1600?–82, was born in Ireland and went to England about 1641, probably living in Hereford. Gervasius of the Blessed Sacrament (Walter Luddington), 1600?–58, made his profession of faith on 29 June 1630 and returned to England in 1638. John Baptist of Mount Carmel (John Rudgeley), 1587–1669, went to England in 1614, before Stock, although he seems to have had no contact with his confrères in the early times. He was imprisoned on several occasions for religious reasons, and at this time was probably living in Wells, Somerset. As to Stock's first confrères, Eliseus of St. Michael had just returned to England (May 1649) and was very ill, Edmund of St. Martin had died in 1635, and Bede of the Blessed Sacrament had died in 1647. (See Zimmerman, *Carmel in England*, 54, 60, 94, 137–60.)

314 Alonso de Cardenas was Spanish ambassador in London from August to December 1655. The letter Stock refers to is no longer in the archives of Propaganda and has probably been lost. This is the same letter to which reference is made in APF, *Acta*, vol. 19, f. 216r, no. 11 (22 February 1649).

# Bibliography

I. MANUSCRIPT SOURCES

*British Library (formerly British Museum), Department of Manuscripts, London [BL]*

*Additional Mss.*

15389    Relatione Dello Stato della Religione Cattolica in Inghilterra Data alla Santità di Nostro Signore Urbano VIII da Gregorio Panzani nel suo ritorno da quel Regno hanno 1637 (ff. 99rv–126rv).

17988    Historia Generalis Carmelitarum in Belgio Congregationis, ab anno 1611 usque ad annum 1682, 17th century.

22465    [Simon Stock]. An Advertisement of old Anonimous Eremita to his noble friend Sir Edward Dearing Knight & Baronet, to correct the multitude of his errors & falsehoods in his booke intituled of fraude, of folly, of foule language, & blasphemy, 1640.

*Egerton Mss.*

2541    Propositions made to Charles I by Robert Hayman concerning Newfoundland, 1628 (ff. 162rv–69rv).

*Royal Mss.*

17 A    [Edward Wynne]. The British India or A Compendious Discourse
LVII    tending to Advancement, 1628.

*Sloane Mss.*

170    Copy of the Charter of Avalon (7/17 April 1623).

3662   An Account of Lord Baltimore's Colonizing Ventures in North
       America, c. 1670 (ff. 24rv–6rv).

3827   George Cottington to Sir John Finet, 7/17 April 1628 (ff. 124rv–
       25rv).


       *Stowe Mss.*


743    George Calvert to John Harrison, Bristol, 5/15 February 1627/28
       (ff. 76rv–7rv).


       *British Library (formerly British Museum), Department of Printed
       Books, London [BL]*


4745.f.11   "Señor. El Doctor Iuan Luis Arias, dize . . . . " [1609]. In *Papeles
(18)        Tocantes la Iglesia Española, 1625–1790.*


       *Lambeth Palace Library, London*


Ms.    Journal of John Guy. 1612 (ff. 406rv–12rv).
250


       *Public Record Office, London [PRO]*


CO 1   Colonial Office Papers. General Series, vols. 1–5.


       *Westminster Diocesan Archives, London [WDA]*


A      Simon Stock to [Sacred Congregation "de Propaganda Fide" in
       Rome]. London, 10 October 1627 (vol. 20, no. 138, pp. 503–4).


       *Public Archives of Canada / Archives Publiques du Canada,
       Ottawa*


MG 11  Colonial Office — London. CO 1, Colonial Papers, General Series.
MG 17  Archives religieuses. A 1, Vatican: Archives Secrétes du Vatican,
       vols. 1–3.


       *Archivio della Sacra Congregazione "de Propaganda Fide," Rome
       [APF]*

———    *Acta*, vols. 1–19.
———    *Scritture Originali Riferite nelle Congregazioni Generali* [*SOCG*],
       vols. 1–417.
———    *Lettere*, vols. 1–27.
———    *Congregazioni Particolari* [*CP*], vols. 1–161.
———    *Congressi, America Settentrionale* vol. 1.

———  *Congressi, America Centrale* vol. 1.

———  *Congressi, America Meridionale*, vol. 1.

———  *Congressi, America Antille*, vol. 1.

———  *Congressi, Anglia*, vol. 1.

———  *Congressi, Missioni*, vol. 1.

———  *Fondo Vienna*, vols. 39–40.

———  *Decreti*, vol. 3.

———  *Miscellanee Diverse*, vols. 20, 22.

———  *Miscellanee Varie*, vols. III, VI, XI, XIII, XIIIa.


*Archivio Segreto Vaticano, Rome [ASV]*

*Segreteria di Stato, Francia*  Simon Stock to Bernardino Spada, London, 22 April 1626, vol. 396, ff. 378rv–9rv.


*Archivio Generale dell'Ordine dei Carmelitani Scalzi, Rome [AOCD]*

———  *Acta Capituli Generalis [Acta CG]*, vols. 1–2.

———  *Acta Definitorii Generalis*, vols. 1–2.

———  *Acta Procurae Generalis*, vol. 1.

Ms. 271.c  "Missiones Europa Anglia. Brevis relatio missionariorum 1614/48."

Ms. 271.d  [Biagio della Purificazione]. "Missiones Europa Anglia. Historia Missionis 1614/83." [1705].

Ms. 271.g  "Missiones Europa Anglia. P. Simon Stock: Litterae & relationes 1622/35."

Ms. 271.h  "Missiones Europa Anglia. P. Beda a SS. Sacr.: Litterae & relationes 1625/27."

Ms. 271.i  "Missiones Europa Anglia. P. Elias a Jesu: Litterae & relationes 1627/41."

Ms. 277  [Biagio della Purificazione]. "Missioni Inghilterra Irlanda Olanda." [1705].

Ms. 317.e  [Simon Stock]. "Sancti Palladii Scotorum Apostoli et Palestinae Monachi Brevis Historia. A Fratris Simone Stocco eiusdem Ordinis, missionario anglo, collecta. [1635].

Ms. 350.i.1  Faculties to Simon Stock and Eliseus of St. Michael, 1621.


## II. REFERENCE WORKS

Allison, Anthony Francis and Rogers, David M. "A Catalogue of English Books in English Printed Abroad or Secretly in England 1558–1640," *Biographical Studies* 3 (1956): 119–220, 220–832 [*sic*].

Ambrogio di Santa Teresa, OCD. "Nomenclator Missionariorum Ordinis Carmelitarum Discalceatorum." *Analecta Ordinis Carmelitarum Discalceatorum* 12 (1942): 15-118; 18 (1943): 9-122, 152-235.

Anstruther, Godfrey, OP. *The Seminary Priests. A Dictionary of the Secular Clergy of England and Wales 1558-1850*, 4 vols., Durham; Upshaw College; Ware; St. Edmund's College; Great Wakering; Mayhew-McCrummon, 1968-77.

[Bartolomeo di Sant'Angelo and Enrico del Santissimo Sacramento, OCD]. *Collectio Scriptorum Ordinis Carmelitarum Excalceatorum Utriusque Congregationis et Sex . . . .* 2 vols., Savona: A. Ricci, [1884].

Biaudet, Henri. *Les Nonciatures Apostoliques Permanentes jusqu'en 1648*. Helsinki: Soumalainen Tiedeakatemia, 1910.

*Biographie Nationale publiée par l'Académie Royale des Sciences, des Lettres et des Beaux-Arts de Belgique*. 28 vols. and 11 supplements, Brussels: 1866-1976.

Bittner, Ludwig and Gross, Lothar. *Repertorium der diplomatischen Vertreter aller Länder seit dem Westfälischen Frieden (1648)*, I: (*1648-1715*). Oldenburg I. O., Berlin; Gerhard Stalling Verlag, 1936.

Chevin, abbé, *Dictionnaire latin-français des noms propres de lieux Ayant certaine notoriété principalement au point de vue ecclésiastique et monastique*. Paris: 1897.

Codignola, Luca. "L'America del Nord e la Sacra Congregazione 'de Propaganda Fide,' 1622-1799. Una introduzione." In L. Codignola, ed., *Canadiana. Storia e storiografia canadese*. Venice: Marsilio Editori, 1979, 33-45.

———— "L'Amérique du Nord et la Sacrée Congrégation 'de Propaganda Fide,' 1622-1799. Etudes", *Bulletin du Centre de Recherche en civilisation canadienne française* 21 (1980): 1-12; also in Pierre Savard, éd., *Aspects de la civilisation canadienne-française*. Ottawa: Editions de l'Université d'Ottawa, 1983, 325-36.

————"L'Amérique du Nord et la Sacrée Congrégation "de Propaganda Fide", 1622-1799. Guide et inventaires", *Revue d'histoire de l'Amérique française*, 33 (1979): 197-214.

————"Roman Sources of Canadian Religious History to 1799." Canadian Catholic Historical Association, *Study Sessions* (1983): 73-88

Cook, Chris, and Wroughton, John. *English Historical Facts 1603-1688*. London and Basingstoke: Macmillan, 1980.

[Cosma de Villiers a Sancto Stephano, OCD]. *Bibliotheca Carmelitana, Notis Criticis et Dissertationibus Illustrata . . . .* 2 vols., Orléans: M. Couret de Villeneuve and Joannes Rouzeau Montaut, 1752.

———— ed. by Gabriel Wessels, OCD. Leipzig and Rome, 1927.

Del Piazzo, Marcello. "Gli ambasciatori toscani del principato (1537-1737)." *Notizie degli Archivi di Stato* 12 (1952): 57-106.

*Dictionari Biogràfic*. 4 vols. Barcelona: Albertì, 1966-70.

*Dictionary of American Biography*. Allen Johnson and Dumas Malone, eds., 20 vols., New York: 1928-37.

*Dictionary of Canadian Biography*, I: *1000 to 1700*. George G. Brown, Marcel Trudel, André Vachon, eds., Toronto: University of Toronto Press, 1966.

*Dictionary of National Biography*. 63 vols. and *Supplement*, 3 vols. Leslie Stephen and Sidney Lee, eds. London: 1885–1903.

*Dictionnaire de Biographie Française*. 13 vols. to date, Paris: Letouzey et Ané, 1933–.

*Dictionnaire d'histoire et de géographie ecclésiastiques*. 18 vols. to date, Paris: Letouzey et Ané, 1912–.

*Enciclopedia Cattolica*. 12 vols. Vatican City: 1948–54.

*Encyclopedia of Newfoundland and Labrador*. ed. by Joseph R. Smallwood. St. John's: Newfoundland Book Publishers, 1981–84, 2 vols. to date.

Fish, Carl Russell, *Guide to the Materials for American History in Roman and Other Italian Archives*. Washington, DC: Carnegie Institution, 1911.

Friedberg, Aemilius, *Corpus Iuris Canonici*. Graz, 1959.

*General Inventory Manuscripts, MG 1-MG 30*. Robert S. Gordon, ed. 7 vols. to date. Ottawa: Public Archives of Canada, 1971–77.

Gillow, Joseph. *A Literary and Biographical History, or Bibliographical Dictionary of the English Catholics from the Breach with Rome, in 1534, to the Present Time*. 5 vols. London: Burn & Oates, 1885–*c*. 1902.

Harben, Henry A. *A Dictionary of London, Being Notes Topographical and Historical Relating to the Streets and Principal Buildings in the City of London*. London: Herbert Jenkins, 1918.

*Hierarchia Catholica . . . .* I: *Saeculum XVI ab anno 1503 complectens quod cum Societis Goerresianae Subsidio . . . .* Ludovicus Schmitz-Kallemberg, ed. Typis Librariae Regensbergianae, 1923.

———.IV: *A pontificatu Clementis PP. VIII (1592) usque ad Pontificatum Alexandri PP. VII (1667)*. Patritius Gauchat, ed. Typis Librariae Regensbergianae, 1935.

Holweck, Frederick George. *A Biographical Dictionary of the Saints. With a General Introduction on Hagiology*. St. Louis, Mo.; London: B. Herder, 1924.

Kallemberg, Paschalis, OCarm. *Fontes liturgiae carmelitanae. Investigatio in decreta, codices et proprium sanctorum*. Rome: Institutum Carmelitanum, 1962.

Kapsner, Oliver R., OSB, *Catholic Religious Orders Listing Conventional and Full Names in English, Foreign Languages, and Latin. Also Abbreviations, Date and Country of Origin and Founders*, Collegeville, MN: St. John's Abbey Press, 1957 (1st ed.: 1948).

Kenneally, Finbar, OFM, ed., *United States Documents in the Propaganda Fide Archives. A Calendar. First Series*. 7 vols. and Index. Washington, DC: Academy of American Franciscan History, 1966–81.

Kowalsky, Nikolaus, OMI. "Inventario dell'archivo [*sic*] storico della S. Congregazione 'de Propaganda Fide," *Neue Zeitschrift für Missionswissenschaft* 17 (1961): 9–23, 109–17, 101–200.

Larkin, James F., and Hughes, Paul L., eds. *Stuart Royal Proclamations of King James I 1603–1625*. Oxford: Clarendon Press, 1973.

*Lexicon Capuccinum. Promptuarium Historico-Bibliographicum Ordinis Fratrum Minorum Capuccinorum (1525–1950)*. Rome: Biblioteca Collegii Internationalis S. Laurentii Brundisini, 1951.

[Magri, Domenico]. *Notizia de' Vocaboli Ecclesiastici, Con la Dichiarazione*

*delle Cerimonie, & Origine delli Riti Sacri, voci Barbare, e Frasi usate da'*
*Santi Padri, Concilj, e Scrittori Ecclesiastici .... Ottava Impressione ....*
Venice: Stamperia Baglioni, 1732.

*New Catholic Encyclopedia.* 15 vols. New York: McGraw Hill, 1967.

*Nouvelle Biographie Universelle depuis les temps les plus reculés jusqu'à nos*
*jours ....* 46 vols., Paris: Firmin Didot, 1857-66.

*Nouvelle Biographie Universelle depuis les temps les plus reculés jusqu'à nos*
*jours ....* 46 vols., Paris: Firmin Didot, 1852-66.

Raimo, John W., ed. *A Guide to Manuscripts Relating to America in Great*
*Britain and Ireland. A Revision of the Guide Edited in 1961 by B. R. Crick*
*and Miriam Alman.* London: Mansell, 1979.

Seary, E. R. *Place Names of the Avalon Peninsula of the Island of Newfound-*
*land,* Toronto: University of Toronto Press, 1971.

Shaw, William Arthur. *The Knights of England. A Complete Record from*
*the Earliest Time to the Present Day of the Knights of all the Orders of*
*Chivalry in England, Scotland, and Ireland, and of Knights Bachelors.* 2
vols., London: Sherrat and Hughes, 1906.

Thériault, Michel. *The Institutes of Consecrated Life in Canada From the*
*Beginning of New France Up to the Present. Historical Notes and refer-*
*ences.* Ottawa: National Library of Canada, 1980

van der AA, A.J., *Biographic Woordenboek der Nederlanden.* Amsterdam:
B.M. Israel, 1969 (1st ed.: 1852)

Zupko, Ronald Edward. *British Weights & Measures. A History from Antiq-*
*uity to the Seventeenth Century,* Madison, WI.: University of Wisconsin
Press, 1977.

## III. PRINTED PRIMARY SOURCES

[Abbot, George, 1562-1633]. *A Briefe Description of the Whole world.*
*Wherein is particularly described all the Monarchies, Empires and King-*
*domes of the same, with their Academies. Newly augmented and enlarged;*
*with their seuerall Titles and scituations thereunto adioyning. The fifth*
*Edition.* London: John Marriot, 1620 (1st ed., of little interest for America,
1599).

*Acts of the Privy Council of England 1621-1623.* London: His Majesty's Stationery Office, 1932.

*Acts of the Privy Council of England 1623-1625.* London: His Majesty's Stationery Office, 1933.

*Acts of the Privy Council of England 1625-1626.* London: His Majesty's Stationery Office, 1934.

*Acts of the Privy Council of England 1627 Sept.-1628 June.* London: His
Majesty's Stationery Office, 1940

*Acts of the Privy Council of England 1628 July-1629 April.* London: Her
Majesty's Stationery Office, 1958.

*Acts of the Privy Council of England. Colonial Series, I: AD 1613-1680.* W. L.
Grant, James Munro, and Almeric W. Fitzroy, eds. Hereford: His Majesty's
Stationery Office, 1908.

Alexander, William, 1567?-1640. *An Encouragement to Colonies*. London: William Stansby, 1624.

Ambrogio di Santa Teresa, OCD. "Regesta Missionaria desumpta ex Actis Definitorii Generalis Ordinis Carmelitarum Discalceatorum", *Analecta Ordinis Carmelitarum Discalceatorum* 20 (1948) 260-311; 21 (1949): 44-104, 193-207.

Anderson, Roger Charles, ed. *The Book of Examinations and Depositions, 1622-1644*. 4 vols., Southampton: Southampton Record Society, 1929-36.

[Bacon, Francis, 1561-1626]. *The Essayes of Counsels, Civill and Morall ....* London: John Haviland for Hanna Barret, 1625.

_____."De Fluxu et Refluxu Maris", in [Francis Bacon], *Scripta in Naturali et Vniversalis Philosophia*, Amsterdam: Ludovicum Elzevirum, 1653, 178-207.

_____ *Scripta in Naturali et Vniversali Philosophia*. Amsterdam: Ludovicum Elzevirum, 1653.

[Birch, Thomas, 1705-1766]. *The Court and Times of Charles the First; Illustrated by Authentic and Confidential Letters, from Various Public and Private Collections ....* 2 vols., London: Henry Colburn, 1848.

_____ *The Court and Times of James the First; Illustrated by Authentic and Confidential Letters, from Various Public and Private Collections*. 2 vols., London: Henry Colburn, 1848.

[Bolìvar, Gregorio, *fl.* 1600-25, OFM Rec], "Der älteste Bericht über Nordamerika im Propaganda-Archiv: Virginia 1625", Josef Metzler, OMI, ed. *Neue Zeitschrift für Missionswissenschaft* 25 (1969): 29-37.

[Briggs, Henry, 1561-1630]. "A Treatise of the Northwest Passage to the South Sea, through the Continent of Virginia and by Fretum Hudson." In [Edward Waterhouse], *A Declaration of the state of the Colony and Affaires in Virginia ....* London: G. Eld for Robert Mylbourne, 1622, 45-50; also in [Samuel Purchas]. *Purchas His Pilgrimes ....* London: William Stansby for Henrie Fetterstone, 1625, 3: 852-53.

Burton, Edwin Hubert, and Williams, Thomas L., eds. *The Douay College Diaries. Third, Fourth and Fifth 1598-1654, with the Rheims Report, 1579-80*. 2 vols. Catholic Record Society, nos. 10-11. Leeds: J. Whitehead, 1911.

[C., T.] *A Short Discourse of the New-Found-Land: Contaynig [sic] Diverse Reasons and inducements, for the planting of that Countrey. Published for the satisfaction of all such as shall be willing to be Adventurers in the said Plantation*. Dublin: Societie of Stationers, 1623.

*Calendar of State Papers and Manuscripts, Relating to English Affairs, Existing in the Archives and Collections of Venice, and in the Other Libraries of Northern Italy*, XV: *1617-1619*. Allen B. Hinds, ed., London: His Majesty's Stationery Office, 1909.

*Calendar of State Papers and Manuscripts, Relating to English Affairs, Existing in the Archives and Collections of Venice, and in the Other Libraries of Northern Italy*, XVI: *1619-1621*. Allen B. Hinds, ed., London: His Majesty's Stationery Office, 1910.

*Calendar of State Papers and Manuscripts, Relating to English Affairs, Existing in the Archives and Collections of Venice, and in the Other Libraries of*

*Northern Italy*, XVII: *1621–1623*. Allen B. Hinds, ed., London: His Majesty's Stationery Office, 1911.

*Calendar of State Papers and Manuscripts, Relating to English Affairs, Existing in the Archives and Collections of Venice, and in the Other Libraries of Northern Italy*, XVIII: *1623–1625*. Allen B. Hinds, ed., London: His Majesty's Stationery Office, 1912.

*Calendar of State Papers and Manuscripts, Relating to English Affairs, Existing in the Archives and Collections of Venice, and in the Other Libraries of Northern Italy*, XIX: *1625–1626*. Allen B. Hinds, ed., London: His Majesty's Stationery Office, 1913.

*Calendar of State Papers and Manuscripts, Relating to English Affairs, Existing in the Archives and Collections of Venice, and in the Other Libraries of Northern Italy*, XX: *1626–1628*. Allen B. Hinds, ed., London: His Majesty's Stationery Office, 1914.

*Calendar of the Patent and Close Rolls of Chancery in Ireland, of the Reign of Charles the First. First to Eighth Year, Inclusive*. James Morrin, ed. Dublin: Her Majesty's Stationery Office, 1863.

*Calendar of State Papers, Colonial Series, [America and West Indies], 1574–1660, Preserved in the State Department of Her Majesty's Public Record Office*. W. Noël Sainsbury, ed. London: Longman, Green, Longman & Roberts, 1860.

*Calendar of State Papers, Colonial Series, America and West Indies, 1675–1676, also Addenda, 1574–1674, Preserved in the Public Record Office*. W. Noël Sainsbury, ed., London: Her Majesty's Stationery Office, 1893.

*Calendar of State Papers, Domestic Series, of the Reign of James I, 1603–1610, Preserved in the State Department of Her Majesty's Public Record Office*. Mary Anne Everett Green, ed. London: Longman, Brown, Green, Longmans & Roberts, 1857.

*Calendar of State Papers, Domestic Series, of the Reign of James I, 1619–1623, Preserved in the State Department of Her Majesty's Public Record Office*. Mary Anne Everett Green, ed. London: Longman, Brown, Green, Longmans & Roberts, 1858.

*Calendar of State Papers, Domestic Series, of the Reign of James I, 1623–1625, with Addenda; Preserved in the State Department of Her Majesty's Public Record Office*. Mary Anne Everett Green, ed. London: Longman, Brown, Green, Longmans & Roberts, 1859.

*Calendar of State Papers, Domestic Series, of the Reign of Charles I, 1625–1626, Preserved in the State Paper Department of Her Majesty's Public Record Office*. John Bruce, ed. London: Longman, Brown, Green, Longmans & Roberts, 1858.

*Calendar of State Papers, Domestic Series, of the Reign of Charles I, 1627–1628, Preserved in the State Department of Her Majesty's Public Record Office*. John Bruce, ed. London: Longman, Brown, Green, Longmans & Roberts, 1859.

*Calendar of State Papers, Domestic Series, of the Reign of Charles I, 1628–1629, Preserved in the State Department of Her Majesty's Public Record Office*. John Bruce, ed. London: Longman, Brown, Green, Longmans & Roberts, 1858.

*Calendar of State Papers, Domestic Series, of the Reign of Charles I, 1629–1631, Preserved in the State Department of Her Majesty's Public Record Office.* John Bruce, ed. London: Longman, Brown, Green, Longmans & Roberts, 1860.

*Calendar of State Papers, Domestic Series, of the Reign of Charles I, Addenda: March 1625 to January 1649, Preserved in The Public Record Office.* Douglas Hamilton and Sophia Crawford Lomas, eds. London: Her Majesty's Stationery Office, 1897.

*Calendar of State Papers Relating to Ireland, of the Reign of Charles I, 1625–1632, Preserved in The Public Record Office.* Robert Pentland Mahaffy, ed. London: Her Majesty's Stationery Office, 1900.

[Calvert, George, 1580–1632], L. B., "The Answere of a Catholike Lay Gentleman, To the Iudgement of a Deuine vpon the Letter of the Lay Catholikes, to my Lord Bishop of Chalcedon." In [Carlos Coloma]. *The Attestation of the Most Excellent, and Most Illustrious Lord, Don Carlos Coloma, Embassadour Extraordinary for Spayne. Of the Declaration made unto him, by the Lay Catholikes of England: Concerning the Authority challenged ouer them, by the Right Reuerend Lord Bishop of Chalcedon* . . . . [Saint-Omer]: 1631, part two, 1–126

*The Calvert Papers, Number One. With an account of their recovery, and presentation to the Society, December 10th, 1888* . . . . Maryland Historical Society Fund Publication, no. 28, Baltimore: 1889

Campeau, Lucien, SJ, éd. *Monumenta Novae Franciae,* I: *La première mission d' Acadie (1602–1616).* Rome: Monumenta Hist. Soc. Jesu, Québec: Les Presses de l'Université Laval, 1967.

_____*Monumenta Novae Franciae,* II: *Établissement à Québec (1616–1634),* Rome: Monumenta Hist. Soc. Jesu; Québec: Les Presses de l'Université Laval, 1979.

Caraman, Philip George, ed. *The Years of Siege. Catholic Life from James I to Cromwell.* London: Longmans, Green & Co., 1966.

Carr, Cecil Thomas, ed. *Select Charters of Trading Companies AD 1530–1707,* London: Selden Society, 1913.

Cauchie, Alfred-Henri-Joseph and Maere, René, éds. *Recueil des instructions générales aux nonces de Flandre (1596–1635).* Brussels: Hayez, 1904

Cell, Gillian T., ed. *Newfoundland Discovered. English Attempts at Colonisation 1610–1630.* London: Hakluyt Society, 1982

[Chamberlain, John, 1553–1627]. *The Letters of John Chamberlain,* 2 vols. Norman Egbert McClure, ed. American Philosophical Society, Memoirs, no. 12, Philadelphia: 1939.

Codignola, Luca. *Calendar of Documents Relating to French and British North America in the Archives of the Sacred Congregation "de Propaganda Fide" in Rome, 1622–1799.* 6 vols., Ottawa: Public Archives of Canada; Université Saint-Paul, 1983 (microfiche edition)

[Coloma, Carlos, 1566–1637]. *The Attestation of the Most Excellent, and Most Illustrious Lord, Don Carlos Coloma, Embassadour Extraordinary for Spayne. Of the Declaration made unto him, by the Lay Catholikes of England: Concerning the Authority challenged ouer them, by the Right Reuerend Lord Bishop of Chalcedon* . . . . [Saint-Omer]: 1631

Cuvelier, Joseph, and Lefèvre, Joseph, éds. *Correspondance de la Cour d'Es-pagne sur Les Affaires des Pays-Bas au XVIIe siècle,* II: *Précis de la Corres-pondance de Philippe IV avec l'infante Isabelle (1621-1633).* Brussels: Librairie Kiessling, 1927

*A Declaration of the State of the Colonie and Affaires in Virginia: With the Names of the Aduenturors, and Summes aduentured in that Action. By his Maiesties Counseil for Virginia. 22. Juny. 1620.* London: T.S., 1620.

[Dering, Edward, 1598-1644]. *The Fower Cardinall-Vertues Of A Carmelite-Fryar, Fraud, Folly, Foul Language, Blasphemy. Discovered by Sir Edward Dering, knight and Baronet. And by him sent backe againe to their Author Simon Stocke, alias Father Simons, alias Iohn Hunt alias Anonymous Eremita.* London: I.R. for R. Whitaker, 1641

[Dodsworth, Roger, and Dugdale, William]. *Monasticon Anglicanum, sive Pandectae Coenobiorum Benedictinorum Cluniacensium Cistercensium Carthusianorum A primordis ad eorum usque dissolutionem . . . .* 3 vols. London: Richard Hodgkinsonne, 1655-73.

Eburne, Richard. *A Plain Pathway to Plantations* (1624). Louis Booker Wright, ed. Ithaca, NY: Cornell University Press, 1962.

Foley, Henry, SJ, ed. *Records of the English Province of the Society of Jesus. Historic Facts illustrative of the Labours and Sufferings of its Members in the Sixteenth and Seventeenth Centuries.* 7 vols., Roehampton: The Han-resa Press, London: Burn and Oates, 1875-83.

Gardiner, Samuel Rawson, ed. *Debates in the House of Commons in 1625,* [London]: Camden Society, 1873.

[Gee, John]. *The Foot out of the Snare: with A Detection of Sundry Late practices and Impostures of the Priests and Iesuits in England . . . .* London: H.L. for Robert Milbourne, 1624.

Gilbert, Humphrey, c. 1537-1583. *A Discovrse Of a Discoverie for a new Pas-sage to Cataia.* George Gascoine, ed. London: Henry Middleton for Richarde Ihones, 1576.

[Goodman, Godfrey, 1583-1656]. *The Court of King James the First by Dr. Godfrey Goodman, Bishop of Gloucester; to which are Added, Letters Illustrative of the Personal History of the Most Distinguished Characters in the Court of that Monarch and his Predecessors. Now First Published from the Original Manuscripts.* John S. Brewer, ed. 2 vols. London: Richard Bentley, 1839.

[Guidi di Bagno, Giovanni Francesco, 1578-1641]. *Correspondence du Nonce Giovanni-Francesco Guidi di Bagno (1621-1627).* Bernard de Meester, éd. 2 vols., Brussels: Palais des Académies; Rome: Institut Historique Belge, 1938.

[Hakluyt, Richard, 1551/2-1616]. *The Principal Navigations, Voiages, Traffiques and Discoueries of the English Nation, made by Sea or ouer-land, to the remote and farthest distant quarters of the Earth, at any time within the compasse of these 1500. yeeres . . . .* 3 vols. London: George Bishop, Ralph Newberie and Robert Barker, 1598-1600.

Hall, Clayton Colman, ed. *Narratives of Early Maryland 1633-1684.* New York: Charles Scribner's Sons, 1910.

[Hall, Joseph, 1574-1656]. *Mercurius Britannicus. Mvndvs Alter et Idem Siue*

*Terra Australis ante hac Semper incognita longis itineribus peregrini Academici nupperime lustrata.* Frankfurt: Haeredes Ascanii de Rinialme, [1605].

Harris, Philip Rowland, ed. *Douai College Documents 1639-1794.* Catholic Record Society, no. 63. St. Alban's: Flarepath Printers, 1972.

Hasted, Edmund. *The History and Topographical Survey of the Country of Kent. Containing The Antient and Present State of it, Ciuil and Ecclesiastical ....* 4 vols. Canterbury: Simmons and Kirkey, 1778-99.

[Hayman, Robert, 1575-1629], R. H. *Quodlibets, lately come over from New Britaniola, old New-found-land. Epigrams and other small parcels, both Morall and Diuine ....* London: Elizabeth All-de for Roger Mitchell, 1628.

Henson, Edwin, ed. *The English College at Madrid 1611-1767.* Catholic Record Society, no. 29. Leeds: J. Whitehead, 1929.

————. *Register of the English College at Valladolid 1589-1862.* Catholic Record Society, no. 30. Leeds: J. Whitehead, 1930.

[Higginson, Francis, 1587-1630]. *New-Englands Plantation. Or, A Short and True Description of the Commodities and Discommodities of that Countrey ....* London: T.C. and R.C. for Michael Sparke, 1630.

Historical Manuscript Commission. *The Manuscripts of the Earl Cowper, KG, Preserved at Melbourne Hall, Derbyshire,* 3 vols. 12th Report, Appendix. London: Her Majesty's Stationery Office, 1888-89.

————. *Report on Franciscan Manuscripts preserved at The Convent, Merchants' Quay, Dublin.* London: His Majesty's Stationery Office, 1906.

[Holinshed, Raphael, ?-1580?]. *The Firste volume of the Chronicles of England, Scotlande, and Ireland ....* London: George Bishop, 1577.

Kelly, Wilfrid, ed., *Liber Ruber Venerabilis Collegii Anglorum de Urbe.* I. *Annales Collegii. Pars Prima. Nomina Alumnorum I: AD 1579-1783.* 2 vols. Catholic Record Society, nos. 37, 40. Leeds: John Whitehead, 1940-43.

Kenny, Anthony, ed. *The Responsa Scholarum of the English College, Rome, 1598-1685,* 2 vols. Catholic Record Society, nos. 54-55. Newport: R.H. Johns, 1962-63.

Kingsbury, Susan Myra, ed. *The Records of the Virginia Company of London. The Court Book, from the Manuscript in the Library of Congress.* 4 vols. Washington, DC: Government Printing Office, 1906-35.

Knox, Thomas Francis, ed. *The First and Second Diaries of the English College, Douay, and an Appendix of Unpublished Documents, edited by Fathers of the Congregation of the London Oratory,* 2 vols. London: David Nutt, 1878-82.

Koci, Josef, Polisenský, Josef Vincent, Cechová, Gabriela, Janácek, Josef, eds. *Documenta Bohemica Bellum Tricennale Illustrantia.* 6 vols. published. Praha: Academia Nakladatelst vi Ceskoslovenské Akademie Ved, 1971-78.

[Lagonissa, Fabio de, c. 1585-1653]. Lucienne van Meerbeck, éd. *Correspondence du Nonce Fabio de Lagonissa Archevêque de Conza (1627-1634).* Institut Historique Belge de Rome, Brussels; Rome: 1966.

Law, Thomas Graves, ed. *The Archpriest Controversy. Documents Relating to the Dissensions of the Roman Catholic Clergy 1597-1602 ....* 2 vols. [London]: Camden Society, 1896-98.

[Lloyd, David, 1635-1692]. *State Worthies. Or, the States-Men and Favourites of England since the Reformation Their Prudence and Policies, Successes and Miscarriages, Advancements and Falls . . . . The Second Edition with Additions.* London: Thomas Milbourn for Samuel Speed, 1670 (1st ed.: 1665).

Lonchay, Henri, and Cuvelier, Joseph, éds. *Correspondance de la Cour d'Espagne. Les affaires des Pays-Bas au XVIIe siècle,* I: *Précis de la Correspondance de Philippe II (1598-1621).* Brussels; Librairie Kiessling, 1923.

Major, Richard Henry, ed. *Early Voyages to Terra Australis, now Called Australia. A Collection of Documents, and Extracts from Early Manuscript Maps . . . .* London: Hakluyt Society, 1859.

[Mason, John, 1586-1635]. *A Briefe Discourse of the New-found-land, with the situation, temperature, and commodities thereof, inciting our Nation to goe forward in that hopefull plantation begunne.* Edinburgh: Andro Hart, 1620.

Morris, John, SJ, ed. *The Troubles of our Catholic Forefathers Related by Themselves.* 3 vols. London: Burns and Oates, 1872-77.

[Morton, George]. *A Relation or Iournall of the beginning and proceedings of the English Plantation settled at Plymoth in New England, by certaine English Aduenturers both Merchants and others . . . .* London: Iohn Bellamie, 1622.

McGrath, Patrick Vincent, ed. *Records Relating to the Society of Merchants Venturers of the City of Bristol in the Seventeenth Century.* Bristol: Bristol Record Society, 1952.

Neary, Peter and O'Flaherty, Patrick, eds. *By Great Waters. A Newfoundland and Labrador Anthology.* Toronto: University of Toronto Press, 1974.

Pacifique de Provins, OFM Cap, 1588-1648. *Le voyage de Perse et Breve relation du voyage de l'Amérique,* Godefroy de Paris, OFM Cap and Hilaire de Wingene, OFM Cap, éds. Assisi: Collegio S. Lorenzo da Brindisi, 1939.

Pasture, Alexandre, abbé, éd. "Documents concernant quelques monastères anglais au Pays-Bas au XVIIIe siècle", *Bulletin de l'Institut Historique Belge de Rome* 10 (1930): 155-223.

[Pendryck, William, OCD, 1583-1650]. *The Application of the Lawes of England for Catholike Priesthood, and the Sacrifice of the Masse. Directed to his Maiesties most Honourable priuie Counsell, Judges, Justices, and other Studients of the Law.* Cullen: 1623.

[Persons, Robert, SJ, 1546-1610]. "Annals of the English College, Seville. With an Account of four other foundations from 1589 to 1595. An unfinished memoir written by Father Robert Persons, SJ, in 1610." In John Hungerford Pollen, SJ, ed. *Miscellanea IX.* Catholic Record Society, no. 14. Edinburgh: Mercat Press, 1914, 1-24.

[Pory, John]. *John Pory's Lost Description of Plymouth Colony in the Earliest Days of the Pilgrim Fathers Together with contemporary accounts of English Colonization Elsewhere in New England and in the Bermudas,* Champlin Burrage, ed. Boston; New York: Houghton Mifflin Company, 1918.

[Purchas, Samuel, c. 1575-1626]. *Purchas His Pilgrimes . . . .* 4 vols., London: William Stansby for Henrie Fetterstone, 1625.

Quinn, David Beers, and Quinn, Alison M., eds. *The English New England Voyages 1602–1608*. London: Hakluyt Society, 1983.

Quinn, D.B. ed., with the assistance of A.M. Quinn and Susan Hillier. *New American World. A Documentary History of North America to 1612*. 5 vols. New York: Arno Press, Hector Bye, 1979.

Quinn, D.B., ed. *North American Discovery Circa 1000–1612*. Columbia, SC: University of South Carolina Press, 1971.

Ritchie, Carson William Alexander, ed. *The New World. A Catalogue of an Exhibition at Lambeth Palace Library 1957*. London: Lambeth Palace Library, 1957.

[Sarmiento de Acuñas, Diego, Count Gondomar]. *Correspondencia oficial de Don Diego Sarmiento de Acuñas conde de Gondomar*. Ed. por Antonio Ballestreros y Berretta. Madrid: Estanislao Maestre, 1943.

Scisco, Louis Dow. "Calvert's Proceedings against Kirke." *Canadian Historical Review* 8 (1927) 132–36.

———. "Kirke's Memorial on Newfoundland," *Canadian Historical Review*, 7 (1926): 46–51.

———. "Testimony Taken in Newfoundland in 1652," *Canadian Historical Review*, 9 (1928): 239–51.

[Smith, John, 1580–1631]. *The Complete Works of Captain John Smith (1580–1631)*. Philip L. Barbour, ed. Chapel Hill, NC: The University of North Carolina Press, 1986, 3 vols.

———. *The Generall Historie of Virginia, New-England, and the Summer Isles, with the names of the Adventurers, Planters, and Gouvernours from their first beginning. An:° 1584. to this present 1624. . . .* London: I.D. for Michael Sparkes, 1624.

[Southcote, John, 1588–1637]. "The Note-Book of John Southcote, DD. From 1623 to 1637." in Catholic Record Society, no. 1, London: Art & Book Co., 1905, 97–116.

Stanfield, Raymund, ed. "The Archpriest Controversy." in *Miscellanea XII*, Catholic Record Society, no. 22. Leeds: J. Whitehead, 1921, 132–86.

Talbot, Clarel, ed. *Miscellanea Recusant Records*. Catholic Record Society, no. 53. Newport: R.H. Johns, 1961.

[Vaughan, William, 1577–1641]. Orpheus Iunior, *Cambrensium Caroleia. Qvibvs Nuptiae Regales celebrantur, Memoria Regis Pacifici renouatur, & Praecepta necessaria ad Rempublicam nostram foeliciter administrandam intexuntur: reportata a Colchide Cambriola ex Australissima Novae Terrae Plaga. . . .* London: William Stansby, 1625.

———, Orpheus Iunior, *The golden fleece Diuided into three Parts, Under which are discouered the Errours of Religion, the Vices and Decayes of the Kingdome, and lastly the wayes to get wealth, and to restore Trading so much complayned of. Transported from Cambrioll Colchos, out of the Southermost Part of the Iland, commonly called the Newfovndland. . . .* London: Francis Williams, 1626.

———. *The Newlanders cvre. As well of those Violent sicknesses which distemper most Minds in these latter Dayes. . . .* London: N.O. for F. Constable, 1630.

---

[Warner, John, 1628–1692]. *The History of English Persecution of Catholics and the Presbyterian Plot.* 2 vol. T.A. Birrell, ed. Catholic Record Society, nos. 47–48. Leeds: John Whitehead, 1953.

[Waterhouse, Edward]. *A Declaration of the state of the Colony and Affaires in Virginia....* London: G. Eld for Robert Mylbourne, 1622.

[Wentworth, Thomas, 1593–1641]. *The Earl of Strafforde's Letters and Dispatches, with an Essay towards his Life by Sir George Radcliffe. From the Originals in Possession of his Great Grandson The Right Honourable Thomas Earl of Malton, Knight of the Bath.* 2 vols. William Knowler, 1699–1773, ed. London: William Bowyer, 1739.

——. *Wentworth Papers 1597–1628.* John Phillips Cooper, ed. Camden Fourth Series, no. 12. London: Royal Historical Society, 1973.

[Whitbourne, Richard, fl. 1579–1626]. *A Discourse and Discovery of New-Fovnd-Land, with many reasons to prooue how worthy and beneficiall a Plantation may there be made, after a far better manner than now it is....* London: Felix Kyngston for William Barret, 1620.

——. *A Discovrse Containing a Loving Invitation both Honourable, and profitable to all such as shall be Aduenturers, either in person, or purse, for the aduancement of his Maiesties most hopefull Plantation in the New-Fovnd-Land, lately vndertaken....* London: Felix Kyngston, 1622.

[Winslow, Edward, 1595–1655]. *Good Newes From New England: Or A true Relation of things very remarkable at the Plantation in New-England....* London: I.D. for William Bladen and Iohn Bellamie, 1624.

Wroth, Lawrence C. "Tobacco or Codfish. Lord Baltimore Makes His Choice", *Bulletin of The New York Public Library* 58 (1954): 523–34.

[Wynne, Edward, fl. 1621–28]. *A Letetr [sic] written by Captaine Edward Winne, to the Right Honourable, Sir George Caluert, Knight, his Maiesties Principall Secretary: From Feryland in Newfoundland, the 26. of August. 1621.* 1621.

——. *A Letter from Captaine Edward Wynne, Gouernour of the Colony at Ferryland, within the Prouince of Aualon, in Newfoundland, vnto the Right Honourable Sir George Calvert Knight, his Maiesties Principall Secretary. Iuly 1622.* [1622].

[Yonge, James, 1647–1721]. *Journal of James Yonge (1647–1721). Plymouth Surgeon.* Frederick Noël Laurence Poynter, ed., London: Longmans, Green & Co., 1963.

[Zaccaria da Saluzzo]. *Orthodoxa Consultatio de Ratione Verae Fidei Agnoscendae et Amplectendae....* Rome: 1635.

## IV. SECONDARY SOURCES

Albion, Gordon. *Charles I and the Court of Rome. A Study in 17th Century Diplomacy.* London: Burn Oates & Washbourne, 1935.

Alexander, H.G. *Religion in England 1558–1662.* London: Hodder and Stoughton 1968.

Alexander, Michael VanCleave. *Charles I's Lord Treasurer. Sir Richard Weston, Earl of Portland (1577–1635).* London; Basingstoke: Macmillan, 1975.

Allison, Anthony Francis. "Bibliographical Notes. Two Carmelites." *Recusant History* 6 (1961): 90–94.

——. "John Gerard and the Gunpowder Plot." *Recusant History* 5 (1959): 43–63.

——. "Richard Smith, Richelieu and the French Marriage. The Political Context of Smith's Appointment as Bishop for England in 1624." *Recusant History* 7 (1964): 148–211.

Andrews, Charles McLean. *The Colonial Period of American History.* 4 vols. New Haven, CN: Yale University Press, 1934–38.

Anstruther, Godfrey, OP. *A Hundred Homeless Years. English Dominicans 1558–1658.* London: Blackfriars Publications, 1958.

Aveling, John Cedric Hugh, OSB. "Documents Relating to the Northern Commissions for Compounding with Recusants 1627–1642." In Clare Talbot, ed. *Miscellanea Recusant Records.* Catholic Record Society, no. 53, Newport: R.H. Johns, 1961, 291–307.

——. *Northern Catholics. The Catholic Recusancy of the North Riding of Yorkshire 1558–1790.* London: Geoffrey Chapman, 1966.

Axtell, James. *The European and the Indian. Essays in the Ethnohistory of Colonial North America.* New York: Oxford University Press, 1981.

——. *The Invasion Within. The Contest of Cultures in Colonial North America.* New York: Oxford University Press, 1985.

Aylmer, Gerard Edward. *The King's Servants. The Civil Service of Charles I, 1625–1642.* London: Routledge & Kegan Paul, 1961.

Banks, Charles Edward. *The Winthrop Fleet of 1630. An Account of the Vessels, the Voyage, the Passengers and Their English Homes from Original Authorities.* Boston: Houghton Mifflin Co., 1930.

Barakat, Robert A. "Some Comments on Lord Baltimore's House at Ferryland, Newfoundland." *Newfoundland Quarterly,* 8 (1976): 17–27.

Basset, Bernard, SJ. *The English Jesuits from Campion to Martindale.* London: Burn & Oates, 1967.

Beales, Arthur Charles Frederick. *Education under Penalty. English Catholic Education from the Reformation to the fall of James II 1547–1689.* London: Athlone Press, 1963.

*Benedictines in Britain.* London: British Library, 1980.

Berkley, Henry J. "Lord Baltimore's Contest with Sir David Kirke over Avalon." *Maryland Historical Magazine* 12 (1917): 107–14.

Bossy, John. *Christianity in the West 1400–1700.* Oxford and New York: Oxford University Press, 1985.

——. *The English Catholic Community 1570–1850.* London: Darton, Longman & Todd, 1975.

——. "The English Catholic Community 1603–1625." In Alan Gordon Rae Smith, ed. *The Reign of James VI and I.* London; Basingstoke: Macmillan, 1973, 91–105.

——. "Reluctant Colonists. The English Catholics Confront the Atlantic." In D.B. Quinn, ed. *Early Maryland in a Wider World.* Detroit: Wayne State University Press, 1982, 149–64.

Browne, William Hand. *George Calvert and Cecilius Calvert, Barons Balti-*

*more of Baltimore*. New York: Dodd, Mead and Co., 1890.

——. *Maryland. The History of a Palatinate*. Boston: Houghton, Mifflin and Co., 1884.

Candide de Nant, OFM Cap. *Pages glorieuses de l'épopée canadienne. Une mission Capucine en Acadie*. Gembloux: J. Duculot, 1927.

Caraman, Philip George. *Henry Morse, Priest of the Plague*. London: Longmans, Green & Co., 1957.

Cell, Gillian T. "The Cupids Cove Settlement. A Case Study of the Problems of Colonisation." In G.M. Story, ed. *Early European Settlement and Exploitation in Atlantic Canada*. St. John's, Nfld.: Memorial University of Newfoundland, 1982, 97–114.

——. *English Enterprise in Newfoundland 1577–1660*. Toronto: University of Toronto Press, 1969.

Chalkin, Christopher William. *Seventeenth-Century Kent. A Social and Economic History*. London: Longmans, Green and Co., 1965.

*Chronique de l'Ordre des Carmélites de la Reforme de Sainte-Thérèse depuis leur introduction en France*. 3 vols. Troyes: Anner-André, 1846–56.

Coakley, Thomas M. "George Calvert and Newfoundland: 'The Sad Face of Winter.' " *Maryland Historical Magazine* 71 (1976): 1–18.

Codignola, Luca. "Notizie dal Nuovo Mondo. Propaganda Fide e il Nord America, 1622–1630." In Luca Codignola, ed., *Canadiana. Problemi di storia canadese*. Venice: Marsilio Editori, 1983, 32–44.

——. "Rome and North America 1622–1799. The Interpretive Framework." *Storia nordamericana* 1 (1984): 5–33.

Connell, Joan. *The Roman Catholic Church in England 1780–1850. A Study in Internal Politics*. Philadelphia: American Philosophical Association, 1984.

Cross, Claire. *Church and People 1450–1660. The Triumph of the Laity in the English Church*. London: Harvester Press, 1976.

Davies, Kenneth Gordon. *The North Atlantic World in the Seventeenth Century*, Minneapolis: University of Minnesota Press; London: Oxford University Press, 1974.

Davis, Richard Beale. *Intellectual Life in the Colonial South 1585–1763*. Knoxville: University of Tennessee Press, 1978.

Del Re, Niccolò. *La curia romana. Lineamenti storico-giuridici*. Rome: Edizioni di Storia e Letteratura, 1970 (1st ed.: 1952).

Dickason, Olive Patricia. *The Myth of the Savage And the Beginnings of French Colonialism in the Americas*. Edmonton: The University of Alberta Press, 1984.

Djwa, Sandra. "Early Explorations: New Founde Landys (1496–1729)." *Studies in Canadian Literature*, 4 (1979), 7–21.

Dodge, Ernest Stanley. *Northwest by Sea*. New York: Oxford University Press, 1961.

Dures, Alan. *English Catholicism 1558–1642*. Harlow: Longman, 1983.

Eagleston, Arthur John. *The Channel Islands under Tudor Government, 1485–1642. A Study in Administrative History*. Cambridge: Cambridge University Press, 1949.

Edwards, Francis O., SJ. *The Jesuits in England. From 1580 to the Present day*. Tunbridge Wells: Burn & Oates, 1985.

Elliott, John Huxtable. *The Old World and the New, 1492–1650.* Cambridge: Cambridge University Press, 1970.

——. "Spain and Its Empire in the Sixteenth and Seventeenth Centuries." In D.B. Quinn, ed., *Early Maryland in a Wider World.* Detroit: Wayne State University Press, 1982, 58–83.

Farley, Edith Chapman. "The Relationships of the Venetian Ambassadors in England with the Royal Family, Privy Council and Parliament, 1603–1629." Ph.D. Thesis, Mississippi State University, 1976.

Faulkner, Thomas. *An Historical and Topographical Description of Chelsea, and its Environs; Interspersed with Biographical Anecdotes of Illustrious and Eminent Persons who have Resided in Chelsea during the three Preceding Centuries.* 2 vols. Chelsea: Tilling, 1829.

[Fisher, Thomas]. *The Kentish Traveller's Companion, In a Descriptive View of the Towns, villages, remarkable Buildings and Antiquities, situated on or near The Road from London to Margate, Dover and Canterbury....* Canterbury: Simmons and Kirby; Rochester: T. Fisher, 1779.

Fishman, Laura Schrager. "How Noble the Savage? The Image of the American Indian in French and English Travel Accounts, ca. 1550–1680." Ph.D. Thesis, City University of New York, 1979.

Flanagan, Thomas. *A History of the Church in England, from the Earliest Period, to the Establishment of the Hierarchy in 1850.* 2 vols. London: Charles Dolman, 1857.

Foster, James W. "George Calvert: His Yorkshire Boyhood." *Maryland Historical Magazine* 55 (1960): 261–74.

French, Allen. *Charles I and the Puritan Upheaval.* London: George Allen & Unwin, 1955.

Galloway, David. "Robert Hayman (1575–1629): Some Materials for the Life of a Colonial Governor and First 'Canadian' Author." *William and Mary Quarterly,* 3rd ser., 24 (1967): 75–87.

Gardiner, Samuel Rawson. *History of England from the Accession of James I. to the Outbreak of the Civil War, 1603–1642.* 10 vols. London: Longmans, 1883–84.

Hall, Clayton Colman. *The Lords Baltimore and the Maryland Palatinate....* Baltimore: John Murphy Co., 1902.

Handcock, W. Gordon. "The West Country Migrations to Newfoundland." *Bulletin of Canadian Studies* 5 (1981): 5–24.

Hardman, Anne. *English Carmelites in Penal Times.* London: Burn Oates & Washbourne, 1936.

Harper, J. Russell. "In Quest of Lord Baltimore's House at Ferryland." *Canadian Geographical Journal* 41 (1960): 106–13.

Hastings, Russel (Mrs.). "Calvert and Darnall Gleanings from English Wills." *Maryland Historical Magazine* 21 (1926): 303–24; 22 (1927): 1–22, 115–38, 211–45, 307–49.

Hervey, Mary Frederica Sophia. *The Life, Correspondence & Collections of Thomas Howard Earl of Arundel "Father of Vertu in England."* Cambridge: Cambridge University Press, 1921.

Higginson, Thomas Wentworth Storrow. *Life of Francis Higginson, First Minister in the Massachusetts Bay Colony, and Author of* New England's

Plantation *(1630).* New York: Dodd, Mead and Co., 1891.

Howley, Michael Francis. *Ecclesiastical History of Newfoundland.* Boston: Doyle and Whittle, 1888.

Hughes, Philip. *Rome and Counter-Reformation in England.* London: Burns Oates & Washbourne, 1944.

Hughes, Thomas Aloysius, SJ. *History of the Society of Jesus in North America Colonial and Federal. Text and Documents.* 4 vols. London: Longmans, Green and Co., 1907-17.

Hurtsfield, Joel. "Gunpowder Plot and the Politics of Dissent." In Howard Stuart Reinmuth, ed., *Early Stuart Studies. Essays in Honor of David Harris Willson.* Minneapolis: University of Minnesota Press, 1970, 95-121.

Ives, J. Moss. *The Ark and the Dove. The Beginning of Civil and Religious Liberties in America.* London: Longmans, Green and Co., 1936.

Jaenen, Cornelius John. *The French Relationship with the Native Peoples of New France and Acadia.* Ottawa: Indian and Northern Affairs Canada, 1984.

———. *Friend and Foe. Aspects of French-Amerindian Cultural Contact in the Sixteenth and Seventeenth Centuries.* Toronto: McClelland and Stewart, 1976.

Jarrett, Bede, OP. *The English Dominicans.* London: Burns Oates and Washbourne, 1921.

Jennings, Francis. *The Invasion of America. Indians, Colonialism, and the Cant of Conquest.* Chapel Hill: The University of North Carolina Press, 1975.

Jones, J.J. *"The Golden Fleece." Cylchgrawn Llyfrgell Genedlaethol Cymru/ The National Library of Wales Journal* 3 (1943): 58-60.

Jowitt, Robert Lionel Palgrave, and Jowitt, Dorothy Marion. *The Isle of Wight.* London: B.T. Batsford, 1951.

Kenny, Hamill. "Baltimore: New Light on an Old Name." *Maryland Historical Magazine* 49 (1954): 116-21.

Kenyon, John Philipps. *The Stuart Constitution 1603-1688. Documents and Commentary.* Cambridge: Cambridge University Press, 1969.

Kinvig, Robert Henry. *History of the Isle of Man.* Oxford: Oxford University Press, 1944.

Krugler, John D. "The Calvert Family, Catholicism, and Court Politics in Early Seventeenth-Century England." *The Historian: A Journal of History* 43 (1981): 378-92.

———. "English and Catholic. Nationalism, Catholicism and the Calverts' Motivation in Founding Their Maryland Colony." Unpublished typescript (1984): 1-29.

———. " 'The Face of a Protestant, and the Heart of a Papist.' A Reexamination of Sir George Calvert's Conversion to Roman Catholicism." *Journal of Church and State* 20 (1978): 507-31.

———. "Lord Baltimore, Roman Catholics, and Toleration. Religious Policy in Maryland during the Early Catholic Years, 1634-1649." *Catholic Historical Review* 65 (1979): 49-75.

———. "Sir George Calvert's Resignation as Secretary of State and the Founding of Maryland." *Maryland Historical Magazine* 68 (1973): 239-54.

———. " 'With promise of Liberty in Religion.' The Catholic Lords Baltimore and Toleration in Seventeenth-Century Maryland, 1634-1692." *Maryland Historical Magazine* 79 (1984): 21-43.

Kupperman, Karen Ordahl. *Settling with the Indians. The Meeting of English and Indian Cultures in America, 1580-1640.* Toronto: J.M. Dent, 1980.

Lahey, Raymond J. "Avalon. Lord Baltimore's Colony in Newfoundland." In G.M. Story, ed., *Early European Settlement and Exploitation in Atlantic Canada*. St. John's: Memorial University of Newfoundland, 1982, 115-37.

———. "The Role of Religion in Lord Baltimore's Colonial Enterprise." *Maryland Historical Magazine* 72 (1977): 492-511.

Lenhart, John M., OFM Cap. "The Capuchin Prefecture of New England (1630-1656)." *Franciscan Studies*, new ser., 3 (1943): 21-46, 180-95, 306-13.

———. "An Important Chapter in American Church History (1625-1650)." *Catholic Historical Review* 8 (1929): 500-24.

Leys, Mary Dorothy Rose. *Catholics in England, 1559-1829. A Social History.* London: Longmans, Green and Co., 1961.

Lindley, K.J. "The Lay Catholics of England in the Reign of Charles I." *Journal of Ecclesiastical History* 22 (1971): 199-211.

Lunn, David. *The English Benedictines, 1540-1688. From Reformation to Revolution.* London: Burn & Oates; New York: Barnes & Noble, 1980.

Lunn, Maurus, OSB. "Benedictine Opposition to Bishop Richard Smith (1625-1629)." *Recusant History* 11 (1971): 1-20.

McCaffrey, Patrick Romaeus. *The White Friars. An Outline of Carmelite History with Special Reference to the English-speaking Provinces.* Dublin: M.H. Gill, 1926.

McElwee, William Lloyds. *The Wisest Fool in Christendom. King James I and VI.* London: Faber and Faber, 1958.

McKinnon, M.H.M. "Parnassus in Newfoundland. The First Fruits of Britaniola." *Dalhousie Review* 32 (1952): 110-19.

Marchant, Roland Albert. *The Church under the Law. Justice, Administration and Discipline in the Diocese of York, 1560-1640.* Cambridge: Cambridge University Press, 1969.

Mathew, Arnold Harris, and Calthrop, Annette. *The Life of Sir Tobie Mathew Bacon's Alter Ego.* London: Elkin Mathews, 1907.

Mathew, David. *Catholicism in England. The Portrait of a Minority: Its Culture and Tradition.* London: Eyre & Spottiswoode, 1936.

Mattingly, Garrett. *Renaissance Diplomacy.* London: Jonathan Cape, 1955.

Metzler, Josef, OMI. "Francesco Ingoli, der erste Sekretär der Kongregation." In Metzler, J., ed., *Sacrae Congregationis de Propaganda Fide Memoria Rerum*, 1/1: *1622-1700*, Freiburg: Herder, 1971, 197-243.

———. "Francesco Ingoli und die Indianerweihen." *Neue Zeitschrift für Missionswissenschaft* 25 (1969): 262-72.

———. "Orientation, programme et premières décisions (1622-1649)." In Metzler, J., ed. *Sacrae Congregationis de Propaganda Fide Memoria Rerum*, 1/1: *1622-1700*. Freiburg: Herder, 1971, 146-96.

———. *Sacrae Congregationis de Propaganda Fide Memoria Rerum.* 3 vols. Freiburg: Herder, 1971-76.

Meyer, Arnold Oskar. "Charles I and Rome." *American Historical Review* 19 (1913): 13-26.

——. *England and the Catholic Church under Queen Elizabeth*. London: Kegan Paul, Trench, Trübner & Co., 1916.

Nicklin, John Bailey Calvert. "The Calvert Family." *Maryland Historical Magazine* 16 (1921): 50-9.

O'Flaherty, Patrick. *The Rock Observed. Studies in the Literature of Newfoundland*. Toronto: University of Toronto Press, 1979.

O'Neill, Charles Edwards, sj. "North American Beginnings in Maryland and Louisiana." In Metzler, J., ed. *Sacrae Congregationis de Propaganda Fide Memoria Rerum*, 1/2: *1622-1700*. Freiburg: Herder, 1972, 713-26.

O'Neill, Paul. *Upon This Rock. The Story of the Roman Catholic Church in Newfoundland and Labrador*. St. John's: Breakwater Books, 1984.

Parker, Geoffrey. *The Army of Flanders and the Spanish Road 1567-1659. The Logistics of Spanish Victory and Defeat in the Low Countries' Wars*. Cambridge: Cambridge University Press, 1972.

——. *Europe in crisis 1598-1648*. Glasgow: Fontana, 1979.

Parker, John. *Books to Build an Empire. A Bibliographical History of English Overseas Interest to 1620*. Amsterdam: N. Israel, 1965.

Parks, George Bruner. *Richard Hakluyt and the English Voyages*. James A. Williamson, ed. New York: American Geographical Society, 1928.

Pasture, Alexandre, abbé. *La Restauration religieuse au Pays-Bas Catholiques sous les archiducs Albert et Isabelle (1596-1633) principalement d'après les Archives de la Nonciature et de la Visite ad limina*. Louvain: Librairie Universitaire, 1925.

Pecchiai, Pio. *Roma nel Cinquecento*, Bologna: Cappelli, 1948.

Peltier, Henri. *Histoire du Carmel*. Paris: Éditions du Seuil, 1958.

Petrocchi, Massimo. *Roma nel Seicento*, Bologna: Cappelli, 1970.

Phelps, William. *The History and Antiquities of Somersetshire; being A General and Parochial Survey of that Interesting Country. . . .* 4 vols., of which only 2 published. London: J.B. Nichols, 1836-39.

Polisenský, Josef Vincent. *The Thirty Years War*. London: B.T. Batsford, 1971 (1st ed.: 1970).

Porter, Harry Culverwell. *The Inconstant Savage. England and the North American Indian*. London: Gerard Duckworth, 1979.

Prestwich, Henna. *Cranfield. Politics and Profits under the Early Stuarts. The Career of Lionel Cranfield Earl of Middlesex*. Oxford: Clarendon Press 1966.

Prowse, Daniel Woodley. *A History of Newfoundland from the English, Colonial, and Foreign Records*. London: Macmillan, 1895.

Quinn, David Beers. "Documenting Canada's Early White History." *Archivaria* 7 (1978): 86-94.

——. *England and the Discovery of America, 1481-1620. From the Bristol Voyages of the Fifteenth Century to the Pilgrim Settlement at Plymouth: The Exploration, Exploitation, and Trial-and-Error Colonization of North America by the English*. London: Allen & Unwin, 1974.

——. *North America from Earliest Discovery to First Settlements. The Norse Voyages to 1621*. New York: Harper & Row, 1978.

——. *Sir Humphrey Gilbert and Newfoundland on the Four Hundredth Anniversary of his Annexation of the Island to the Realm of England*. St. John's: Newfoundland Historical Society, 1983.

————, ed. *Early Maryland in a Wider World*. Detroit: Wayne State University Press, 1982.

————, ed. *The Hakluyt Handbook*. 2 vols. London: Hakluyt Society, 1974.

Quinn, D.B. and Cheshire, Neil M. *The New Found Land of Stephen Parmenius. The Life and Writings of a Hungarian Poet Drowned on a Voyage from Newfoundland, 1583*. Toronto: University of Toronto Press, 1972.

Quinn, D.B. and Ryan, A.N. *England's Sea Empire, 1550-1642*. London: Allen & Unwin, 1983.

Raffaeli Cammarota, Marina. "L'archivio Guidi di Bagno". *Clio* 12 (1976): 235-43.

Reinmuth, Howard Stuart, ed. *Early Stuart Studies. Essays in Honor of David Harris Willson*. Minneapolis: University of Minnesota Press, 1970.

Reynolds, Ernest Edwin. *The Roman Catholic Church in England and Wales. A Short History*. Wheathampstead: Anthony Clarke, 1973.

Rowe, Frederick W. *A History of Newfoundland and Labrador*. Toronto: McGraw-Hill Ryerson, 1980.

Ruigh, Robert Edgar. *The Parliament of 1624. Politics and Foreign Policy*. Cambridge, MA: Harvard University Press, 1971.

Russell, Conrad. *Parliaments and English Politics 1621-1629*. Oxford: Clarendon Press, 1979.

Salisbury, Neal. *Manitou and Providence. Indians, Europeans, and the Making of New England, 1500-1643*. New York: Oxford University Press, 1982.

Schmidlin, August. "Projekt eines Nordamerik. Missionswegs nach China in der Frühzeit der Propaganda (vor 300 Jahren)." *Zeitschrift für Missionswissenschaft* 15 (1925): 147-49.

Schumacher, Walter Henry. " 'Vox Populi': The Thirty Years War in English Pamphlets and Newspapers." Ph.D. Thesis, Princeton University, 1975.

Sheehan, Bernard. *Savagism and Civility. Indians and Englishmen in Colonial Virginia*. New York: Cambridge University Press, 1980.

Sheppard, Lancelot Capel. *The English Carmelites*. London: Burns Oates, 1943.

Signorini, Antonella. "Un carmelitano scalzo e l'America, 1623-1636. Una selezione dalle lettere di Simon Stock, nell'archivio della Sacra Congregazione de Propaganda Fide." Tesi di laurea, Università di Pisa, 1980.

Silverio de Santa Teresa, OCD. *Historia del Carmel Descalzo en España, Portugal y America*. 15 vols. Burgos: Tipografia Burgalesa, 1935-52.

Smith, Alan Gord Rae, ed. *The Reign of James VI and I*. London; Basingstoke: Macmillan, 1973.

Smith, Bromley. "George Calvert at Oxford." *Maryland Historical Magazine* 26 (1931): 109-30.

Spini, Giorgio. *Autobiografia della giovane America. La storiografia americana dai Padri Pellegrini all'Indipendenza*. Turin: Einaudi, 1968.

Steinberg, Sigfrid Heinrich. *The "Thirty Years War" and the Conflict for European Hegemony 1600-1660*. London: Edward Arnold, 1966.

Steiner, Bernard Christian. *Beginnings of Maryland 1631-1639*, Baltimore: Johns Hopkins University Press, 1903.

————. "The First Lord Baltimore and His Colonial Projects." *Annual Report of the American Historical Association* (1905): 109-22.

Stommel, Henry. *Lost Islands. The Story of Islands that have vanished from National Charts*. Vancouver: University of British Columbia Press, 1984.

Story, George Morley, ed. *Early European Settlement and Exploitation in Atlantic Canada. Selected Papers*. St. John's: Memorial University of Newfoundland, 1982.

Sweet, William Warren. *Religion in Colonial America*. New York: Charles Scribner's Sons, 1953.

Taylor, Eva Germaine Rimington. *Late Tudor and Early Stuart Geography 1538-1650. A Sequel to Tudor Geography, 1485-1583*. London: Methuen, 1934.

———. *The Mathematical Practitioners of Tudor & Stuart England*. Cambridge: For the Institute of Navigation at the University Press, 1954.

———. *Tudor Geography 1485-1583*. London: Methuen, 1930.

Thaddeus, OFM. *The Franciscans in England 1600-1850 Being an Authentic Account of the Second English Province of Friars Minor*. London and Leamington: Art and Book Co., 1898.

Thomas, David Lleufer. "Iscennen and Golden Grove." *Transactions of the Honourable Society of Cymmrodorion* (1940): 115-29.

Thompson, E. Margaret. *The Carthusian Order in England*. New York: Macmillan, 1930.

Ting Pong Lee, Ignacio, "La actitud de la Sagrada Congregación frente al Regio Patronato." In Metzler, J., ed., *Sacrae Congregationis de Propaganda Fide Memoria Rerum*, I/1: *1622-1700*. Freiburg: Herder, 1971, 353-438.

[Tootell, Hugh]. *The Church History of England, From the Year 1500, to the Year 1688. Chiefly with regard to Catholicks*. . . . 3 vols. Brussels: 1737-42.

Trigger, Bruce G. *Natives and Newcomers. Canada's "Heroic Age" Reconsidered*. Montreal: McGill-Queen's University Press, 1985.

Tuck, James A. "Looking for a Colony of Avalon." In Jane Sproull Thomson and Callum Thomson, eds. *Archaeology in Newfoundland and Labrador 1984*. St John's: Newfoundland Museum, 1984, 378-97.

Turner, Olga. "Some Aspects of the Life and Works of don Carlos Coloma 1566-1637." Ph.D. Thesis, University of London, 1950.

Wallis, Helen. "England's Search for the Northern Passages in the 16th and Early 17th Centuries." Paper read at the Conference of The History of the Discovery of the Arctic Regions as Seen through the Descriptions of Travellers and the Work of Cartographers from Early Antiquity to the 18th Century, organized by the Comité Arctique de Monaco, Rome, 5-9 October 1981.

Walsh, Richard and Fox, William Lloyd, eds. *Maryland. A History 1632-1974*. Baltimore: Maryland Historical Society, 1974.

Wedgwood, Cicely Veronica. *The Thirty Years War*. London: Jonathan Cape, 1938.

White, Arthur Wilson, Jr. "Suspension of Arms. Anglo-Spanish Mediation in the Thirty Years War, 1621-1625." Ph.d. Thesis, Tulane University, 1978.

Wilkinson, Henry C. *The Adventurers of Bermuda. A history of the Island from Its Discovery Until the Dissolution of the Somers Island Company in 1684*. London: Oxford University Press, 1933.

Willaert, Léopold, SJ. "Négociations politico-religieuses entre l'Angleterre et les Pays-Bas catholiques (1598-1625) d'après les Papiers d'État et de l'Audience conservés aux Archives Générales du Royaume de Belgique à Bruxelles," *Revue d'histoire ecclesiastique* 6 (1905): 47-54, 566-81, 811-26; 7 (1906): pp. 584-607; 8 (1907): 81-101, 305-11, 514-32; 9 (1908): 56-61, 736-45.

Williams, Michael E. *The Venerable English College Rome. A History 1579-1979*. London: Associated Catholic Publications, 1979.

Williams, E. Ronald, "Cambriol. The Story of a Forgotten Colony." *Welsh Outlook* 8 (1921): 230-33.

Willson, David Harris. *King James VI and I*. London: Jonathan Cape, 1956.

——. *The Privy Councillors in the House of Commons 1604-1629*. Minneapolis: University of Minnesota Press, 1940.

Wright, Louis Booker. *The First Gentlemen of Virginia. Intellectual Qualities of the Early Colonial Ruling Class*. San Marino, CA: Huntington Library, 1940.

——. *Religion and Empire. The Alliance between Piety and Commerce in English Expansion 1558-1625*. Chapel Hill: University of North Carolina Press, 1943.

Zimmerman, Benedict, OCD. *Carmel in England: A History of the English Mission of the Discalced Carmelites. 1615 to 1849. Drawn from Documents preserved in the Archives of the Order*. London: Burns & Oates, 1899.

## V. ATLASES, MAPS, CARTOGRAPHICAL STUDIES

### a. Atlases, Maps

[Briggs, Henry, 1561-1630]. "The North part of America Conteyning Newfoundland, new England, Virginia, Florida, new Spaine, and Nova Francia, wth ye riches Iles of Hispaniola, Cuba, Jamaica, and Porto Rieco, on the South, and upon ye West the large and goodly Iland of California. The bonds of it are the Atlantick Ocean on ye South and East sides ye South Sea on ye west side and on ye North Fretum Hudson and Buttons baye a faire entrance to ye nearest and most temperate passage to Japan & China." "R[eynold/enier] Elstracke sculpsit." In [Samuel Purchas], *Purchas His Pilgrimes....* London: William Stansby for Henrie Fetterstone, 1625, 3: 852-53.

[de Jode, Cornelis, 1568-1600]. "Americae Pars Borealis, Florida, Baccalaos, Canada, Corterealis. A Cornelio de Iudaeis in lucem edita...." In [Gerard de Jode], *Specvlvm Orbis Terrae*. Antwerp: Arnold Coninx, 1593.

[de Jode, Gerard, 1521-1591]. *Specvlvm Orbis Terrae*. Antwerp: Arnold Coninx, 1593.

——. *Specvlvm Orbis Terrarvm*. Antwerp: Gerard Smits, [1578].

——. "Totivs orbis cogniti Vniversalis Descriptio. Cui etiam eandem orbis terrae delineationem, duorum circulorvm capacitate, huius descriptionis mundi longitudinem documentum admirantibus, adiecimus." 1589. In [Gerard de Jode], *Specvlvm Orbis Terrae*. Antwerp: Arnold Coninx, 1593.

[Gilbert, Humphrey, *c.* 1537-1583]. "A General Map, Made Onelye for the

Particvler Declaration of This Discovery." In Humphrey Gilbert, *A Discouvrse Of a Discouerie for a new Passage to Cataia*, George Gascoine, ed. London: Henry Middleton for Richard Ihones, 1576.

[Hondt, Josse de, 1563–1612], Hondius, Jodocus. "America Descrip." In [Samuel Purchas], *Purchas His Pilgrimes.* . . . London: William Stansby for Henrie Fetterstone, 1625, 3: [858].

[Keer, Peter, 1571–1646]. "Americae Nova Descriptio. . . . Abraham Goos, Sculpsit." Amsterdam: 1614.

[Mason, John, 1586–1635]. "Newfovnd Land described by Captaine Iohn Mason an industrious Gent: who spent seuen yeares in the Countrey." In Orpheus Iunior [William Vaughan], *Cambrensivm Caroleia.* . . . London: William Stansby, 1625; also in Orpheus Iunior [William Vaughan], *The golden fleece.* . . . London: Francis Williams, 1626.

Ortelius, Abraham, 1527–1598. "Americae Sive Novi Orbis, Nova Descriptio." 1587. In [Ortelius], *Teatro del mondo.* . . . Antwerp: Giovanni Battista Vrintio, 1608.

———. *Teatro del mondo di Abrahamo Ortelio: Da lui poco inanzi la sua morte riueduto, & di tauvole nuoue, et commenti adorno, & arricchito, con la vita dell'Autore, Translato in Lingua Toscana dal Sig.r Filippo Pigafetta.* Antwerp: Giovanni Baptista Vrintio, 1608.

———. *Theatrvm Orbis Terrarum.* Antwerp: Aegidius Coppenius Diesth, 1570.

———. "Typvs Orbis Terrarvm." 1587. In [Ortelius], *Teatro del mondo.* . . . Antwerp: Giovanni Battista Vrintio, 1608.

[Speed, John, 1522?–1629]. "America with those known parts in that unknowne worlde both people and manner of buildings Discribed and inlarged by I.S. . . . Abraham Goos Amstelodamensis sculpsit." [London], G. Humble, 1626; also in Speed, *A Prospect of the Most Famovs Parts of the World.* . . . London: John Dawson for George Humble, 1627.

———. "A New and Accvrat Map of the world Drawne to ye truest Descriptions latest Discoueries & best Obseruations yt haue been made by English or Strangers." [London]: George Humble, 1626; also in Speed, *A Prospect of the Most Famovs Parts of the World.* . . . London: John Dawson for George Humble, 1627.

———. *A Prospect of the Most Famovs Parts of the World with These Kingdomes therein contained, together With all the Prouinces, Counties and Shires, contained in that large Theater of Great Britaines Empire. . . . .* London: John Dawson for George Humble, 1627.

### b. Cartographical Studies

Bagrow, Leo. *History of Cartography.* Ed. Raleigh Ashlin Skelton. London: C.A. Watts, 1964.

Cumming, William Patterson. *British Maps of Colonial America.* Chicago: University of Chicago Press, 1974.

———, Skelton, R.A., D.B. Quinn, *The Discovery of North America.* New York: American Heritage Press; London: Paul Elek, 1971.

Fite, Emerson David, and Freeman, Archibald, eds., *A Book of Old Maps*

*Delineating American History from the Earliest Days down to the Close of the Revolutionary War*. Cambridge, Mass.: Harvard University Press, 1926.

Ganong, William Francis. *Crucial Maps in the Early Cartography and Place-Nomenclature of the Atlantic Coast of Canada*. Theodore E. Layng, ed. Toronto: University of Toronto Press, 1964.

Harrisse, Henry. *Découverte et évolution cartographique de Terreneuve et des pays circonvoisins 1497–1769. Essais de Géographie historique et documentaire*. Paris: H. Welter; London: Henry Stevens, Son & Stiles, 1900.

———. *Notes pour servir à l'histoire, à la bibliographie et à la cartographie de la Nouvelle-France et des pays adjacents 1545–1700*. Paris: Librairie Tros, 1872.

Howgego, James, *Printed Maps of London circa 1553–1850*. Folkestone: Wm. Dawson, 1978.

Howse, Derek. *Greenwich Time and the Discovery of the Longitude*. Oxford: Oxford University Press, 1980.

Lehner, Ernst, and Lehner, Johanna. *How They Saw the New World*. Gerard L. Alexander, ed. New York: Tudor Publishing Co., 1966.

Lister, Raymond. *How to Identify Old Maps and Globes with a List of Carthographers, Engravers, Publishers and Printers Concerned with Printed Maps and Globes from c. 1500 to c. 1850*. Hamden, Conn.: Archon Books, 1965.

Marguet, Frédéric Philippe. *Histoire de la longitude à la mer au XVIIIe siècle, en France*. Paris: Augustin Challanel, 1917.

O'Dea, Fabian. *The 17th Century Cartography of Newfoundland*. Cartographica, no. 1. Toronto: York University, 1971.

Perrin, W.G. "The Prime Meridian." *Mariner's Mirror* 13 (1927): 109–24.

Skelton, Raleigh Ashlin. *Explorers' Maps. Charters in the Cartographic Record of Geographical Discovery*. London: Routledge and Kegan Paul, 1958.

Tyacke, Sarah. "Map-sellers and the London Map Trade *c* 1650–1710." In H. Wallis and S. Tyacke, eds. *My Head Is a Map. Essays & Memoirs in Honour of R.V. Tooley*. London: Francis Edwards and Carta Press, 1973, 63–80.

van Ortroy, Fernand. *L'Oeuvre cartographique de Gérard et de Corneille De Jode*. Université de Gand, Recueil de Travaux publiés par la Faculté de Philosophie et Lettres, 44 (1914).

Wagner, Henry R. *The Cartography of the Northwest Coast of America to the Year 1800*, 2 vols. Berkeley: University of California Press, 1937.

Wallis, Helen, and Sarah Tyacke, eds. *My Head is a Map. Essays & Memoirs in Honour of R.V. Tooley*. London: Francis Edwards and Carta Press, 1973.

Wallis, Helen. "The Map Collection of the British Museum Library." In H. Wallis and S. Tyacke, eds. *My Head is a Map. Essays & Memoirs in Honour of R.V. Tooley*. London: Francis Edwards and Carta Press, 1973, 3–20.

### VI. WORKS BY SIMON STOCK

#### a. Printed

1618    *The Practise how to finde Ease, Rest, Repose, Content, and Hap-*

---

*pines. Written By a Religious man of the Congregation of S. Elias, &*
*of the Order of our Blessed Ladie of Mount Carmell. The First Part.*
*Contayning Directions, how to make Mentall, or Spirituall Prayer.*
*The Second Edition.* At Dovay By Iohn Higham, with permission of
Superiors. 1618.

1619    *The Practise how to finde Ease, Rest, Repose, Content, and Hap-*
*pines. Written by a Religious man of the congregation of St. Elias*
*the Prophet, and of the Order of our Blessed Lady of mount Carmell,*
*restored by the Blessed mother Teresa. The Second Part. Containing*
*directions how to end all Controuersies, and take away all discon-*
*tentments, and euils, and attaine vnto true ioy of minde, and content*
*of heart, and all good.* At Roan. By Iaques Foüet, with permission
of Superiors. 1619.

1620    *An hvmble appeale to the Kings most excellent maiestie. Wherein is*
*proued, that our Lord and Sauior Iesvs Christi, was Author of the*
*Catholike Roman Faith, which Protestants call Papistrie. Written*
*by Iohn Hvnt, a Roman Catholike, in defence of his Religion*
*against the Calumniations and persecutions of Protestant Ministers.*
Printed with permission of Superiours. 1620.

1621    *A briefe discouerie of the crafte & pollicie Which Protestant Minis-*
*ters vse in seducing theire Followers By Preaching and Publishing*
*theire owne words for the word of God. Written by Iohn Hunt a*
*Romaine Catholique, in defence of the true Gospell or Word of God.*
Printed with Permission of Superiours M.DC.XXI.

1623    *Iesvs Maria Joseph. The Practise of the Presence of God, and how to*
*seeke, finde, and enjoy him, who is the peace, rest, repose and happy*
*life of Man. Written by S.S. of the Congregation of S. Elias the*
*Prophet, and of the order of our blessed Lady of Mount Carmel,*
*restored by the blessed Mother, and Virgin Saint Theresa. The Third*
*Part.* Roan. By Jaques Foüt, with permission of Superiors,
M.DC.XXIII.

1637    *Of the Visible Sacrifice of the Chvrch of God. The First Part. Writ-*
*ten by Anonymvs Eremita.* At Brvxelles. By Hvbert Antony Velpius,
Printer to his Maiestie. 1637.

1638    *Of the Visible Sacrifice in the Chvrch of God. The Second Part.*
*Written by Anonymvs Eremita.* At Brvxelles. By Hvbert ·Antony
Velpius, Printer to his Maiestie, 1638.

Stock's works have been reprinted by Scolar Press in the series "English Recusant Literature," edited by D.M. Rogers, in a facsimile edition, according to
the following order:
1618, no. 16 (1970)
1619, no. 17 (1970)
1620, no. 54 (1970)
1621, no. 62 (1971)
1623, no. 375 (1978)
1637, no. 135 (1973)
1638, no. 135 (1973)

### b. Manuscript

[1635] "Sancti Palladii Scotorum Apostoli, et Palestinae Monachi Brevis Historia. A Fratris Simone Stocco eiusdem Ordinis, missionario anglo, collecta." AOCD, Ms. 317.e.

[1640] "An Advertisement of old Anonimous Eremita to his noble friend Sir Edward Dearing Knight & Baronet, to correct the multitude of his errors & falsehoods in his booke intituled of fraude, of folly, of foule language, & blasphemy." BL, *Add. Mss.* 22 465.

In his manuscript work of 1640 Stock refers to Edward Dering's book printed in 1641 (see Bibliography, III. Printed Primary Sources). Obviously, Stock knew the manuscript version of Dering's book prior to its publication.

# Index